# The Political Thought
of
# Ibne Taymiyah

# The Political Thought
## of
# Ibne Taymiyah

Prof. **Qamaruddin Khan**

# ADAM PUBLISHERS & DISTRIBUTORS
New Delhi-110002, INDIA

**Adam Publishers & Distributors**
(Exporters & Importers)
1542, Pataudi House, Darya Ganj,
New Delhi-110002
Ph.: (O) 23282550, 23284740, 23267510
Tele Fax : 23267510
E-mail : apd@bol.net.in
          syedsajid_ali@rediffmail.com

Edition: 2007

ISBN : 81-7435-224-4
Price:

Printed & Bound in India
Published by :
Syed Sajid Ali, for,
**Adam Publishers & Distributors**
1542, Pataudi House, Darya Ganj,
New Delhi-110002

# CONTENTS

# CONTENTS

# PREFACE

This book: The political Thought of Ibne Taymiyah, is perhaps the first attempt at presenting a systematic and objective study of the political philosophy of Ibne Taymiyah, one of the very few great original political thinkers in Islam. As a background to the main study of thought analysis of the growths and development of political ideas and theories in Islamic history has been given in the introductory chapters. The work is very carefully documented from original Arabic sources and hardly a proposition has been made in it without a reliable authority being cited as its basis.

It may however be pointed out that the present study has been undertaken in a most critical and scientific spirit to clear up age long misconceptions and misrepresentations of Islamic political ideas, hence the author expects that readers will go through the following pages with scholarly patience and open-mindedness, for his only aim is to arouse honest and sincere thinking in those who are interested in the main problems of Islamic polity and society.

Further that this precious treatise has been lastly published by our Establishment Adam Publisher, New Delhi in 1992. But observing, now, a fresh demand in International Market, we are pleased to prepare and present an Improved Edition in accordance with the latest standereds of publication including an excellent recomposing and proof Reading, exclusively for our esteemed clients.

# FOREWORD

The great Hambalite Imam, Ibne Taymiyah, has been source of inspiration for all the Muslim Thinkers who ever cared to restore Islam to its pristine purity. Honest and sincere, as he has been, Ibne Taymiyah's harsh criticism, and sometimes even exaggerated and extremely severe remarks, were never attended to by such scholars as closely followed him in their zeal of making an effort to uplift to the Muslim Society. Critical studies of a number of his works have already seen the light of the day. But his political ideas have not, so far, been adequately dealt with for readers in the English language. Mr. Qamaruddin Khan, formerly Reader in Islamic Research Institute, Islamabad, deserves our congratulations and admiration for producing an excellent critical study of Ibne Taymiyah's Political Thought.

I am glad that by the joint efforts of some of my colleagues in the Institute, and employees of the Press, this valuable contribution of Mr. Khan is now in the hands of the readers. Mr. Mahmud Ghazi, Investigator, has prepared a general index of names and important political terms which has been added at the end.

The system of transliteration of Arabic words in this book is the same as that adopted in the series of the English publications of the Institute.

M. Saghir Hasan Ma'sumi
*Director*

# INTRODUCTION

Ibne Taymiyah (661-728H./1263-1328A.C.) has written voluminously, and almost on every aspect of Islam. Much of his work is certainly lost, because of the colossal opposition he faced from the different classes of *'Ulama'* the Sunni the Raw and, the mystics and the *Ahl al-bid'ah* (innovators) whom he severely criticized, and also because of the constant political persecution to which he was subjected by the state. Also, much of his surviving work remains to be uncovered and published. However, what is published and available is immense in bulk as well as in value. The present inquiry is based on the available sources.

Most of the writing of Ibne Taymiyah is the consequence of his reaction to some wrong or evil affecting the general mass of the believer. He was most systematic and thought in his treatment of subjects. When he opposed a thesis, he attacked it from all directions possible; thus a book or tract written by him often contains very important and basic information, but the title may not indicate it, and hence the difficulty of assembling his total thought on a particular subject. In writing the present outline of his political thought I have made an effort to discover these sources as best as I could within reasonable time. The aim has been to concentrate on this specific topic, namely, the political thought of Ibne Taymiyah and a concise and objective estimate of it.

As regards the external sources about him there is

abundant material in the numerous histories; and literary and religious compilations[2]; but these with few exceptions, are entirely biographical and discuss his intellectual worth sparingly and uncritically; they have, therefore, given me little help in the present exploration. Even his exclusive biographies[3] do not enlighten us much.

His works are regarded as having been greatly instrumental in the rise of Wahhabism and reformist movements in general in modern Islam; this has given great incentive to their study by Muslim scholars and orient lists alike. Muslim writers, like Abu Zaharah,[4] Abul-Hasan 'Ali al-Nadwi[5] and Muhammad 'Umar al-Kukani,[6] have, however, largely produced books of eulogies (*Manaqib*) on the pattern of Ibne al-Jawzi, and there is no method in their work. In the West, the most serious and exhaustive study of Ibne Taymiyah has been made by Henri Laoust.[7] His *"Les Doctrines Socials at Politiques d' Ibne Taymiiyah"* is, indeed, very scientific and methodical, yet it is often tinged with the proverbial bias of orientalism.[8] Moreover, the book does not, in reality, primarily deal with the political and social doctrines; it is an encyclopedic work about Ibne Taymiyah, a critical analysis of all that he has written. The part that treats of his strictly political ideas does not comprise more than forty pages. Nevertheless, I have taken much help from it, particularly in the preparation of the last chapter of my book.

Ibne Taymiyah's principal political ideas about the state are found in his famous *Minhaj al-Sunnah al-Nabawiyah fi naqd Kalam al-Shiah wa 'l-Qadariyah* (The Path of the prophetic Sunnah in Refutation of the Belief of the Shi'aites and the Qadarites), written in refutation of Ibne al-Mutahhar al-Hilli's *Minhaj alKaramah fi ma 'rifat al-Imamah* (The Path of Nobility; on the knowledge of the Imamate). As its very name indicates, it is not a systematic work on politics, but a book of polemics;

necessarily, therefore, the political ideas are intricately interwoven with hair-splitting discussions on scholastic theology, Qur'anic and *Hadith* texts, jurisprudence, philosophy and mysticism. In reproducing his arguments, therefore, I have has to indicate the principal original context in which these arguments are set by Ibne Taymiyah, for if they were taken out of context they would become unintelligible.

His second important and exclusive work on political thought is *Al-Siyasah al-Shari'yah* (Political System of the Shari'ah, Government by the Shari'ah). It was written primarily about the Islamic rules of administration rather that politics, yet it contains very important ideas on political theory as well. But the terminology used in this book is after equivocal, and certainly it is deliberately so, for on many issued Ibne Taymlyah did not want to commit himself openly; so must be taken in translating the text for reference. For instance, he uses the word *Wilayah* in the sense of a responsible function, and not in the traditional sense of rulership or governorship. Thus a woman exercises *Wilayah* over the house and the children of her husband, a slave over the discussing the *Wilayah* in *Al-Siyasah al-Shar'iyah*, he is not referring to the *Imamate* or caliphate but to the different functions of state organization. Similarly, he frequently umara, but by '*Ulama*' he does not mean the scholars of religion alone; he includes others who possess some kind of expert knowledge that might be conducive to the upkeep and growth of the state. Again, when he is talking of the supremacy of the Shari'ah he does not necessarily mean state power, but also visualizes a situation in which the community might be called upon to act without the state-machinery.

The third important work of Ibne Taymiyah is *Al-Hisbah fi'l Islam*. Inspection of Public Morality in Islam. It deals with the application of the principle of ordering the good and forbidding the evil, especially with reference to state administration, and contains some important statements about the nature and functions of the state.

The *Kitab al-Ikhtiyarat al-Ilmiyah* (The Book of Independent Juridical Rulings) has also several notable discussions on political theory, especially on the judiciary.

Interspersed causal discussions on the meaning, purposes and functions of the state are to be found throughout his works, particularly in his tracts (*Rasa'il*) which number several hundred. Ibne Qayyim, the illustrious pupil of Ibne Taymiyah, has also written a book, *Al-Turuq al-Hukmiyah ft'l-Siyasah al-Shar'ah*, but it deals mainly with judicial procedure rather than with political theory or administration. His *I'lam al-uruwaq* is another work which contains important material on judicial theory, but it does not concern us here.

As for the method, I have tried to translate Ibne Taymiyah's ideas into the political language of today. It is, however, not always easy to do so, partly because of the change of historical circumstances and party because of the special genius of the Islamic civilization.

This brief critical study of one of the most important political thinker in Islam has an obvious modern relevance, for if Ibne Taymiyah's thought is studied carefully, it could remove much confusion from political thinking in the present day Muslim world, and help clear many issues which are troubling the Muslim mind today. If, therefore, the present study can provoke some independent and dynamic thinking, so urgently required in these times, it shall have been more that amply rewarded.

At the end I have given a complete bibliography of the known published and unpublished works of Ibne Taymiyah. The full index given after the bibliography will also be found useful for ready reference.

## Notes

1. Ibne Hajar, al-Kaminah fr a'yan al-mi'ah al-thaminah, Hyderabad (India), 1348 H., vol. 1, p. 144.

2. Ibne Rajab, Dhayl Tobaqat al-HanSbilah. Vol. I, p. 337; al-Dhahabl, Tadhkirat al-huffaz, Vol. 4, p. 278-279; Ibne Kathir, al-Bidayah wa'l-nihayah, vol. 14, p. 132-141; Ibne Shakir nl-KutubT, Fuwat al-Wafayto, Vol. 1. p. 35-45; al-Yafi'i, Mir'at al-Jinan. vol. 4, p 277-278; al-Shswkanf, al-Badr ai-Tail', vol. 1, p. 63-72, 'Umar Rida Kahhsiah, Mu'jam al-Mu'allifin, vol. 1, p. 261-262 etc.

3. Muhammad bin 'Abd al-Hedi, *al-'Uqud Al-Dwriyah; Mar'I al-Karami, al-Kawakib al-Durriyah fi mantiqib Ibne Taymiyah; TaqI al-din al-Subkl, al-Durrat al-Mudlyah fi al-radd'ala Ibne Taymiyah; Nu'man al-Alusi, Jila' al-'Aynayn bi Muhakamat al-Ahmadayn etc.*

4. Abu Zahrah, Ibne Taymiyah; Hayatuh wa'asruh, Cario, 1952.

5. Abu'l-Hasan 'Ali al-Nadwi, *Tarikh Da'wat wa 'Azimat* (in Urdu), *vol. 2 (Ibne Taymiyah), Lucknow, 1956.*

6. Muhammad *Yusuf Kokan 'Umari, Imam Ibne Taymiyah,* Lahore, 1960

7. Henri Laoust, *Les Doctrines Socials et Politiques d' Ibne Taymiyah,* Cairo, 1939.

8. A few examples of this bias would suffice. Making general remarks on Ibne Taymiyah's concept of state Laoust observes: "We shall see that the doctrines of Ibne Taymiyah, however, democratic they might be, do not conceive political organization except on the image of a religious and political oligarchy". "Les Doctrines, p. 202. Again, commenting on Ibne Taymiyah's recommendation to Muslims about the treatment of non-

Muslims Laoust remarks, "In addition to this distant and disdainful respect the Muslims have the first duty to maintain a sort of systematic aloofness from the Christians and the Jews in the midst of the community, "and to oppose systematically their way of thinking and acting", Ibid, p. 269.

9.  Al-Hili died in 726/1326'A.C.

# CHAPTER I

## LIFE AND CHARACTER OF IBNE TAYMIYAH

Taqi ad-din Ahmad Ibne Taymiyah was born in 661 H./ 1263 A.C., in Harran, in Syria, into a famous family of scholars and theologians. He was, however, only seven years old when Harran was attacked by the Mongols, and he had to flee away to Damascus along with his parents. In this journey, because of the great panic that had overtaken southern Syria, the family experienced immense hardship and suffering. This tragic event left a permanent stamp on the sensitive mind of young Ahmad. Thus when he grew up, his aversion to the Mongols also grew and he was instrumental in collecting big armies to fight against them, even though they had already embraced Islam. He had seen the evil and the tyranny they had spread, so he thought that even if they had become Muslims they were ac-tually rebels, and war against them was a religious duty.[2]

Taymiyah was the name of a clan; it is, however, not known whether this clan was Arab or non-Arab, most probably they were Kurds.[3] The Kurds were a sturdy and brave people and possessed great moral integrity and sharpness, qualities which were abundantly reflected in the character of Ibne Tay-miyah, although he was brought up in the serene and quiet atmosphere of scholars. He was, naturally, associated with the Kurdish people who in the sixth and seventh centuries of the Hijrah stood up as the main defenders of Islam and the Muslims, and bore the brunt of the attack by the Crusaders; indeed, it was they who broke the might of the Christian in vaders and paved the way for the Egyptian Mamluks to push the Crusaders back to Europe.[4]

Since his parents and relations had resettled in Damascus he got all his education there. His father, Shihab ud-din, was a noted teacher of *Hadith* and a renowned preacher in the central mosque of the city. His uncle Fakhr ad-din, too, was a reputed scholar and writer. Taqi ud-din bin Taymiyah was, therefore, educated in the school of his own father and in the scholarly tradition of his own house. He also benefited from other leading scholars in Damascus. His studies were not confined to the Qur'an, *Hadith* and *Fiqh;* he also studied mathematics, history and literature and mastered them all. He paid special attention to the Hanbalite Law, of which his father was an eminent exponent.

At this Juncture of history the Muslim world was on the retreat. The eastern lands were overrun and devastated by the Mongols; and in the west the Muslims were completely and finally ousted from Spain. Most of the scholars in these regions, therefore, fled away to safer places for protection. Cairo and Damascus were the two great centres and havens of peace where they flocked. Ibne Taymiyah's own parents and relations had taken refuge in Damascus, where they rose to prominence because of their devotion to Islamic learning. Thus, although the times were disturbed, they offered Ibne Taymiyah an excellent opportunity to learn from the multitude of *'Ulama'* of different schools whom fortune or misfortune had accidentally brought into the city.

The most important branch of study, to which Ibne Taymiyah devoted himself resolutely, was that of theology (*'Aqa'id*), and there were historical reasons for this. The

Ayyubids, who ruled over Syria and Egypt a little before the advent of Ibne Taymiyah, were staunch supporters of Ash'arism, they said: This is the *Sunnah* which must be followed and this is the path of religion which every one must walk. Besides, Ash'arism had already spread widely in the east and the west, and faced no opposition except from the Hanbalites, whose method of study in theology was the same as their method in the study of law (*Fiqh*) i.e. they derived the articles of faith from the Scriptural texts (nusus) in the same way as they derived the details of law from the texts, because religion in their opinion consisted in combining these two things. Anyone who followed the first method had also to follow the second method, i.e. to derive his theology also from the Qur'an and the *Sunnah*. For example, there are verses in the Qur'an relating to the attributes of God, which apparently resemble the attri-butes of creatures; in *Ahadith*, too, there are such statements. Now, the Hanbalites explained these passages according to their philological requirements, sometimes in a literal sense and sometimes in a figurative sense. On the other hand, the Ash'arites adopted the rational and logical method in explain-ing the principles of faith, because their leader, Abu'l-Hasan al-Ash'ari, was brought up as a Mu'tazilite, who had first mastered the method of the Mu'tazilah and then opposed them with their even argument and logic, the same method with which they had established themselves. Thus the method of the Ash⁴arites was the same as that of the Mu'tazilites, although they were opposed in their conclusions. This difference of approach led to a sharp conflict between the Ash'arites and the Hanbalites, and the latter were often accused of anthropo-morphism with regard to the attributes of God.

Ibne Taymiyah witnessed these intellectual disputes in the schools where he was educated; he acquired high proficiency in the subjects taught there, and became master of the techniques, the rational-philosophical and the traditional. (Just as al-Ghazzali had studied philosophy to destroy the work of the philosophers) so did Ibne Taymiyah study rational theo-logy to refute both the Mu'tazilah and the Asha'irah. By nature he was a man of perception, insight and deep under-standing; by education he disciplined his mind and became one of the most brilliant and consistent thinkers in Islam. Islam in itself is a consistent and coherent philosophy of life, so that no independent philosophy can develop within its fold. Consequently, the great thinkers in Islam have devoted their genius mainly to the exposition of this philosophy. Among these men Ibne Taymiyah is perhaps the most prominent; he is the one who presents the purest and most rational image of Islam. He takes his fundamentals from the Qur'an and the Sunnah and the practice of the Companions of the Prophet, and defends them stoutly with the weapons of rationalism and philosophy, as his opponents defend their theses. In short, his academic training was consummate for his age and for the work he was going to undertake in life. With this serious preparation he started his career, and influenced his generation deeply and became the most dynamic reformer of his age.

He had just completed his studies when his father died in 682 H./1283 A.C. He was then twenty-one years old. A year later he was appointed to the chair of *Hadith* which his father occupied in a number of leading *Madaris* in Damascus, and soon began to rival the fame of leading traditionists of the time, such as Ibne Daqiq al-'Id, Kamal ad-din al-Zimlikani and Shamsad-din al-Dhahabi.[5] He soon be-gan to teach and preach in the Central (Umayyad) Mosque and attracted increasingly large audiences, among whom were students, friends, adherents of different schools, his supporters and opponents. His name was frequently and reverently mentioned in the intellectual circles within the Mamluk dominions as well as outside. His lectures covered all subjects of Islamic learning, but their central theme was one: the revival of the spirit of the age of the Prophet and his Companions, when Islam was pure and was not contaminated by strange ideas and heretical beliefs. Since he was convinced that his view was in conformity with the beliefs and practice of the pristine Islam, he defended it with all his logic and marshalled in its favour powerful arguments based on his vast and intelligent study of the Qur'an, Sunnah, history, and other branches of learning, in a language that was extremely effective. But his struggle to revive Islam shorn of all accretions aroused both admiration and opposition. His followers and supporters were numerous but his enemies were not few. His admirers raised him to the status of the highest authority on *Ijtihad*, but his detractors pulled him down, and called him a mere mediocrity and even questioned his faith. There were indeed some people, who maintained the balance, yet the conflict was sharp and Ibne Taymiyah lived all his life in a state of serious commotion.

The chief causes of opposition to his views are said to be his short temper, his harsh expression and determined fight against his foes. There is, indeed, some truth in such state-ments, but these qualities were not inherent in him; they were the result of the bitter polemics in which he was involved with his contemporaries.[6] The men who opposed him belonged to the establishment mostly fighting for vested interests. Hence he was bitter when he knew that what he was trying to establish was the faith and practice of the virtuous early muslims (*Al-salaf al-salih*), and the really great scholars of the day recognized it to be so while his opponents were only defending selfish interests. His times were notorious for the spiritual acrobatics of the mystics, their extreme in-dulgence in heretical interpretations, absolute imitation (*Al-taqlid al-mutlaq*) in matters of belief and in the method of understanding, and in the acceptance of the rules of the *Shari'ah* and their derivation. For a man like Ibne

Taymiyah, who proclaimed freedom from all 'imitation' except that of the Qur'an, the Sunnah and the practice of the early Muslims, smooth sailing was impossible under these conditions, and, therefore, conflicts were inevitable, especially when his contemporaries, belonging to different sects saw that he was bent upon exposing their beliefs and opinions. His intellectual stature, linguistic attainments and polemical skill were universally recognized, but these very qualities also made him a man to be feared. His opponents took shelter behind the walls of their sectarianism and ignorance. But Ibne Taymiyah was not content with lecturing to his classes and to his audience in the Central Mosque; he also frequently gave legal opinions (*Fatawa*), which were written out in the form of books and tracts and were widely circulated. This was perhaps the principal cause of conflict with the other *'Ulama'* and the government, for these opinions, based on the Qur'an, the *Sunnah* and the practice of the pious early Muslims was often opposed to current beliefs and usages. They were frequently responsible for religious and social explosions in different regions. The result was that the *'Ulama'* and the government for more than forty years relentlessly persecuted Ibne Taymiyah, from the time he came into prominence until his very death. It should, however, he noted that he was not persecuted by the people at large but only by the higher officials, especially by the Hanafite judges of Damascus and Cairo, aided by certain interested noblemen. The masses of the people in Syria were his strong admirers and they supported him in most situations. Even in Egypt, the common people were opposed to him only during the early years of his persecution when they were not aware of his intellectual and moral qualities.

The political life of the country was mainly controlled by the Turkish Mumluk nobility, while the civil service, especially the judiciary, was entirely in the hands of the Arabs.

The jurists as a class were very powerful and exercised great influence on the day-to-day administration and effectively dominated the religious life of the people. As already indicated above, the three main Sunni schools of law had adopted the Ash'arite theology but the fourth school, the Hanbalites, opposed Ash'arism vehemently. Since Ibne Taymiyah was the chief spokesman of Hanbalism, a clash with the other schools was inevitable. Since, however, Ahmad bin Hanbal was a pupil of al-Shafi'i the Shafi'ites, maintained a soft heart for Ibne Taymiyah and did not approve or encourage his persecution.

The trouble began early when, in 698 H./1298/99 A.C., the people of Hamah asked him for a legal opinion (*Fatawa*) about the attributes of God mentioned in the Qur'an. He gave his opinion in the form of a tract, *Al-Risalah al-Hama-wiyah*, which at once sparked off the opposition of the fuqaha' headed by the Hanafite *Qazi* Jalal ad-Din of Damascus. Ibne Taymiyah was brought before a council of distinguished judges and jurists to defend the views expressed in the *Risalah*. There was a heated debate but Ibne Taymiyah won the day; the incident was a pointed indication to the great polemical battles, which were to follow.

These religious bickerings were, however, suddenly inter-rupted by the Mongol invasion of Syria in 699 H./1299/1300 A.C. The country was actually occupied by the enemy for some time, but they vacated it after a few months for military reasons. The Mongols however, entered Syria again and again and continued to press against the Mamluk Empire until they were finally routed in the battle of Shaqhab in 702 H./1302-3, A.C. When peace returned to the Mamluk dominions, however, the persecution of Ibne Taymiyah recom-mencec. There were a number of reasons for this[7].

1.    The Mongols were defeated and thrown out of the

country mainly because of the efforts of Ibne Taymiyah; after this event, therefore, he won great respect in the eyes of the people and the government alike. His popularity kindled the fire of jealousy in his opponents, who became more active in undermining his position.

2. The *'Ulama'* and *'Fuqaha'* were mostly stipendiaries of the state, so that those of them who enjoyed favour with the sultan exercised great influence on him in the appointment of the *'Ulama'* and the fixation of their stipends, Ibne Taymiyah, never joined the government service; he was content to remain a guide and a preacher and an effective teacher all his life. Because of this self-denial he was highly respected by the government and often consulted in the selection of the *'Ulama'* to preside over important educational institutions and to be appointed to high offices in the judiciary. For the same reason he was equally esteemed by the people, who reposed their faith in him and found their guidance in his leadership, submitted to his opinions and responded to his call (*Da'wah*). The other *'Ulama'* made little effort to qualify for this unique honour and only envied and tried to discredit him. Commenting on this issue, Ibne Kathir writes: "Among the jurists there was a group which was jealous of *Shaikh* Taqi ad-din, because of his distinguished position with the state, his exclusive role in commanding the good and forbidding the evil, the submission of the people to and their love for him, the great number of his followers, his defence of truth, his knowledge and his conduct."[8]

3. He was a sworn enemy of innovation; hence all the heretical sects were united against him, especially the Assassins, the Ahmadiyah and the Kisrawaniyin. He,

however, uprooted, most of them from their settlements and persuaded the state army to exterminate as many of them as possible. [9] We shall explain the real cause of this extreme bitterness further on in this chapter.

4.  He also waged a relentless war against the mystics; spoke and wrote incisively against their foremost leader (*Imam*) and philosopher, Muhiyy ud-din Ibne al-'Arabi; made a determined effort to counter his thought and opinions. He persuaded the rulers to put an end to their impostures and trickeries. This was the age not only of political but a general decline of the Muslims; in such times people are prone to believing in the efficacy of magic, legerdemain, miracles and all sorts of supernatural' possibilities. The decadence of Ibne Taymiyah's age carried all these evils with it. The mystics—the Sufis— were the foremost in exploiting these weaknesses of the people. Their mischief did not end there; they utterly perverted the Islamic faith and ghari'ah by inculcating the philosophy of pantheism (*Wahdat al-wujud*) and union (*Wahdat al-Shuhud*)[10] and asserted that the texts (*Nusus*) of the Qur'an and the *Sunnah* and the injunctions (*Ahkham*) have an external meaning and a hidden one; their *Shuyukh* (teachers) being the only ones to know the hidden one. These views had taken a firm grip over the minds of the ignorant masses, especially in Egypt, where Ibne Taymiyah's influence was not very powerful during the early years of his persecution. The Sufis were equally active in Syria, but Ibne Taymiyah had almost broken their cower there. The nobility in Cairo had, however, in their own interest, made an alliance with the mystics. The crowning event of this period is that poli-tical intrigues forced Sultan al-Nasir Ibne Qala'un to abdicate in 708 H./1308 A.C. in favour of al-Malik

al-Muzaffar Baybars al-Jashangir, who was a votary of *Shaikh* Nasr al-Manbiji, a great champion of the school of Ibne al-'Arabi. With the help of the state, therefore, the mystics started a great campaign to capture the conscience and obedience of the people, and aroused the determined hostility of Ibne Taymiyah.

5. It has already been noted that the Hanbalites formed one faction and all the other jurists and *'Ulama'* formed another, following Abu'l-yasan al-Agh'an and Abu Mansur al-Maturidi, in the definition and understanding of faith. When Ibne Taymiyah came on the scene, he set himself to defend the method of the Hanabalities. He denied that they were anthropomorphists (*Mujassimah*) or 'comparers' of God with man (*Mvshabbihah*), and asserted that they followed the Tradition (the Qur'an and the *Sunnah*) in understanding the faith (*'Aqa'id*) as well as the law (*Furu'*). And the high status and reputation that he enjoyed enabled him to strengthen their power and influence in the government and the country; this again provoked the other jurists to oppose and fight them.

6. Lastly, it must be noted that there certainly was vehemence in his manners and in his tongue. Sometimes when he was annoyed by the objections of his opponents or by the uproar that they created at some opinion expressed by him, he used very harsh language against them, such as, "this is sheer ignorance", "this is the result of lack of understanding," etc. His opponents were equally vocal, and a bitter conflict was, therefore, inevitable.

All these causes collectively constituted a formidable force against Ibne Taymiyah and subjected him to almost permanent persecution (*Mihnah*). A good deal of his life was spent in prison, where he wrote some of his important works. This perpetual conflict, his indomitable courage to fight against falsehood and heresy, and his frequent incarceration, combined with his rare intelligence, deep thinking, universal interest and total devotion to God, gave him a personality that was unique. Through study, fighting and suffering he developed a character that stood only for truth and that could dash against any evil, irrespective of the consequences. It is indeed difficult to give even a bare survey of his life in this introduction, yet it would greatly help us in understanding and analyzing his political thought if we depict here, however summarily, the main features of his personality and character.[12]

The foremost of his personal qualities was a powerful memory, which was the subject of universal recognition and praise in his day. A retentive memory is essential to learning, for it is the repository of basic information. The quality of a scholar is determined by the amount of this information and by the ability with which he can draw upon it in need. This was very commonly demonstrated in Ibne Taymiyah's daily lectures; meanings flowed down his tongue when he required them, without labouring and deliberating. This eloquence was hereditary in his house; his father was an excellent speaker; among his ancestors there were many renowned preachers (*Khutaba*), one of them was in charge of the Friday sermon in the central mosque of Baghdad, and his grandfather was a reputed author. He acquired this unique skill from extensive reading and memorizing the Qur'an and the entire corpus of the *Sunnah*, as well as from the frequent encounters and theological debates he had with his contemporaries. And when he was engaged in a debate he silenced his opponents easily with the great knowledge he possessed and with the singular spontaneity with which he could recall things from memory. His opponents were inferior to him in these qualities and therefore could not refute him except after long deliberation and consultation of the original sources. They indeed feared him on account of this quality in him; no one ever gained a victory over him in a dispute or argument. He was several times brought before the High Court at Damascus and the Supreme Court at Cairo but no charge could ever be established, nor could any one plead against him.

He deliberated over problems very seriously and deeply, sometimes devoting whole nights to the consideration of one single problem; and he would not leave it until he had solved it to his satisfaction. He considered the verses of the Qur'an, the traditions of the Prophet (P.B.U.H.) and the judgments of reason, and weighed them and compared them again and again till at last the truth emerged before him clearly. That is why he is regarded as one of the most critical and competent scholars who could derive rules and injunctions from traditions and the verses of the Qur'an.

Independence of thought was no less important a quality, which helped his mental development and built up his intellectual personality, and gave him superiority over his contemporaries. Whenever Ibne Taymlyah was faced with a problem or was asked a question he studied it in the light of the Qur'an, the *Sunnah* and the traditions ('athar) of the virtuous early Muslims. And whatever he found there he accepted it and invited others to accept it, not minding in the least whether the people supported or opposed him. He thus did not follow what the scholars of his day said or what the people believed, but depended on the results of his own inquiry into the pristine teaching of Islam. For instance, from his studies he found that there was no evidence in the *Shar'* for appealing to the Prophet for help, so he declared his finding unhesitatingly and suffered grievously on account of it but did not retract his opinion. This in fact was the quality which helped him in the revival (*Tajdid*) of Islam, because, while others saw things with borrowed reason, this great reformer and thinker saw with his own vision and was influenced by nothing but the Qur'an, the *Sunnah*, the companions of the Prophet, and some of the Successors. This is how he cleared away the dust of later accretions, which had settled over Islam through the course of the ages.

His character was clean and untarnished by selfish desires; his sole aim in life was to know the religion and explain it to the people. It is in the nature of reality that it bestows its light on the sincere person and makes him see things straight without deviation. Nothing deludes reason and seduces it from the right path mope than selfishness and personal ambition; such an attitude warps reason and makes it impossible to penetrate into reality. Not so with Ibne Taymiyah; God had given him utmost sincerity. He sought the truth sincerely in the name of God and found it, and devoted himself whole-heartedly to the service of religion, and God made his name echo through his age before he died. All the succeeding generations have clearly found this sincerity in his writings and works.

Ibne Taymiyah was above all a brave man, and with the quality of bravery, he combined the two subsidiary qualities of patience and endurance. These qualities were the natural complement of his independence of thought. This was reflected in all aspects of his life, and he was not content with sitting in his cloister or mosque and giving lectures to his pupils or engaging himself in literary discussions. Following the *Sunnah* of the early Muslims he was a soldier and commander of the armed forces when the existence of the community (*Ummah*) was in danger, and in the battle-field his bravery was superior to that of the other generals because it had originated from the sincerity of heart and devotion, and not from any military training. [13]

His literary courage was equally great, and the cause of most of his persecutions. As has been pointed out already, he never hesitated from pronouncing the truth in the face of most stiff opposition from the *'Ulama'*, the nobility and the sultan. He did not abandon his position, even if at times the masses were infuriated against him. And when he was persecuted for his bold opinions and imprisoned, he neither regretted nor retracted, but endured cheerfully and bravely. He continued to write even in jail, not wanting to waste one moment of his life in idleness. And when he was completely deprived of the means of studying and writing, he bade farewell to this unkind world. [14]

His unusual insight and intelligence could be seen in every problem to which he addressed himself. When he saw the Mongols he at once realized that they were not the same fighting machine that they were when they started their invasion of Syria, for indulgence in luxury and sophisticated living had corroded them from the inside. Ibne Taymiyah saw that they over-awed their enemies with their past achievements and not with their present strength, and firmly predicted that the Egyptian and Syrian forces would certainly vanquish the Mongoss.[15] History unfolded itself as he had predicted. Similarly, whenever he spoke before a gathering he intuitively knew how to bring them round to his opinion. This quality is indispensable to persons who embark upon a reform of communities and nations; Ibne Taymiyah was singularly gifted with this quality.

Furthermore, God had endowed him with a personality that impressed everyone who met him; one always felt that one was standing in the presence of a great man. It was this awe that often saved him from the mischief of the common people who were frequently incited against him by his enemies. He was often threatened with physical harm but never took any precaution to defend himself and none ever dared to attack him. The jurists were very bitter against him but were terribly afraid to face him. He met the Sultan in Cairo several times and always addressed him in a frank and effective language. Similarly, when he met the Mongol Emperor, Qazan Khan, he spoke to him in the harshest language: his followers thought that he would be beheaded immediately, but the Emperor was simply overawed by the scholar and treated him with politeness and dignity.[16]

The combination of all these qualities in a single personality is rare in history. Yet Ibne Taymiyah was not altogether without a serious drawback; both in writing and speech he often developed an undesirable heat and stiffness, which sometimes made him appear personal rather than, objective. In his arguments against the *'Ulama'* he was in the right, yet he did not hesitate to call them ignorant and stupid when they refused to accept his logic. Surely, it does not behave a great thinker to abuse his opponents in this way. Ibne Taymiyah's opponents claimed that they followed the *Sunnah* and that he was an innovator. He, on his part, asserted that he was the champion of the *Sunnah* and his opponents were its violators. This naturally led to a clash, which generated heat on both sides. Ibne Taymiyah felt that he was in the right, and, therefore, answered the prejudice and malice of his opponents with harsh words, but a dignified silence would have been more effective on these occasions. It must be stressed, that this defect, however serious it may be could not detract much from the qualities of this great man. But it is a fact that a man of such exceptional merit cannot live in peace in any age. Ibne Taymiyah's lot was no better; most of the jurists and *'Ulama'* of his age were extremely jealous of him and harassed and persecuted him as often as they could; he died in prison in 728 H./I328 A.C.[17]

So far we have tried to delineate Ibne Taymiyah's character in general, now we shall discuss briefly the historical circumstances, which had a profound effect on his thinking, especially his political ideas. He was born in the Mamluk empire, which composed the present-day Egypt, Syria, Lebanon and Palestine. This was the only great power in the Muslim world of that period. To the east of this Empire all the Muslim lands had been conquered and occupied by the Mongols. By the time of Ibne Taymiyah the Mongols had embraced Islam, but only in name; for their devastation of the world of Islam and its peoples continued unabated.[18] In all other parts of the world where the Muslims lived they were divided into small potentates and continually engaged in fighting among them-selves. Islam at the moment faced three grave dangers: the Crusaders, the Mongols and internal dissensions.[19]

After the battle of Yarmuk, during the reigns of Abu Bakr (R.A.) and 'Umar (R.A.), the Muslims rapidly occupied Syria and Egypt, and soon became the political masters of western Asia. Later, the Umayyad and 'Abbasid Empires grew so extensive and powerful that the Byzantine Empire almost completely shrank away from Africa and Asia and was permanently kept at bay. But when the great Muslim Empires were reduced to small states and the Muslims were involved in their internal problems and their might was wasted in internecine feuds, the Byzantines availed of this opportunity and started to take revenge on Islam. They thought they had a juridical claim to the provinces they had lost to the Muslims in Asia and Africa. It was, therefore, their right as well as their duty to liberate these areas. This war of revenge they called the Crusade-fight for the freedom and Protection of the Holyland of Palestine, containing the Holy Sepulchre and other remains of jesus Christ— and incited the might and fanaticism of entire Europe to help them in this 'sacred' cause. The Crusaders marched into

Syria and Palestine in great hordes, massacred the Muslims, took them captives, perpetrated most inhuman crimes in the conquered areas and established a number of small States on the Mediterranean coast, under the protection of France and other European powers. When the Crusades started in 1095 A.C. the Muslim world was, politically, in a virtual state of disintegration; the 'Abbasid Caliph in Baghdad was a mere puppet in the hands of the Saljuqs; the Saljuq empire was itself divided into a number of potentates perpetually fighting among themselves; the Fatimids in Egypt had allied themselves with the Crusaders; [21] North Africa (*Al-Maghrib*) wars groaning under the tyranny of the Muwahhidun, who had no interest in eastern Islam; and the Muslims in Spain were only waiting for their final liquidation. The Mamluks of Syria and Egypt faced by the Atabeks of Mawsil and of the later Crusades the fury of the first Crusades. This latter drama took place in the time of Ibne Taymiyah. The determined effort of united Christian Europe to conquer Palestine, Syria and Egypt— traditional lands of Islam— the total inability of the 'Abbasid Caliph to meet the challenge, the general disintegra-tion of the Saljuq empire on the eve of the Crusades, the utter helplessness of the Muslim world to stop the advance of the Cross, the great havoc, plunder and massacre carried out in these lands by the Crusaders, the treachery of the Fatimids, the spectacular rise of the Atabeks— the Zangids and the Ayyubids— and the turning of the tables in favour of Islam— all this had a tremendous influence in shaping Ibne Taymiyah's political views.

Ibne Taymiyah was born five years after the sack of Baghdad by the Mongols under Hulagu Khan. The fall of the 'Abbasids was neither an incidental affair, nor the mere end of a dynasty; it stands as one of the most fateful events in the history of Islam, and marks the final collapse of Muslim power and the complete supremacy of the Mongols in the East. With the fall of Baghdad the whole of the Muslim world plunged into darkness and despair, nobody could conceive a greater calamity. The Mongols got a clear charter to march across the land with fire and sword.[22] People in large numbers fled away to Syria and Egypt to escape massacre. But after consolidating themselves in Iraq the Mongols advanced upon Syria, of course, intending to bring western Islam also under their heels. Even the apparently crushing defeat inflicted on them by the Mamluks, at *'Ayn Jalut*, in 658 H.[23] proved no deterrent to them. They continued their pressure with increased intensity, and gradually occupied most of eastern Syria. It was one of these campaigns that compelled Ibne Taymiyah's parents to abandon their home-city, Harran, for Damascus with their children and relations; he was then only six years old.

One far-reaching result of the Mongol invasion was that the political integrity of the Muslim world was completely shattered, and utter chaos prevailed allround for a number of years. In 659 H./1261 A.C., however, al-Zahir Baybares restored the Caliphate in Cairo by recognizing al-Mustansir Billah, one of the surviving 'Abbasid princes, as the Caliph of Islam. This Caliphate was in mere name, the real authority being wielded by the Mamluk sultans themselves. But it helped to maintain the historical fiction that politically and spiritually the Muslim world was one because the Caliph was supposed to be the vicegerent of the Prophet (P.B.U.H.). Moreover, the Caliph invested the Mamluk sultan with real authority, so that the sultan obtained the juridical right to proclaim suzerainty over all the Muslim princes and *Umra'*. This unity and this right were urgently required to defend the Muslims against the Mongols and the Crusaders both.

The Mamluks established an absolute hereditary rule, yet Ibne Taymiyah saw in them the only hope and, therefore, regarded them as defenders of the faith. That is why he gave them his whole-hearted support and was prepared even to overlook grievous errors committed by them.[24] This strange situation influenced his political thinking deeply, and compelled him to make certain drastic changes in evolving the concepts of State and government.

The internal dissensions, which influenced his political thinking, were no less serious than the external factors we have just discussed. The great empire of the Saljuqs fell to Pieces in 1092 A.C. with the death of Malik Shah. Thereafter the entire dominion of the 'Abbasid Caliphate was divided into a number of Saljuq and Turkish princes who fought against one Another continually, and weakened the over-all war potential of the Muslim world. This situation was one of the immediate factors, which emboldened the European Crusaders to attack Palestine. And this was the state of affairs when the Mongols fell upon the 'Abbasid caliphate and tore it to shreds.

But the greatest disruptive force in the fourth, fifth and sixth centuries of the Hijrah was Shi'ism. The rise of the Fatimids in 297 H./909 A.C., in North Africa, and the establishment of the Fatimid Caliphate in Fustat in 361 H./972 A.C., the capture of power at Baghdad, in 334 H./946 A.C. by the Buwayhids, and then the emergence of the Batimyah and the Qaramitah rent the world of Isalm asunder from end to end. It is an open fact of history that the Buwayhids imposed a Shi'ite regime on the Sunnite Caliphate in Baghdad and destroyed the whole social and political structure of society, and stubbornly prevented the Caliph from helping the Muslims in Syria when the Byzantines attempted to reconquer their lost provinces in the east in the tenth century.[25] It is equally well-known how the Qaramitah, an extremist Isma'ilite sect, basing their faith on a system of communism, formed themselves into strong bands of marauders and ravaged Yaman, Iraq, Syria and Khurasan, during the tenth and eleventh centuries, and drenched the whole area with blood, and carried away the Black Stone from the Ka'bah in 930 A.C.[26] Writing about the Assassins, a modern historian says: "Their secret organization, based on Isma'ilite antecedents, developed an agnosticism which aimed to emancipate the initiate from the trammels of doctrine, enlightened him as to the superfluity of Prophets and encouraged to believe nothing and dare all[27]". The Assassins and the Fatimids in Egypt rendered most valuable help to the Crusaders and constituted the most serious internal danger to the Muslims.[28] Finally it was a Shi'ite al-'Alqami, the grand vizier of al-Musta'sim, who invited Huiaku to attack Baghdad.[29]

After the Mongols had conquered the whole of the eastern Caliphate, the Shi'ites entered into their service in large numbers and completed the work of destruction. They won such rapid influence in the Mongol court that within a few decades their masters had to embrace Shi'ism. And these early Shi'ite Mongol emperors were extremely bigoted, particularly Uljayta Khan, for whom Ibne al-Mutahhar al-Hilli wrote his *"Minhaj al-Karamah fi ma'rifat al-itnamah."*[30] This book is a complete distortion of Islam and its early history. It was to refute this that Ibne Taymiyah wrote his famous *"Minhaj al-Sunnah al-Nabawiah fi naqd Kalam al-Shi'ah wa'l-Qadariyah"*

All these factors collectively had a tremendous impact on the mind of Ibne Taymiyah and went a long way in shaping and determining his political concepts. This also, incidentally, explains why his ideas arc found mostly scattered in his polemical writings, and not in his principal work on political science, *Al-Siyasah al-Shar'iyah.*

### Notes:

1.    Muhammad bin Shakir al-Kutubi, Fawat al-Wafayat, Cairo 1951, vol. I, p. 62.

2.  Ibne 'Abd al-Hadi, al-'Uqud al-durriyah, Cairo 1938 A.C., p. 120. This fatwa (legal opinion) of *jihad* is an important document in which Ibne Taymiyah establishes conclusively, in the light of the Qur'an and Sunnah, that the Mongols were not Muslims, although they had nominally embraced Islam, and that war against them was a religious obligation. This fatwa was occasioned by the reluctance of many ulama, to permit the Muslims to fight against the Mongols on the plea that the latter had entered the fold of Islam.

3.  Abu Zuhrah, Ibne Tayniyah, Cairo 1962, p. 18.

4.  Ibid., p. 19.

5.  Ibid., p. 94.

6.  Ibid., -pp. 49-53.

7.  Ibne Kathir, al-Bidayah wa'1-nihayah, vol. 14, p. 37.

8.  Ibid., p. 36,. Ibne 'Abd al-Hadi, pp. 181-83.

9.  Wahdat al-Shuhud is the opposite of pantheism. Some sufis believe that the love and sincerity of the creature for the Creator can unite it with Him. This state of the soul they call effacement or the dissolution of the mortal self into the immortal self of God.

10. Ibne Kathir, vol. 14, p.

11. Abu Zuhrah, pp. 96-110.

12. Ibid., p. 105.

13. Ibne Kathir, vol. 14, p. 136.

14. Ibne Kathir, vol. 14, p, 28.

15. Ahmad bin Hajar, al-Durar al-Kaminah f a'yan al-mi'ah al-thaminah, Hyderabad 1949, vol. 4, p. 154; Saf. al-din al-Hanaf, al-Qawl al-jali fi tarjamat al-Shaykh Taqi uddin bin Taymiyah al-Hambali, Bulaq 1881, pp. 162-3.

16. Ibne Kathir, vol. 14, p. 135.

17. Ibne 'Abd al-Hadi, p. 121.

18. Ibne al-Athir, Tarikh al-Kamil, Cairo 1873, vol. 12. p. 147.

19. Rene Grousset, Histoire des croisedes, Paris 1934, vol. I, pp. v, vi, XVIII.

20. Ibne al-Athir, vol. 10, p. 94, Ibne Taymiyah, Minhaj vol. 3, p. 244, In 1163 A.C. the Fatimid caliph made a formal alliance with Amory, the Christian King of Jerusalem and a vassal of France. The idea was to push the forces of Nur ud-din Zangi in Syria from three directions, from the east, from the west and from the northern sea-cost. The struggle continued until 1169 A.C., when Salah ud-din, the famous general of Nur ud-din, liquidated the Fatimid caliphate and occupied Egypt on behalf of his master. If the alliance had perchance materialized it would have been disastrous for the world of Islam. (Rene Grousset, vol. 2, pp. 443-533).

21. The rosy pictures of these conquests painted by Shi'ite historians of the Mongol court, like Mirkhwand in his Rawdat al-Safa' and Rash'd al-din Fad! Allah in his Tarikh Mubarak-e-Ghazni, are wholly untrue and sheer forgery. These writers themselves admit that the Mongol hordes even after embracing Islam, often wrought great bloodshed and wide-spread havoc in the Muslim lands of western Asia.

22. Ibne Kathir, vol. 13, 220-21.

23. Abu Zuhrah, p. 141.

24. Rene Grousset, vol. Im p. VII. The author further comments; "In reality the Buwayhids had well decided never to cross the Euphrates: the Iranian dissent, the devastation of the caliphate by the Iranian princes left the Syrian Islam to its own resources."

25. Miskawayh, Tajaribal-Umam, ed. Amedroz, vol. I, p. 201; Ibne al-Athir, vol. 8, pp. 513-14; art. "Karmatians", Encyclopaedia of Islam; Phillip K. Hitti, History of the Arabs, pp. 441-5.

26. Phillip K. Hitti, p. 446.

27. Ibne al-Athir.vol. 10, p. 94.

28. Ibne Kathir, vol. 13, p. 201-2; Mir Khwand, Teheran 1932, vol. 5, pp. 237-38, 250; Abu 'l-Fida', Tarikh, vol. 3, pp. 1934.

29. Ibne Taytniyah, Minhaj vol. I, p. 1.

# CHAPTER II

## ORIGIN AND NATURE OF THE STATE

The Qur'an abounds in references to power and authority in different contexts, but gives no indication as to the defini-tion of an ideal state.[1] The words *Khalifah, Khulfa'* and many other politically charged terms do occur in the Book; however, they, only refer to the possibility of political power being realized by the Muslims in the world, and do not prescribe any political principles as part of the fundamentals of religion for organizing a state. The *Sunnah* is equally silent on the issue. And this explains why the immediate successors of the Prophet (P.B.U.H.) had to adopt different principles of political organization.

The first question, therefore, in this inquiry arises as to how the idea of the state originated in Islam. Muslim thinkers have raised this problem in a different form, namely: Is the institution of the *Imamah* (the political authority) a religious obligation? All the political controversies in Islam have arisen around this question. For example, the orthodox Sunnite view, as given by al-Iji, declares, "the *Imamah* is not one of the fundamentals of faith and religious practice, as the *Shi'ah*tes believe; but according to us it is one of the details (*Fura'*) connected with the acts of the believers, because we think the appointment of the *Imam* is enjoined on the *Ummah* by *al-sama'* (tradition)".[2] Tradition comprises the Qur'an and the *Sunnah* and includes *Ijma'* (consensus). Clarifying this definition, al-Iji says: "We accept this argument for two reasons, First, because the Muslims, in the earliest era after the death of the Prophet, were agreed not to allow any time to be free of a <u>Kh</u>alifah or Imam, And, secondly, because the *Imamah* is instituted to ward off expected harm, and to ward off expected harm is binding on men, by consensus, if they have the ability to do so. In other words, we know that the Lawgiver (the Prophet) has given laws about practical matters, marriage, *Jihad* (Holy war), punishment of crimes and compensations, and about the public status of the symbols of the *Shara'* relating to 'Ids and Fridays, and that the benefits of all this accrue to mankind in this world as well as in the hereafter. But this purpose cannot be realized without an *Imam*, appointed in place of the Lawgiver, to whom all may refer in case of dispute."[3]

This particular statement of the Sunnite political theory, though very late, faithfully represents the orthodox classical school. . In this enunciation we find first, that the origin of the state is not traceable in the Qur'an and the *Sunnah*. This is precisely the reason why sharp differences arose about the meaning and necessity of the *Imamah* in early Islam, Secondly, 'it is to be noted that the argument of "religious necessity" is nothing but the rationalistic theory of the state developed by the Mu'tazilah. But what strikes one most is that the Muslim thinkers have, as a rule, made no systematic sociological app-roach to this problem. Ibne <u>Kh</u>aldun (808 H./1406 A.C.) remains a rare exception; in this he is neither preceded nor followed by anyone else. The Muslim philosophers, like al-Farabi, Ibne Miskawayh, Ibne Rushd and others, did come to the issue in a more naturalistic speculative manner, but they were so much pre-occupied with reconciling the theory of *Nubuwwah* to the Greek and neo-Platonic theories of knowledge that they produced nothing tangible that could be assimilated into the categories of Islamic political thought.

Further, giving an exact definition of the *Imamah*, al-Iji says: "[It] is the General State, governing affairs of religion and of the world; but it would be better if it is said: it means representing the Prophet in establishing the religion."[4] The concept deen (religion) includes many other facts— such as the *zakat* (Poor-due); yet the author is anxious to exclude "worldly affairs" from the definition. In fact, all standard definitions of the Sunnite theory from al-Ash'ari (330 H./942 A.C.) to Shah WaliyAllah (1176 H./1762 A.C.) are couched in similar language. The inference, or rather the result is that the Sunnite thinkers take no interest in the theoretical study, e.g. the natural evolution of the state, and do not inquire at all into many important aspects of it, like sovereignty, fundamental rights, principle of resistance, etc., and their ideas often seem to be incoherent and irrational.

The Mu'tazilite view of the problem is entirely opposed to the Sunnite; in general, it holds that the necessity of the *Imamah* is proved by reason. That is, the obligatoriness of the institution of the *Imamah* is discovered by our reason and not revealed to us by God. This controversy is ably illustrated by al-Shahrastani (548 H./1153 A.C.) who remarks: "The Sunnites say that all obligations are based on tradition (*Sama'*) and all learning on reason (*'Aql*); and reason does not render anything good or bad, nor does it make any demand or create any obligation, while tradition does not inform, that is, does not create knowledge but creates obligation."[4] According to the Mu'tazilah, therefore, all that is demanded by reason is obligatory; and since God (Providence: *al-Mun'im*) has endowed us with reason, thankfulness is due to Him even before the advent of the *Shari'ah*. This, thankfulness amounts, among other things, to recognizing the necessity of the *Imamah* even before the message of the Prophet was received.[5] When the Sunnites say that the institution of the *Imamah* is demanded by *ijma'*, they mean that there is no *Nass* (text) for it in the Qur'an or the *Sunnah*, but the general spirit of the *Shari'ah* makes it an absolute imperative, because the Companions of the Prophet, before making arrangements for his burial, agreed unanimously to elect an *Imam*. Moreover, the *Ummah*, they say, has in no period of history ever decided to remain without an *Imam*; on the eontrary, it has always insisted to have an *Imam* even if he were unjust and wicked. It is clear, however, that this argument of *Ijma'* is based on reason. But the Sunnites answer that *Ijma'* is nothing but an opinion derived from the general understanding of the *Shari'ah* and is not the result of absolute speculation. As against this the Mu'tazilite position is that the principles of the State are discovered by reason alone, without reference to the *Shari'ah*.

The difference between the two views is vital, because a function that is not demanded by the *Shari'ah*, but is only based on reason, carries wide latitude for interpretation and adjustment. But despite this freedom the Mu'tazilah were not able to develop and elaborate anelaborate rational theory of the State, and in practice fell back to the position of the *Ahl al-Sunnah wa'l-Jama'ah* (people of the *Sunnah* and of the Community). And the idea of the necessity of the *Imam* assumes so much importance with them that Abu Bakr al-Asamm (c. 200 H./815 A.C.) reports: "Wasil (131 H./748 A.C.) maintained that the community exists only if it is unanimous as to the election of the *Imam*."[6] This opinion is obviously directed against the *Shi'ah*tes, because it is known that the *Ummah* was not agreed on the *Imamah* of 'Ali. Notwithstanding this, it strongly corroborates the Sunnite view that the *Imamah* is a religious necessity.

But with all this emphasis on the rational necessity of the *Imamah* the Mu'tazilah can visualize a situation in which the community (*Ummah*) can live without an *Imam*. Higham al-Fuwati (c. 218 H./1043 A.C.), one of the great Mu'tazilites, says, "If the community has reached an accord, and refrained from injustice and corruption, then it requires an *Imam*, to govern it; but if it transgresses and sins and kills the *Imam*, the *Imamah* cannot be instituted for anyone in these conditions."[7] But another famous Mu'tazilite, al-Asamm, holds the contrary view on the issue and says: "If people refrain from mutual tyranny they certainly require no *Imam*."[8] In fact with the exception of the Rawafid all schools of opinion are agreed "it is permitted that the earth may have no *Imam* until one is instituted under proper conditions."[9] This view is, for example, supported by the orthodox Sunnite al-Iji (756 H./1355 A.C.), "If they [the Muslims] do not institute the *Imam*, because it is impossible to do so, and because there is none to fulfil the conditions of the *Imamah*, this does not amount to abandoning the obligation, since the obligation does not exist under these conditions,"[10]

There are two schools of thought among the Mu'tazilah: (1) the School of Basrah and (2) the School of Baghdad. The Baghdad School is heavily inclined towards *Shi'aism*.[11] Their ideas on this issue will be included in the *Shi'ah* view, which we shall discuss shortly. The Mu'tazilite opinions which we have just discussed mainly pertain to the Basrah School, led by Wasil, al-Asamm, Hisham al-Fuwati, al-Jubba'i (303 H./ 915 A.C.) and his son Abu Hashim (321 H./933 A.C.).[12] The Basris generally support the Sunni stand,[13] although, of course, from a different point of view. The similarity is only formal, because the difference between the two approaches is basic. Moreover, when the Sunni theory was finally enunciated y Ash'ari, namely, that the necessity of the *Imamah* is established by the *Shari'ah* and then supported by reason, it completely reversed the Mu'tazili view.[14]

The Shi'ah also rejected reason as unsatisfactory and

said that the *Imamah* is the "*Lutf*" (grace) of Allah towards His people.[15] "And all that brings the believers near to obedience and keeps them away from sins is technically termed lutf. From this it is clear that the necessary and effective appointment of the *Imam* is a grace (of God) towards the realization of the obligatory responsibilities."[16] So the Shi'ah stand is: since God is the absolute ruler of the universe and has placed certain responsibilities on mankind for the good of His creation, it is, therefore, incumbent on Him to appoint someone (an *Imam*) to enforce His law and execute His decrees, because He does not look into all these affairs personally.[17]

The Khariji position in this controversy is very interesting. They attach no importance to the question whether the *Imamah* is ordained by reason or revelation. They are interested only in the application of the *Shara'*. If the community without the help of a superior authority can apply this law there is no need for an *Imam*. The Khawarij as a whole "allow that there may be no *Imam* in the world at all."[19] And the *Najdat* are agreed that the people have no need for an *Imam* at all; for it is their duty to do justice to one another. But if they see that this aim cannot be realized without an *Imam*, who may compel them to do justice, and they actually appoint one, it is permitted."[20] In fact, the presence and absence of the *Imam* are both justified according to the extent of observance and sanctity of moral values prevailing in the community at a particular time.[21]

In actual practice, the Khawarij, too, were forced to recognize the necessity of the state, to elect a caliph and to set up a government, however rudimentary and predatory in nature. Their samous slogan, "There is no rule but of the God", at first sight suggest that there may be no government; but what they really mean is that all matters must be decided only by reference to the Qur'an.[22] So their acceptance of the Caliphate is not doctrinal but born out of practical necessity.

In this controversy Ibne Taymiyah agrees with the majority of the *Ummah* "that the administration of the affairs of men is one of the greatest obligations of religion; rather the fact is that religion cannot exist without it."[23] But he does not follow the usual method of arguing from *Ijma'*. He has two other arguments to put forward:

1)   The nature of the religon (*Deen*) demands that there must be an organized social order where it may function properly. This is apparently the argument of the Mu'tazilah. But whereas they take their authority from reason, Ibne Taymiyah takes his cue from the nature of religion itself and combines it with the sociological argument, later on developed in great detail by Ibne Khaldun. He says, "The good of mankind cannot be realized except in a social order, because everyone is dependent on others, and society requires, indispensably, someone to direct it."[24] This argument is developed in greater detail in another place where he observes:

"The good of mankind cannot be realized in this world or in the hereafter, except in society and by cooperation and mutual help. Cooperation and mutual help are required to cultivate the good and to ward off harm. And it is for this reason that it is said: man is social by nature. And when men are organized it is certain that they will be faced with things which they will do to realize their good and with things which they will not do because they breed evil. And they will submit to the commander who upholds these aims and to the prohibitor who prohibits these evils. So the whole of mankind must submit to some commander or prohitbitor."[25]

He goes on to say that all the people of the world,

whether they have a revealed religion or an unrevealed one, and even if they have no religion at all, obey their kings in matters, which bring good to them in this world. The people of the entire world are agreed that human action is always accompanied by its moral consequences in this life. No one questions that the ultimate result of tyranny is pernicious and the final consequence of justice is commendable. "It is for this reason that it has been reported: Allah helps the just government even if it is infidel, and does not help the tyrannical government even if it is Muslim."[26]

The influence of Hellenistic thought and al-Faribi, as Rosenthal remarks, is here undeniably obvious;[27] yet these ideas are not particularly the outcome of Greek genius. They are the common heritage of mankind; all human societies have been conscious of them before Aristotle and after him. So far as Muslim philosophers are concerned, Greek thinkers undoubtedly influenced them. But even if they had no knowledge of the Greek legacy, they would have independently arrived at these ideas because the sense of the *Jama'ah* and collective responsibility is so strong in the fundamentals of Islam that no great effort was required to discover and formulate them. That is why they are much more eloquently expounded by Ibnee Sina (428 H./ 1037 A.C.), al-Ghazzali (505 H./1111 A.C.), Miskawayh (421 A.H./1030 A.C.) and Ibne Khaldun than by Aristotle and Plato. It must also be borne in mind that the idea of the state as an emphatic expression of the will of the *Ummah*, and a necessary instrument to implement its ideology, did not exist among the Greeks. The concept of the *Ummah* bound by the supreme law of an allpervading *Shari'ah* is exclusively Islamic. Here, Ibne Taymiyah who was well read in Greek philosophy, must have been influenced by it, but not as strongly as Rosenthal suggests. The nature and content of the Islamic religion were sufficient to inspire him with the sociological approach to the theory of the state; for the way in which he develops this methodology to explain the political philosophy of Islam is much more profound than that of his predecessors.

Ibne Taymiyah believed that when it is proved that the state is a necessity, the best thing is to accept the authority of Allah and His Prophet (P.B.U.H.); for Allah orders good and forbids evil, and permits the use of clean things and prohibits the use of unclean ones. Acceptance of all this, he holds, is obligatory on all mankind, and these functions cannot be realized without power and authority.[28] "Similarly, all the obligations of religion, like *Jihad*, justice, arrangement for *Hajj* and *'Id* and Friday congregations, extending help to the oppressed and the enforcement of the penal provisions of the Qur'an, cannot be fulfilled without power and authority."[29] To establish this authority Allah has 'revealed the Book and created iron', as He says; "We have sent Our Prophets with the clear signs and revealed to them the Book and the Balance so that (with their help) the people may establish justice; and We have sent down (created) iron, which embodies great power and profit for mankind."[30]

These requirements and this verse of the Qur'an, therefore, prove the imperative nature of the state. Hence Ibne Taymiyah depends neither on *Ijma'* nor on the theory that the state is required as a defensive measure against harm and injustice. He takes the direct view that it is needed to achieve the positive aims enumerated above. In fact, he is so much possessed with the idea of the necessity of authority that he gives admiring credence to the sayings: "Indeed the sovereign is the shadow of God on earth",[31] and that "sixty years of rule under a tyrant *Imam* are better than a night without an *Imam*."[32] Like the earlier Muslim jurists and theologians Ibne Taymiyah, too, is haunted by the fear of anarchy and disintegration of the Muslim community, and, therefore, recommends that even the worst form of tyranny may be preferred to disorder and chaos.

2)   The other argument is based on the *Sunnah*. When the necessity of the state has been established by the Book and by sociological arguments, it is no longer difficult to see how "the Prophet (P.B.U.H.) has ordered his *Ummah* to appoint their administrators to govern their affairs and has ordered the administrators to return the trusts to whom they are due and to adjudicate with justice when they sit in judgement on them."[33] For the Prophet (P.B.U.H.) have said, "When three of them go out on a journey they should appoint one of them as their leader."[34] Now if the smallest party of men was ordered to appoint an *Amir* for itself it follows a fortiori that "bigger parties must do the same."[35] "Therefore, the institution of the *Imarah* (*Imamah*) is obligatory, religiously and from the viewpoint of seeking nearness to Allah."[36] And if a ruler accepts his job as a religious duty and fulfils the obligations to the best of his ability, this would be esteemed a most virtuous act.[37]

In short Ibne Taymiyah thinks that the establishment of the *Imamah* is a doctrinal as well as a practical necessity, and conforms to the classical view of al-Ash'ari and others, but be arrives at his conclusions from a fresh line of approach. He does not go into the details of dogmatic theology and juridical hair splitting, but strongly feels that the Prophet had not come only to preach and give a few rules of conduct. Rather he came to create a social order on the basis of certain divinely inspired, permanent and universal principles. These principles are enshrined in the Book of Allah. The true religion must possess "the guiding book and the helping sword" (*Al-kitab al-hadi wa'l-sayf al-nasir*).[38] This very idea, in a highly accentuated from, appears at another place where Ibne Taymiyah says: "Allah has made the benefits of religion and the benefits of this world depend on the rulers, irrespective of whether the *Imamah* is one of the fundamental facts of religion or not."[39]

Here an apparent contradiction in the views of Ibne Taymiyah on the necessity of the *Imamah* requires special consideration.

In *Al-Siyasah al-shar'iyah* he says that "the *Wilayah*, the government of the affairs of men, is one of the greatest obligations of religion (*min a'zam wajibat ad-deen*)."[40] But in the Minhaj he presents what appears to be an apparently opposite view. Commenting on the *Shi'ah* claim that the *Imamah* is one of the pillars of faith, he writes; "The Prophet (P.B.U.H.) has explained *Iman* (faith) and described its categories but neither has God nor the Prophet mentioned *Imamah* as one of the pillars of faith."[41] Furthermore, in the famous tradition where in Gabriel appeared before the Prophet and asked him to define *Iman, Islam* and *Ihsan* (sincerity of belief), the latter replied: "And *Iman* is that you believe in Allah, in His books, in His Prophets and in the Last Day, and in the resurrection after death, and you believe in predestination, in its good as well as its evil." Here, too, there is no mention of *Imamah*.[42] Then, setting aside *Hadith* as an argument in this case, since it is subject to controversy and doubt, he draws a number of arguments from the Qur'an itself. For instance, Allah says, 'The believers are those whose hearts, when the name of Allah is mentioned, tremble; and when His verses are read to them their faith increases, and they rely on their Lord; and who establish the prayer and give charity from what we have given to them. These are believers, in truth."[43] Here Allah has testified to their faith but made no mention of the *Imamah*.[44] Again, He says: "Indeed the believers are those who believe in Allah and His Prophet, and do not doubt, and struggle in the way of Allah with their possessions and their lives; these are the truthful people."[45] Allah calls them true in faith but makes no mention of the *Imamah*.[46] Further, Allah says, "There is the Book, there is no doubt in it. It is a guidance to the god fearing, who believe in the unseen, and establish the prayer, and give in charity from what We have bestowed on them; and to those who believe in what is revealed to you [the Prophet] and what is revealed before you, and have faith in the Last Day. These are on right guidance from their Lord and these are those who flourish."[47] He calls them guided and flourishing but makes no mention of the *Imamah*.[48]

Thus, we know that, if the *Imamah* were one of the pillars of faith, the Prophet must have pointed to it; but we certainly know that he did not do so. And if it is agrued that it is included in the general spirit of the *Nass* (Qur'an-or-*Hadith* text), or that it is one of the obligations established by some text, then it may be answered that even if all this were true, it would only mean that the *Imamah* is one of the minor issues of religion (*Min ba'd furu' al-din*) and not one of the pillars of faith.[49]

Now what Ibne Taymiyah is obviously anxious to point out is that the state is not one of the constituents of religion, but a matter of practical necessity though it is, nevertheless, an institution to help the cause of religion.[50] The necessity of this institution is indeed, great, as he remarks in *al-Siyasah*, but, however, great the necessity, it remains simply a subsidiary issue as far as it is connected with religion. Hence, there is no contradiction between the two views expressed in the two books quoted above.

He makes this concept clearer at the end of *al-Siyasah* and says that if the ruler, with his power and authority, endeavours his best to realize the good of the Muslims and thereby seeks the pleasure of Allah, he will not have to account for his failures; "because the basis of religion is the Guiding Book and the Helping Tradition."[51]

This concept is developed in much greater detail in the *Minhaj*. First he argues historically and says that the Prophet fought against the infidels until they repented from their infidelity and witnessed that there is no God but Allah and that Muhammad (P.B.U.H.) is His Prophet, but he never mentioned the *Imamah*.[52] And a large number of people entered the fold of Islam in his life-time, and whenever they intended to do so he explained to them the meaning and object of Islam but did not even hint at the *Imamah*.[53] "Further, if one is convinced that Muhammad (P.B.U.H.) is the Prophet of Allah and obedience to him is obligatory, and exerts one's utmost to obey him, then if it is said he would enter paradise, it is proved that he has no need of *Imamah*. And if it is said that he would not enter paradise, this would go against the text of the Qur'an; for Allah has guaranteed paradise to one who obeys Allah and His Prophet, on many occasions in the Book."[54] Then he adopts a more positive tone and says, "The Qur'an is full of the mention of the unity of God and of the mention of His names, attributes, verses, angels, books, prophets, and of the Last Day, and of anecdotes, of commands and prohibitions, of the ordinances against crimes, and of the laws of inheritance, but there is no mention of the *Imamah*."[55] How could Allah omit to mention such an important problem if it were really of the fundamental of religion?[56]

Ibne Taymiyah is here considering the ultimate end of region. For him the establishment of state power is neither one the fundamentals i.e. end nor a necessary adjunct of religion. It must not be thought, however, that Ibne Taymiyah perhaps advocated an Islam that was to prosper under the protection of *Kufr*. It is true that He does not preclude the existence of Muslim minorities under non-Muslim rulers. As a matter of fact, in one of his writings he actually refers to such a situation. The island of Cyprus, off the coast of Syria, was ruled in his days by an independent Christian king; but it also contained a considerable

Muslim minority. These Muslims had originally gone there as prisoners of war. They were first made slaves and then freed but compelled to remain there as hostages. Ibne Tymiyah once received a report that the Christian king of the island Sajwas, was treating his Muslim subjects very harshly. He was moved by this report and addressed a lengthy letter to the king, reminding him that the Islamic State was always very just and tolerant to its Christian subjects, whose number was quite large, and telling him that if he reciprocated in similar terms, his conduct would be much appreciated by the Muslims.[57] Now this incident while it assumes the possibility of a Muslim minority, nevertheless indicates that in the opinion of Ibne Taymiyah Muslims cannot live up to their ideals as a minority; they must endeavour to become the majority wherever they happen to be, so that they might orient the social order according to their ideology.

To this subject he has dedicated a comprehensive work: *Iqtida al-sirat al-mustaqitm*. In this book he discusses in great detail that the Muslims must maintain their distinct identity as a religious community, and take extreme care not to merge themselves into other religious groups by imitating or associating themselves with their ways, customs, festivals, beliefs, etc. For the ultimate end of Islam is to encompass the whole of mankind and to build a common society based on a single faith and a single law. Therefore, if the Muslims are scattered in small groups in non-Muslim lands, they must endeavour to become numerically superior in these areas so as to be able to capture the reins of political power there; without such a situation they would not be normally able to mould their destiny, as their religion requires. In any case Ibne Taymiyah does not conceive the situation where the Muslims would live as a free people and yet not be able to control the social order of their day. Islam is not a mere set of ritual whose performance entitles one to the pleasure of God or offers spiritual satisfaction to the performer. It embraces the whole of life, and the life of the individual is but a drop in the life of the community. Ibne Taymiyah conceives not only of a free but also a powerful community. The individual Muslim, therefore, must not exist as a fossil reflecting certain ideas of the past; tie should be dynamic and incessantly working, alone as well as in company, to capture the whole world for Islam.

Discussing the theory of *Jihad* Ibne Taymiyah writes: "So there are two things which can establish and sustain religion; the Qur'an and the sword."[58]a

The Quran precedes the Sword, that is, *Da'wah* or propagation of Islam is necessary before resort is made to force. Hence the Muslim minorities must continue to propagate their faith until they become powerful enough to take the reins of government in their own hands. Amplifying the idea further he observes:

> "It is mentioned in a tradition that when a sin is hidden it harms only the door of it. But if it is open and is not condemned, it does universal harm. That is why the *Shari'ah* has enjoined war against the infidels. However, it is not obligatory until full preparations have been made to fight against them."[58]b

Ibne Taymiyah is obviously advocating a permanent struggle against the disbelievers. The Muslims may happen to be minority in different lands, but they must not remain contented and disabled. They must endeavour to become powerful and master of their situation by means of a determined and sustained *Da'wah*.

Some western writers, e.g. Henri Laoust and E.J. Rosenthal have tried to infer that, in his political thinking, Ibne

Taymiyah was inclined towards Kharijism, because the denial of the principle of the *Imamate* naturally leads to an anarchic state of affairs. They say that in fact he never supports the Khariji concept of the state explicitly; on the contrary, he condemns the Khawarij as misguided people. Yet his political ideas lead to the same kind of negation that is ascribed to them.[59] This view seems to be sheer injustice to Ibne Taymiyah, who could be the last man on earth to advocate chaos and anarchy. In the name of law and order, in fact, he was prepared to support even the worst form of government; nay, he even preferred the rule of a *Kafir* to disorder. Moreover, he is firmly of the view that political organization is a necessity for mankind—an absolute necessity for the proper working of Islam—that the ruler is the shadow of God on earth under whose protection all His creatures live, and that one night of rule is better than sixty nights of no-rule. How can a man who feels so strongly about the necessity of the state can deny its existence altogether, even by implication or inadvertence? No one can gainsay that Ibne Taymiyah had a complete understanding of Kharijism; nor is any particular evi-dence required to show that he condemned it outright. To assert that he supported its most important principle—the theory of no state—unconsciously is to do open violence to his intelligecne and scholarship.

In his writings Ibne Taymiyah pays no special attention to the Khawarij because as a religious force they had practically vanished from history and left behind nothing except a few ideas, which had been incessantly condemned by the *Ahl al-Sunnah* throughout the preceding centuries. But, even though he ignores them, he is deeply influenced by them in the literal conception of the law and its rigid application. His literalism of courses, the direct legacy of the Hanbali tradition, yet it ultimately goes back to and is rooted in Khariji dogma. He also resembles the Kharijis in several other aspects, as we shall point out later on. (see p. [42]).

The chief cause of misunderstanding about Ibne Taymiyah is his vehement opposition to the *Shi'ah* doctrine that the *Imamah* is an article of faith. For him, too, the *Imamah* is an absolute necessity for the maintenance of the *Shari'ah*—because "the world is to serve the religion"[60]— but he insists, and rightly so, that the *Imamah* is not one of the essentials of faith, **it is only an instrument to serve the faith**. In the introductory passages of the *Minhaj* where he quotes the Qur'an profusely to establish that the *Imamah* is not mentioned anywhere in connection with faith (*Iman*), he is really concerned to refute the *Shi'ah* doctrine. But there is no indication to show that he is absolutely opposed to the institution of the state as such. All the confusion has arisen due to his claim that the *Imam*ah is only a "minor issue" in religion. The real faith, according to all sections of the orthodox community (*Ahl al-Sunnah*) is belief in Allah, His Prophet, His Book, the Day of Judgement and the angels. The *Shari'ah* follows from the acceptance of these ideas; and any of the ensuing ideas is certainly minor compared to the major principles of faith just narrated. This is exactly what Ibne Taymiyah means: he does not minimize the importance of the *Imamah* but only clarifies the issues between Sunnism and *Shi*'aism by saying that the state is not one of the fundamentals of faith. It is in this special context that he uses the word "minor"; for otherwise he is equally anxious to emphasize the necessity of state-power to assist religion, since he firmly believes that Islam aims at creating a social order in which the basic values given by the Qur'an and the Sunnah are realized. But this social order cannot be ideally realized without the state. That is why on one occasion he remarks that there can be no religion if there is no state. The idea is not that the two are equivalent but that the state-authority is indispensable for the complete realization of the religious order. In plain language the state is not a matter of faith but a matter of necessity.

Hence when he treats the principles of the state with reference to the Muslim *Ummah* in general his attitude is quite different; he is no longer haunted by the *Shi'ah* claims of the infallible *Imam* and other preposterous ideas based on it. Now he feels strongly that the duty of enforcing the religion lies squarely on the shoulders of the *Ummah*, which may and should be capable of carrying out its obligations. This function the *Ummah* cannot perform without the backing of state-power. The *Imam*, however, is only the executive head charged with the duty of enforcing the *Shari'ah*, and carries no sanctity or privilege of any kind with his person. In short, the state is not a sacred institution, even though it is indispensable for the fulfilment of Islam. Thus the two statements quoted above, if viewed in this light, do not seem to be contradictory, but are both true in their special contexts.

Further, it must be noted that Ibne Taymiyah is basically not interested in the institution of the *Imamah*; he only wants the supremacy of religion. This idea is so deeply rooted in his mind that he admires the *Al-Salaf al-Salih*, the virtuous Muslims of the early period, that "they......order the doing of good and forbid the doing of evil, and believe that arrangements must, be made for the *Hajj* and *Jihad* and for the Friday and the 'Id congregations, under the supervision of rulers whether they be virtuous or wicked."[61] The form and structure of the government have little or at best secondary importance for him; he is essentially interested in the enforcement of the *Shari'ah*. For the same reason he has completely ignored the discussion of the traditional *Khilafah* in his writings. He has written a number of tracts to define the faith of Islam. In each of these, he lays great emphasis on the unity and integrity of the *Jama'ah*, but there is only passing reference, or none at all, to the state or government. For instance, he writes: "And as regards the *Ahl al-sunnah wa'l-jama'ah* they hold fast to the rope of Allah,"[62] and, "indeed the *Jama'ah* is blessing and the dissension is punishment."[63] The Qur'an and the Sunnah also enjoin very strongly to stick to the *Jama'ah*. Now Ibne Taymiyah is not unaware that the maintenance of the integrity of the *jama'ah* requires the establishment of institutions and agencies which have to promote, organize and regulate its affairs, but these are secondary matters, and their nature, their form and constitution, can be determined only by times and circumstances. The permanent entities are the *Jama'ah* and its ideology. By its very definition this *Jama'ah* or *Ummah* is supraterritorial. It potentially encompasses the whole of the globe. Within it there may be one state, there may be more states. But if there is one state it cannot be co-extensive with the *Ummah*, until the whole world has entered the fold of Islam. This is obvious, because if a part of the world remains non-Muslim it might contain within it Muslim minority groups, which would certainly be constituents of the *Ummah,* but would remain outside the jurisdiction of the universal Islamic state. What Ibne Taymiyah is anxious to convey is that the effective section of the *Ummah* must endeavour to establish the state, otherwise the religion would disappear. Refuting the <u>Shi</u>'ai claim that the *Imam* is required to protect the <u>Shari</u>'*ah*, he observes; "we certainly do not admit that it is obligatory on the *Imam* to protect the <u>Shari</u>'*ah*, but that it is obligatory on the *Ummah* to protect the *Shari'ah*, and the protection of the <u>Shari</u>'*ah* can be achieved by the whole *Ummah* as well as one person."[64] What is important is the presence of the state, the sword-arm of religion; how it comes into being and what shape it acquires are of no interest to Ibne Taymiyah.

As regards the <u>Kh</u>ariji view of the state, Ibne Taymiyah does not even consider it, because he dismisses the <u>Kh</u>awarij summarily as *Ahl al-bid'ah*[65] (the Innovators). Yet they unconsciously influence him. In the first place, the <u>Kh</u>awarij did not believe in anarchy as is generally alleged; they really wanted a rule in strict conformity with the law of God. But their misfortune was that they could not evolve a consistent and articulate theory of state. Ibne Taymiyah, too, wanted a similar state but he was able to develop its concept and give it a concrete and practicable shape. Like them he believes that ordering the good and forbidding the evil is the fundamental aim of the *Ummah*, and, in fact, the chief purpose of religion. Again like them, as we have already noted, he regards it as the foremost duty of the <u>*Ummah*</u> to enforce the <u>*Shari'ah*</u>. He, of course, does not clearly talk of the institution of the *Imamah*, but believes that it automatically follows from the establishment of the *Shari'ah*, and, therefore, takes it for granted. Finally, it must be observed that he is greatly impressed by the republicanism of the <u>Kh</u>awarij. (see Chapt. 5, p. 145).

It is also necessary to explain that some of the views of the *Sunni* theologians, quoted earlier in this chapter, referring by implication or because of ambiguity to the nonnecessity of the state, are really not meant to be taken in that light. As a matter of fact, when al-Iji and other standard writers of *Kalam* (theology) talk of the necessity of the *Imamah* to realize the purposes of religion, they visualize the whole of human life within it. That is why they insist on using the words *Umur al-dunya* (matters of religion) in the definition of the state and often exclude the mention of *Umur ad-deen* (matters of the world), because, for them, outside the purview of deen there exists nothing.

In developing his political theory, however, Ibne Taymiyah considers in great detail the *Shi'ah*te concept of the state. In the midst of these details he gives his own positive views about the subject. Therefore, it will be necessary to examine briefly his criticism of the Shi'ah view.

The first problem is the necessity of the state. This necessity has been explained by the *Shi'ah*te al-Hilli as follows:

> "The *Imarmis* say that Allah is just and wise. He does no evil and does not interfere with what is obligatory. His actions are always directed towards good and wisdom. He practices neither tyranny nor does anything purposeless; and that He is kind and merciful to His creatures and does for them only that which is best and most beneficial. He has placed on them responsibility which is optional and not imposed. He has promised them rewards and warned them of punishments through His infallible messengers and the Prophet, to whom it is not permissible to attri-bute error, forgetfulness or disobedience, otherwise the veracity of their words and deeds could not be guaranteed and the benefit of their mission would not be realized. Then He started the institution of *Imamah* after the death of the Prophet (P.B.U.H.), and appointed His infallible trustees so that the people may be saved from the commission of error and...the world may not become deprived of His grace (*Lutf*) and mercy."[66]

In simpler language this theory means that Allah has placed on man certain responsibilities, which he cannot fulfil without the light of divine guidance. And since Allah will not come into the world in physical form, and since the institution of Prophecy is abolished after Muhammad (P.B.U.H.), it is incumbent on Him to initiate a new series of infallible guides, to save mankind from error and damnation. This act of Allah is called *Lutf* (grace) and this series is called the *Imamah*. It is further claimed that under orders from Allah the Prophet designated 'Ali as the first *Imam*, and 'Ali designated his successor, and the successor of his successor, until the twelfth *Imam*, Muhammad, was reached. Muhammad disappeared from the world alive, (in 261 H.) when he was only a few years old. Since then, so it is claimed, he has been guiding mankind from his hiding. He is "the expected one" (*al-Muntazar*) who is to reappear when the world is filled with tyranny; he will then fill it with justice.

Ibne Taymiyah has written four big volumes of the *Minhaj al-sunnah* to refute this theory. For our purpose, however, it would suffice to give a few of his arguments advanced against those salient features of the theory which concern our present investigation.

The first thing is the theory of grace. If it means that Allah appoints His trustees (the infallible *Imams*) and actually gives them power and authority over man so that the latter might benefit by it, it is an open lie.[67] But the Shi'ah do not say this; they say that the *Imams* were oppressed and tyrannized, were helpless and possessed no power, authority or control, and they know also that Allah has not bestowed on them rule or kingship as He bestows it on good Muslims or on infidels and evildoers. So the intended *Lutf* (grace) is not actually realized by this appointment.[68]

But if this appointment means that Allah has enjoined on mankind obedience to the *Imams*, that is, if to obey them means to be rightly guided, then the historical fact that they have been disobeyed clearly shows that by this act of God neither grace nor mercy was realized; people only rejected the *Imams* and rebelled against them. And even those who believe in the expected *Imam* (*al-muntazar*) do not receive any grace or any other profit, in spite of their love and longing for him. So the net result is that no grace or good is secured either for the believer or the disbeliever in the expected *Imam*.[69]

"As regards the other infallible *Imams*, they have benefited mankind as other men of religion and learning have done. But, the benefit required of the *Imams* possessed with authority and military might has not been obtained from any of these infallibles; so it is clear that the mention of grace and mercy with their appointment is mere fraud and falsehood."[70]

Now when the purposes of the *Imamah* have not been realized, because most of the conditions leading to their realization were not fulfilled, how can it be rationally known that it is obligatory on Allah to create an infallible *Imam*—an *Imam* through whom all the good of mankind has to be reali-zed? And how can it be known especially when the one He did create was helpless and unable to realize this good; rather he became the cause of much evil that would not have been but for him?[71]

There are two opinions about the acts of Allah. One is that He does no evil, and, therefore, all that He does is good, or that in any case He is under no obligation to do anything at all. The other is that He must do only justice and mercy. In either case it follows that He does no tyranny and does not omit to do the obligatory. Now if He does what is obli-gatory on Him, and yet does not create the conditions under which the *ma'sum* (the infallible *Imam*) may realize the universal good, so that the good is not realized, then it follows that his creation is not obligatory on Allah. And if the realization of the good is dependent on the creation of the *Imam* and of other necessary conditions, which however, are not created by Allah, it again follows that the creation of the Ma'sum is not obligatory on Him.[72]

So much about the necessity of the state of *Lutf* as the *Shi'ah*s call it. The second point in the theory is that Allah must appoint the *Imam*, because election leads to litigation and evil. And 'Ali is the only person whose appointment is proved by *Ijma'* (consensus).

Ibne Taymiyah rebuts this claim in detail. He begins by saying that no such *Ijma'* on 'Ali is known in history, rather there is a better *Ijma'* on Abu Bakr. He goes on: *Imamah* is either mansus (nominated) or not mansus (not nominated). If the first statement is true the argument of *Ijma'* does not stand. If the second is admitted then the basic claim that the appointment of the *Imam* is obligatory on Allah fails. In fact the real argument for nomination (*Nass*) is the word of the person for whom '*Ismah* (infallibility) is claimed, al though as yet neither '*Ismah* is established for him nor *Nass*. That is, he should say: I am the infallible and I am the proof of my own appointment, "which is the highest folly,"[73]

Again, the assertion that the absence of appointment would lead to litigation and evil is not borne out by history. No such thing occurred during the regimes of Abu Bakr (R.A.) and 'Umar (R.A.) but it occurred on a gigantic scale during the regime of the (allegedly) appointed (*mansus*) *Imam*.[74]

Finally if somebody had really been nominated by the Prophet in the Shi'ah sense, that is, accompanied by '*Ismah*, he would have become the source of religion, and the finality of the Prophet would have been cancelled.[75]

The third point in the *Imami* theory is that there must be an *Imam* to protect the *Shari'ah*, after the death of the Prophet (P.B.U.H.). This is further necessitated by the fact that the Qur'an and the *Sunnah* contain no details about the working of the Shan'ah, so there must be an infallible *Imam* who may meet the requirements of time and circumstance, and would not allow anyone to modify or change the Shan'ah.[76] Ibne Taymiyah replies: "We certainly do not admit that there must be an *Imam* to protect the *Shari'ah*, but that it is obligatory on the *Ummah* to protect the *Shari'ah*, and the protection of the *Shari'ah* can be achieved by the whole *Ummah* as well as by one person."[77]

If the *Imams* can protect the *Shari'ah*, one after another, then who has been protecting it through these long centuries after the disappearance of the 12th *Imam*? And how do you know that this is the same Qur'an that was revealed to Muhammad (P.B.U.H.)? And how do you know anything about the Prophet (P.B.U.H.) himself, because your *Imam* who could have given you correct reports about these matters, has had no contact with you for more than four hundred years? That time if you say: a large body of men has reported it from the last *Imam*, then we say: a very much larger body has reported it from the Prophet (P.B.U.H.) himself.[78]

Finally, as regards the functions of the Prophet (P.B.U.H.), Allah has defined these clearly:

1.   And we have sent no messenger but with the language of his people so that he might explain to them clearly.[79]

2.   So that the people may have no plea against Allah after the (coming of) messengers.[80]

3.   The duty of the messenger is only to deliver (the message). [81]

     Now if the truth of religion is not established by the explanation (*Tabligh*) of the Prophet (P.B.U.H.) these verses carry no meaning.

Ibne Taymiyah concludes: "We do not admit the necessity of appointing an infallible *Imam*, because the infallibility of the *Ummah* is independent of his infallibility. And this is what the scholars have observed about the wisdom of the infallibility of the *Ummah*. They say: whenever the former nations changed their religion Allah sent among them a new prophet to explain the truth, But this *Ummah* shall have no prophet after her Prophet i.e. (Muhammad) (P.B.U.H.) so that her infallibility shall stand in place of Prophecy (*Nubuwwah*). It shall not be possible for anyone among them to change any part of religion. If anyone does so, Allah will surely send someone to expose the falsity of his deviation, because the *Ummah* shall not agree on an error, as the Prophet has pronounced."[82]

In short, Ibne Taymiyah is most bitter against the *Shi'ah* concept of the *Imamah,* and regards it not only as irrational but wholly opposed to the fundamental tenets of Islam.

So far we have discussed the meaning and necessity of the state and its relation to religion, including Ibne Taymiyah's ideas on the subject and his criticism of the opinions of the main political schools in Islam. As regards his positive contribution to political theory and its chief features, we shall consider these in detail in the chapters that follow.

## Notes:

1. Ibne Taymiyah, *Minhaj*, vol. 1, pp. 17, 23; al-Ghazal', *Fada'ih al-Batiniyah,* Leiden 1956, p. 64.
2. *Minhaj*, vol. 1, p. 26. al-Juwayni, K. al-Irshsd, p. 410. al-Iji, al-Mawaqif with al-Jurjani's commentary, vol. 8, p. 344.
3. Al-Iji, op. cit., p. 346.
3a. Ibid., p. 348.
4 Al-Shahrastani, *al-Milal wa'l-nihal,* vol. 1, p. 153 (on the margin of Ibne Hazm's al-Fisal).
5. Ibid. p. 154
6 Albert N. Nader, Le *Systeme Philosophique des Mu'tazilah.* L'Institute de Letters Orientale de Beyrouth, 1956, p. 323; 'Abu al-Qahir al-Baghdadi, al-farg bayn al firaq, Cairo 1948, p. 99.
7. Abd al-Qahir, op. cit., p. 99; Al-Shahrastan, op. cit., pp. 192-93.

8    Abu'1-Hasan al-Ash'ari, *Maqalat al-Islamiyin.* Cairo 1950, vol. 2, p. 133.

9.   Ibid., p. 134.

10.  Al-Iji, op. cit., p. 348.

11.  Albert N. Nader, op' cit., p. 324.

12.  Ibid., p. 323.

13.  Al-Shahrastani, op. cit., p. 107.

14.  Elie, Abid Salem, *Political Theory and Institutions of the Kkawarij*, p. 51.

15.  Al-Iji,op. cit., p. 348.

16.  Khwajah Nasir ul-din al-Tusi, Risalah *Imam*ah Teheran 1335 H. p. 16; Fakhr al-din Al-Razi has here verbally quoted the opinion of al-Sharif al-Murtada, the great *Shi'ah* scholar and theologian.

17.  Al-Tusi op. cir., p. 19.

18   *Political Theory and Institutions of the Kkawarij* op. dt., Ibne Khaldun. al-'Ibar, vol. 1, p. 160.

19.  Al-Shahrastani ed. by Muhammad b. Fathallah Badran, Cairo, 1910, vol. I, p. 200.

20.  Al-Shahrastani, (ed. Fathllah), vol. 2, p. 216; al-Iji, op. cit., p. 349.

21.  Al-Razi, op. cit., p. 427.

22.  Political Theory and Institutions of the Khawarij, p. 49.

23.  Ibne Taymiyah, *al-Siyasah al-Shar'iyah*, Cairo 1951. p. 172.

24.  Ibid., pp. 172-173.

25.  Ibne Taymiyah, Majmu' Rasa'il, al-Hisbah, Cairo 1323 H., p. 36.

26.  Ibid.p. 37

27.  E.I.J. Rosenthal, Political thought in Medieval Islam, Cambridge 1958. p. 53.

28. Al-Hisbah, p. 37.
29. Al-Siyasah, p. 173.
30. Ibid. p. 174
31. Al-Qur'an, ch. 57:25.
32. Al-Siyasah, p. 173
33. Ibid.: Minhaj, vol. 2, p. 146.
34. *Al-Hisbah.* p. 37.
35. Abu Da'ud, Ma'alim al-Sunan.
36. Minhaj. vol. 1, p. 148; at-Hisbah. p. 37; al-Siyasah. p. 173.
37. Al-Siyasah, p. 174.
38. Al-Hisbah, p. 37.
39. Minhaj, vol. 1, p. 142.
40. Ibid., p. 24.
41. Al-Siyasah, p. 172.
42. Minhaj. vol. 1, p. 25.
43. Quotation: Al-Qur'an
44. AI-Qur'an, ch. 8:2.
45. Minhaj, vol. 1, p. 26.
46 AI-Qur'an, ch. 49:15.
47 Minhaj. vol. 1, p. 26.
48 Al-Qur'an, ch. 2:2.
49 Minhaj, vol. 1, p. 26.
50 Ibid., p. 23.
51 Al-Siyasah. p. 178.
52 Ibid., p. 179.
53 Minhaj, vol. 1, p. 17,
54 Quotation: Al-Qur'an
55 Ibid., p. 20.
56 Ibid.,p. 20.

57    Al-Siyasah, p. 179.

58    Ibne Taymiyah, Risalah Qubrusiyah.

58a.  Al-Siyasah (Urdu translation, Lahore), p. 41.

58b.  Ibid., p. 167.

59.   Rosentbal writes, "He (Ibne Taymiyah) ignores the problem of the Khilafah altogether, denies its necessity (though for other reasons than the Kharijites) and is very critical of its theoretical foundations" (*Political Thought in Medieval Islam*, p. 52). Laoust remarks, "Thus there is to be found incorporated in the system of Ibne Taymiyah the last of the doctrines which came to be, in itself situated in his conciliatory synthesis, the Khsrijite doctrine, one of whose characteristics is to deny the obligation of the community to have a caliph at its head" (*Essai sur les doctrines sociales et politiques*, p. 282).

60.   Al-Siyasah, p. 179.

61.   Ibne Taymiyah, Majmu'at ol-rasa'il al-Kubra, al-A'qidah al-Wasitiyah, Cairo, 1322 H., vol. 1, p. 405.

62.   Ibid., *al-Wasiyah al-Kubra*, p. 308.

63.   Ibid.p. 308

64.   Minhaj, vol. 3, p. 270.

65.   Ibne Taymiyah, K. al-Nubuwwat, Cairo, 1346, pp. 129-30; Minhaj, vol. 1, p. 15.

66.   Minhaj, vol. 1, p. 30, quoted from the Minhaj al-Karamah of Ibne al-Mutahhar al-Hilli, written for the pleasure of the Mongol Empreor Uljaytu Khan Khudabandah, the grandson of Hulaku Khan. Most of Ibne Taymiyah's political views are expressed in refuting the opinions of al-Hilli, the great champion of *Shi'ah*sm.

67.   Minhaj, vol. 1, P- 32.

68.   Ibid. p. 33

69.   Ibid. p.33

70. Ibid. p. 34
71  Minhaj, vol. 3, pp. 250-51.
72. Ibid., p. 253.
73. Ibid., p. 266.
74. Ibid., p. 267.
75. Ibid., 268.
76  Ibid., p. 270, quoted from al-Hilli.
77. Ibid., p. 271.
78. Ibid., p. 272
79. Al-Qur'an, ch. 14:14.
80. Ibid., ch. 14:164.
81. Ibid., ch. 5:99.
82. Minhaj. Vol. 3, p. 272.

# CHAPTER III

## THE PROPHETIC "STATE"

The use of the word "state" in the title of this chapter is only provisional, because Ibne Taymiyah argues that the Prophet (P.B.U.H.) did not establish any state. It is, however, certain that the Prophet (P.B.U.H.), in Madinah, did establish some kind of a social order, which clearly resembles a state. Therefore, a fuller inquiry into the subject is essential before any final conclusion can be drawn on the matter. Moreover, it is necessary to examine and analyse Ibne Taymiyah's views on the issue to understand his influence on the later development of the political theory in Islam.

In the very opening passage of his *Minhaj*, Ibne Taymiyah comments on Ibne al-Mutahhar's book which the latter wrote to persuade Uljaytu Khan, the Mongol emperor, to embrace Shi'ism, and observes that these people make only a hypocritical show of Islam, but are in fact a species of the Batiniyah heretics, "who do not enjoin submission to the faith of Islam, and do not prohibit submission to other religions, but regard the different religions as different schools of thought and varieties of politics which may be suitably adopted, and who regard prophecy as a kind of just polity, evolved for the common good in this world. Now this kind of people appears and abound when blind ignorance and its votaries increase."[1] This passage is apparently confusing; it seems to mean that Ibne Taymiyah is denying the claim that the purpose of prophecy is the establishment of a political order. His real intention is, however, just the opposite: he does believe in the dire necessity of the state, but does not regard it as the principal aim of prophecy. For the Shi'ites the *imamate* is the first article of faith, and the whole of religion depends on the profession of this dogma. Ibne Taymiyah refutes this concept in the strongest of terms and points out that faith, and not state, is the foremost consideration in religion, and that the state is a necessary consequence of the acceptance of faith and not vice versa. Similarly, he condemns the preoccupation of the Muslim philosophers with the thesis that the only aim of the prophet (P.B.U.H.) was to create a just political order. Ibne Taymiyah is dot in the least prepared to identify Prophethood with state-craft, although he regards it as essentially generating a social and political order which should sustain its message. The two approaches are basically different; according to the one the institution of the *Imamah* is the central function of prophecy, according to the other it is of secondary importance.

The real mission of the Prophet is defined by the Qur'an itself, "Certainly Allah conferred on the believers a favour when he raised among them, from amongst themselves, a Prophet who recites His verses to them and purifies them and teaches them the Book and the wisdom."[2] The state is not specifically mentioned, though it is certainly envisaged in the over-all teaching of the Book. This is the real force of Ibne Taymiyah's argument. He does not belittle the importance of the state-institution at all, but after a thorough consideration of the matter regards it only as an instrument, though of the highest necessity, for the fullest realization of the purposes religion. This view he declares again and again and always argues from the famous Qur'anic verse: "Certainly We sent our Messengers with clear arguments, and sent down with them the Book and the balance, that men may conduct themselves with equity. And We created iron, wherein is great might and advantages for men, and that Allah, Who is unseen, may know who helps Him and His Messengers."[3] Commenting on this verse he writes: "So the right religion must have in it the Guiding Book and the Helping Sword."[4] Thus the real import of the strong, words used by Ibne Taymiyah against the Shi'ahs and the philosophers is that religion (*Deen*) cannot be reduced to a mere system of polity. Polity is indeed essential to religion but it is not itself the religion.

A detailed discussion of this issue as we have already pointed out in the previous chapter, is to be found in the *Minhaj*. In this discussion Ibne Taymiyah apparently builds up a thesis, which seems to deny that the *Imamah* is an essential element in religion, or that the Prophet (P.B.U.H.) established any *Imamah* at all. We shall, therefore, follow his argument in detail and try to see what principles he does actually want to enunciate with regard to the institution of the state.

Once again, his principal thesis is that the Prophet (P.B.U.H.) was only a Prophet, that all his activities were inscribed within the function of Prophecy, and that the institution of the *Imamah* was not something external to this function nor did it constitute an article of faith. To establish this he argues as follows:

The infidel becomes a believer by only professing that there is no God but Allah and that Muhammad (P.B.U.H.) is His Prophet. It is primarily for the recognition of these two principles that the Prophet (P.B.U.H.) fought against the disbelievers. Hence, "belief in God and His Prophet is more important than the problem of the *Imamah*"[5] Ibne Taymiyah strengthens his argument by quoting a famous *Hadith*: "I have been ordered to fight the people until they witness that there is no God but Allah and that I am the Prophet of Allah, and establish the prayer and pay the *Zakat*. And when they have done this they have saved their blood and possessions from me, except when they are charged against a right (of Islam), and their account would be with Allah."[6] This is the *Hadith* quoted by 'Umar to challenge the decision of Abu Bakr to take action against certain tribes who believed in Islam but refused to pay *Zakat* poor-due to the Islamic state. Here was a clear instance in which a mere profession of faith did not suffice: the apostates were doing positive harm to the organized life of the community and hence were declared enemies of Islam.

Arguing in the same vain he further quotes the Qur'an: "When the forbidden months have passed, slay the infidels wherever you find them, and encircle them and lie in wait for them in every ambush. But if they repent and establish the prayer and pay the *Zakat* leave them alone."[7] Accordingly, wherever the Prophet went among the infidels he spared their blood if they repented from their *Kufr* (disbelief), but never mentioned the *Imamah* to them. Again, referring to the infidels Allah says, "And if they repent and establish the prayer and pay *Zakat* then they are your brethern in faith."[8]

He makes them brethern in faith on mere repentance. And during the life-time of the Prophet (P.B.U.H.) when the infidels entered the fold of Islam he instructed them in the injunctions of Islam but never mentioned the *Imamah*. In all these examples Ibne Taymiyah is only denying the Shi'ah concept, of the *Imamah* and not rejecting it altogether. He continues his argument thus; it is certainly a fact also that the Muslims who lived during the age of the Prophet (P.B.U.H.) had no need to obtain the knowledge of the *Imamah*; the problem of knowing and establishing it arose only after his death.[9] But if it was the most fundamental element of faith, what would we say about the Companions who died during the life-time of the Prophet (P.B.U.H.) without any knowledge of this truth? This is obviously directed against the Shi'ah and does not prove that the *Imamah* is not essential. Further, if it is argued that the Prophet (P.B.U.H.) was *Ab initio imam* in his life-time, it may be answered that even so the *imamate* was not a primary issue in Islam; for:

> "First...it was important at some times but at other times it had no importance: and specially during the best of times—the Prophetic era—it was neither the most urgent requirement of religion nor the highest problem of the Muslims.

Secondly, it can be said that belief in Allah and in His Prophet has been in every age, more important than the problem of the *Imamah*.

Thirdly, it can be said that it was obligatory on the Prophet (P.B.U.H.) to explain this problem for the generations of the *Ummah* which were to come, as he explained to them the problems of prayer, *Zakat*, fasting and *Hajj* and defined the obligation of belief in Allah and His unity and in the hereafter. But it is certainly known that the problem of the *Imamah* has not been explained in the Book and the *Sunnah* along with these other principles."[10]

Now these statements must be accepted only in their proper context. Ibne Taymiyah himself writes, subsequently in this very chapter, that ultimately the Prophet (P.B.U.H.) became the bead of a political order in Madinah; so the import of his argument is the refutation of *The Divine Theory* of the *Imamate* and not the rejection of the "historical fact that the Prophet was a real *Imam*. The second argument is also certainly correct; the Muslims have indeed never placed anything above faith, but the problem of a free and independent political society of the Muslims has never been unimportant in history, and of all the people Ibne Taymiyah gives it the greatest importance. The third argument is also admitted, but there was no need that all the details of state-craft should have been mentioned in the Qur'an. Ibne Taymiyah himself argues frequently that the very nature of Islam requires the setting up of a strong political order to realize its aims and purposes. All these aims are clearly laid down in the Book, like the dispensation of justice, removal of evil, collection of *Zakat*, organization of *Jihad*, etc.; to achieve them the institution of the *Imamah* is naturally essential. As regards constitutional provisions, it was in the fitness of things that the Qur'an did not mention them, and left them to be provided by special historical situations.

In the abovequoted paragraph, therefore, Ibne Taymiyah is not denying the necessity of the state in Islam. On the contrary, he is proving that the state is essential but that it must be dynamic and progressive in its nature and constitution. Finally, he is trying to convey that if the form and structure of the state were divinely ordained, as the Shi'ahs claim, it must have been mentioned in the Qur'an. In fact, in the first chapter of the first part of the *Minhaj*, Ibne Taymiyah has not only made a great endeavour to refute the Shi'i theory of the *Imamah*, but has also incidentally made remarks on the general political theory in Islam, which, if not interpreted properly, may lead to serious misunderstanding. In these preliminary discussions he has brought out two very important facts. One of these we have treated already in detail above, namely that the *Imamah* is not the highest and most fundamental issue in religion. The second fact is that, according to Ibne Taymiyah, the regime of the Prophet (P.B.U.H.) was a Prophecy (*Nubuwwah*) and nothing else. He is not prepared even to call Muhammad (P.B.U.H.) the Prophet *Imam*; for him the *Imamah* came into being only after the death of the Prophet (P.B.U.H.). He has strong reasons to differentiate between the Prophetic regime and the Islamic state, which came into being after him. A sovereign claims the obedience of his people to himself in virtue of his being the sovereign. But Ibne Taymiyah argues: it is certainly known that obedience was due to Muhammad (P.B.U.H.), not because he was the head of a state, but because he was the Prophet of Allah. And this obedience is due to him for all time, as it was due to him in his life-time. But an ordinary *Imam* does not enjoy this privilege; he is obeyed only as long as he is alive and in office (and acting, as long as, in accordance with Kitabullah and *Sunnah* of the Holy Prophet (P.B.U.H.)). [11] Moreover, the Prophet received his mandate from Allah and was not made *Imam* by the people possessing power, or by his helpers, nor was he nominated to the *Imamah* by a predecessor. In short, obedience to him is not due because he has received his sovereign authority from some human agency, but only because Allah has made it obligatory to obey him. And obedience would have been due to him even if he had no helpers and sympathisers; it was due to him even during his early career in Makkah, when he had none by his side to fight against his opponents. [12] Thus, according to Ibne Taymiyah, conditions of earthly sovereignty were not realized in the regime of the Prophet (P.B.U.H.), so that this regime cannot be called anything but *Nubuwwah*.

But there seems to be a serious drawback in Ibne Taymiyah's reasoning here. In political theory it does not matter how power has been attained; the de facto wielder of supreme authority over a people is certainly the sovereign of that people. Now it is certainly known and admitted by Ibne Taymiyah that the Prophet (P.B.U.H.) ultimately succeeded in establishing his political sovereignty over the Arabs. Necessarily, therefore, in political language it will be said that he founded a state. The nature, form and constitution of the state do not matter, for in these respects it can be classified into numerous categories.

He further contends that while in Makkah the Prophet (P.B.U.H.) neither possessed a territory nor the coercive force of state-power nor get a people to support his authority, yet he was obeyed by his followers. Hence his authority cannot be compared with that of a worldly ruler. This contention is again not well-founded. It is true that the obedience to the Prophet (P.B.U.H.) in the present instance was purely moral in character and not induced by the fear of a political power. But in Makkah in fact he held no political authority. Moreover, for purposes of political theorizing we are not concerned with this period of the Prophet's (P.B.U.H.) life; what concerns us relevantly in this discussion is that in the later part of his life the Prophet (P.B.U.H.) was able to demonstrate that his religious ideology could fully blossom through the basis of a social and political order. And just as his physical nature was similar to the nature of other men so also the state that he built was similar in function to other states that have existed in history. A political scientist cannot call it anything but a state. The moral greatness of a Prophet (P.B.U.H.) can idealize the working of a state, but it remains a state nevertheless. For reason and experience both have shown that it is an indispensable necessity for social living of which Islam is a great champion. Also there can be no moral objection or contradiction in political theory in regarding Muhammad (P.B.U.H.) as the Prophet *Imam*, since according to the Qur'an at least two of the great Prophets, David and Solomon (P.B.U.H.), were Kings. Of course what is understandable is that in this case the function of the *Imam* cannot possibly be extricated from the function of the Prophet. Therefore any state builder in the Islamic *Ummah* can never possess all those attributes, which the Prophet *Imam* did, and yet this fact cannot detract anything from the regime of Muhammad (P.B.U.H.) being a state.

Ibne Taymiyah however continues his argument: "If it is said that he adjudicated in such-and-such a case and gave his decree in favour of so-and-so, and applied the penal injunctions of the Qur'an to so-and-so, and sent such-and-such military expedition, so necessarily he has to be counted as a sovereign, we say: yes, all this is true yet he was not a sovereign. His obedience shall be binding in similar situations until the Day of Judgment, but this cannot be said of any temporal authority."[13] Here he is in very clear words refusing to call the Prophet a sovereign-ruler. But this is quite against what he has written elsewhere in the *Minhaj* and other works. Discussing the sociological concept of the state in the *Hisbah* he writes; "When the presence of a commander and forbidder is indispensable it is better to enter into the obedience of God and His Prophet."[14] Again a little further in the same book he remarks: "When the basis of religion and governments is commanding and forbidding then the purpose for which God sent His messenger was just the same, i.e., commanding the good and forbidding the evil, and this is the attribute of the Prophet and the Muslims." He at one place even goes to the extent of identifying religion with state-power. But since the institution of prophecy, is a divine arrangement, Ibne Taymiyah is not willing to call the order built by the Prophet a state. This judgment is, however, arbitrary, for the state, if it carries all the attributes, which characteristically pertain to it, remains a state, irrespective of the person who founds it and the way it is founded. Perhaps what is troubling his mind is that the Prophet could not be brought down to be compared with worldly rulers; for in that case his stature would very much diminish, since as an empire builder he does not occupy any great place in world history. Moreover, his principal aim was not to build an empire but a social order based on the special ideology that he had brought. The state, though a necessary function of this social order, is yet subservient to it and not dominant over it.

We shall consider a few more of his arguments before we draw any final conclusions. Insisting on his idea that the prophet is only a prophet and not a sovereign, he writes; "If it is said that he is an *Imam* and by this is meant an *Imamah* which is external to prophecy, or an *Imamah* that is qualified by conditions which do not apply to prophecy, or *Imamah* which envisages obedience without enjoining obedience to the Prophet; all this is absurd, because on whatever grounds he is obeyed it is all inscribed in his prophecy, and he is obeyed only as a messenger of Allah."[15] In this passage he indirectly admits that the *Imamah* is included in prophecy and is not external to it. In the same way it can be asserted that in every age the *Imamah* shall remain one of the prominent functions of the Islamic religious order. He further writes; "If it is asserted that he (the Prophet) is obeyed because of his *Imamah* which partakes of his prophecy, the answer is that this is utterly ineffective, because his prophecy is alone sufficient to enjoin obedience. But the *Imam* can claim no obedience in his own right, since he becomes an *Imam* only when he is helped to power by his supporters and friends; otherwise he is a mere individual like other men of learning and religion."[16] Ibne Taymiyah has here failed to differentiate between moral obedience and political obedience. Moral obedience is self-imposed. Those who obeyed the Prophet (P.B.U.H.) in Makkah, where he possessed no physical power to enforce his decrees, did so out of their own will; but those who preferred to disobey him he could do nothing against them. As against this, in Madinah, where he became the head of a state, even the Jews and the pagans had to obey him as his subjects. Similarly, the obedience that the Muslim *Ummah* has offered to the Prophet, from his death to this day, is purely moral in character, and to inculcate it in the believers is the principal function of prophecy. To compare the Prophet in this respect with other non-Prophet *Imam*s is simply irrelevant. But the Prophet had also other functions to perform, the most important of which was certainly to translate his message into practice by building a social order based on it. The highest form of the social order is the stale; the Prophet actually succeeded in establishing it and showing to his followers by his example how to orient the whole world on this pattern.

Finally Ibne Taymiyah writes, "If it is said that when the Prophet attained power in Madinah he was also invested with the *Imamah* to enforce justice, the answer is that even after that he only remained a Prophet, but was then helped by his supporters and sympathisers who carried out his decrees and fought his opponents; and as long as there are in this world people who believe in Allah and His Messenger they shall be the helpers and supporters of the Prophet and they shall enforce his decrees and fight his enemies. Hence, he did not utilize his helpers to achieve things, which he required to add to prophecy, like his becoming an *Imam* or a ruler or a governor, as all these things were inherent in his prophecy. But with the helpers he attained efficient power which obliged him to set up some kind of rule and organize *Jihad*, things which were not obligatory on him when he possessed no power."[17] This passage is certainly the clearest admission on the part of Ibne Taymiyah that the institution of the *Imamah* developed as one of the functions of prophecy and that the Prophet (P.B.U.H.) indeed established a state. From all this discussion we conclude that according to Ibne Taymiyah:

1.    The institution of the *Imamah*, though not a constituent; part of the faith, became one of the main functions of the Prophet in his later life.

2.    The *Imamah* is not external to prophecy but inscribed and inherent in it.

3.    The Prophet actually rounded a state, yet it is not proper to call him a sovereign or his state a state; his regime was a prophecy and he was only a Prophet.

4.   The *Imamah* came into being only after the death of the Prophet.

With the last two conclusions we do not agree. We have already commented on them in detail in this chapter, and have also tried to explain the real import of these assertions by Ibne Taymiyah.

In fact, his contention is not that the Qur'an does not enjoin on the believers to establish an ideological state, but that it gives no fixed constitution of any kind. And although there is no express command to institute the *Imamah*, its immediate necessity and obligatoriness are prescribed within the scope of the important Qur'anic injunctions. So when Muhammad was commanded to establish his prophecy, his commission primarily included the establishment of the *Imamah*. By denying the fixed provisions of the constitution Ibne Taymiyah hits at the *Sunnis* and the Shi'ah both; for according to him there is no basis in the Qur'an or the *Sunnah* for the traditional theory of the Khilafah or the divine theory of the *Imamah*. He in fact visualizes Islam as a social order where the law of Allah must reign supreme. As a result he is not interested at all in the state and its formation, but simply accepts the state as a religious necessity, that is, according to him any form of government where the authority of the *Shari'ah* is supreme is the required Islamic state.

## Notes

1.   Minhaj, vol. 1, pp. 2-3.
2.   Al-Qur'an, ch. 3:164.
3.   Ibid., ch. 57:25.
4.   Minhaj, vol. 1, p. 142.
5.   Ibid., p. 17.
6.   Muslim, al-Sahih, K. al-iman.

7. Al-Qur'an, ch. 9:6.
8. Ibid., ch. 9:11.
9. Minhaj, vol. 1, p. 17.
10. Ibid. p. 17.
11. Ibid., p. 18.
12. Ibid. p. 19.
13. Ibid., p. 19.
14. Al-Hisbah fi'I-Islam, in Majmu' rasa'il, Cairo, 1323 A. H., p. 37.
15. Minhaj, vol. 1, p. 19.
16. Ibid., p. 20.
17. Ibid. p. 21.

# CHAPTER IV

## PROPHETIC SUCCESSION
### (KHILAFAT MINHAJ AL-NUBUWWAH)

The Orthodox Caliphate that was set up after the death of the Prophet is regarded by Muslim jurists, theologians and political thinkers as the ideal manifestation of the Islamic polity. It is also worth noting that while discussing the Islamic political theory these authorities invariably refer to the institution and practice of this Caliphate, but seldom refer to the Prophetic era, as if no state existed in that period. Thus they seem to confirm Ibne Taymiyah's view that the Prophet (P.B.U.H.) did not preside over any *Imamah* and that he commanded and was obeyed only as a prophet; "And from amongst those who survived the Prophet no one had the need to submit to the authority of the *Imamah* except after his death."[1] We have contended against this view and also tried to discover the real motives of his opinion in the previous chapter. What we want to emphasise here is the scant attention that the Muslim political thinkers have paid to the study of the nature and form of the Prophetic regime.

But what is most perplexing in this context is the confusion that has been created between the terms *Imamah* and *Khilafah*, Muslim writers generally use the term *Imamah*, in place of *Khilafah*, which simply means the state and may be applied to the Prophetic regime also, though it has never been applied in fact. The term *Khilafah*, however, strictly refers to the post-prophetic era. Despite this distinction, most writers indiscriminately employ the terms. And in recent times this confusion has become even greater with the word *Khilafah* being made to mean the ideal Islamic State as is supposed to be conceived in the Qur'an and realized in the practice of the Prophet and the Orthodox Caliphs (*al-Khulafa' al-rashidun*).

It must also be noted that, barring the present times, the word *Imamah* has been exclusively used, throughout the course of Islamic history, to denote the idea of the state in all juristic, theological, political and philosophic speculation. The reason for this is two fold. One is that the word *Imam* is borrowed from the term *Imam al-salah* (leader of the prayer), signifying one entrusted with enforcing the *Shari'ah* and guiding the Muslims in all their affairs. In other words, the *Imam* is the executive head of the community. The word *Khalifah* means only the person who succeeds or represents the Prophet as head of the *Ummah* to perform his administrative functions. But the word *Imam,* being politically and religiously more meaningful, gained wider currency and technical recognition at the hands of all those who made the systematic study of the Islamic political philosophy. Defining these two terms Ibne *Kh*aldun writes:

> "We have (just) explained the real meaning of the institution (of the caliphate). It substitutes for the Lawgiver (Muhammad (P.B.U.H.)) in as much as it serves, like him, in preserving the religion and to exercise (political) leadership of the world. The institution is called the caliphate or the *Imamate*. The person in charge of it is called 'the caliph' or 'the *Imam*."

> "The name *Imam* is derived from the comparison (of the caliph) with the leader (*Imam*) of prayer, since (the caliph) is followed and taken as a model like the prayer leader.  Therefore (the caliph) is called 'the great *Imam*.' "The name caliph (*Khalifah*) is given to the

caliph, because he 'represents' (*Khalf*) the Prophet of Islam, One uses 'Caliph' alone, or 'Caliph of the Messenger of God.' Three is a difference of opinion concerning the use of 'caliph of God.' Some consider the expression) permissible as derived from the general 'caliphate' (representation of God) of all the descendants of Adam, implied in the verse of the Qur'an, 'I am making on earth a caliph,' and the verse, 'He made you caliphs on earth.' But, in general, it is not considered permissible to use the expression 'caliph of God', since the verse quoted has no reference to it (in connection with the caliphate in the specific sense of the term). Abu Bakr forbade the use of the expression 'caliph of God' when he was thus addressed. He said 'I am not the caliph of God, but the caliph (representative, successor) of the Messenger of God.' Furthermore, one can have a caliph (representative, successor) of someone who is absent, but not of someone who is present (as God always is)." [2]

Ibne Khaldun is of course a late authority on the subject there are many earlier references to it as well. For instance, al-Baladhuri writes: "Then 'Ali came out and said: O Abu Bakr! Did you see no right for us in this matter (caliphate)? He said: 'why not, but I feared civil dissension (al-fitnah), and (I am aware that) I hold a high office (of responsibility).' Then 'Ali said: 'Of course I do know that the Prophet appointed you to lead the prayer and that you were one of the two in the cave; (despite all this) we were entitled to a right but you did not consult (us)."[3] In another passage he reports, "Some people delayed in swearing allegiance to Aba Bakr (R.A.) where upon he said: 'who deserves this office (caliphate) more than I? Am I not the first who led you in prayer, am I not, am I not?' and mentioned things which he had done together with the Prophet."[4]

In yet another passage he says, "When Abu Bakr was sworn in and the people had given their oath of allegiance to him, he stood up and declared thrice: 'O people! I have authorized you to break your oath for me'; then 'Ali said: 'by God, we will neither break our oath for you nor demand your resignation; the Prophet made you (above all the rest) the leader of prayer. After that what can keep you away from the caliphate?"[5] Similarly, discussing the election of Abu Bakr at Saqifah bani Sa'idah, Ibne Jarir al-Jabari writes; "Then Abu Bakr said, 'this is 'Umar and this is Abu 'Ubaydah, swear allegiance to anyone of the two you like.' But the two men said: 'By God we will not accept this office above you, because you are the best of the *Muhajirin* (Immigrants), the second of the two in the cave and the deputy of the Prophet in prayer, and the prayer is the best thing in the religion of the Muslims. So who is it that can precede you or occupy this office above you?"[6] These passages are enough to prove that the political connotation of the word *Imam* was certainly derived from the *Imam* of the prayer.

The second reason is that the Shi'ah gave a special meaning to the word *Imamah,* and built a most complex and challenging theory around it, changing the entire concept of Islam and its political requirements. The *Sunnis*, in self-defence, took up the same word and gave it a definite meaning of their own.

It is, however, certain that during the first two centuries of the *Hijrah* the word *Imam* was not used as an official term; and even unofficially it did not have wide circulation in literature or general usage of the day. By the middle of the second century, however, it had found a place in the *Fiqh* books and is frequently mentioned in Abu Yusuf's al-Radd '*ala siyar Al-Awza'i*. But it is used in a very loose sense; it denotes a scholar and a jurist, a political leader of the community (*A'Immat al-Muslimin*), commaders of the armies and also the heads of state.[7] It is worth noting that by the close of the second century this word became very popular and is almost exclusively used for the Head of the state in the works of Abu Yusuf (189 H./804 A.C.), although it had received no official recognition as yet. These two men use the word *Imam* only for the caliph; for commanders of armies they use the word *Amir,* and seem political leaders and the *'Ulama'.* This change in the use of the word *Imam* definitely seems to have come as a strong reaction against the Shi'i theory of the *Imamate* which had been by now fully developed. It can be safely aussumed that when in the beginning of the third century, al-Ma'mum adopted *Imam* as an official title it was largely in order to rebut the Shi'ah and also to work up their own theory of the *Imamate.*

As regards the institution of *Khilafah,* no serious scholar has ever argued that its obligatoriness is demanded by the Qur'an or the *Sunnah.* Necessarily, therefore, it follows that the word *Khalafa* and its derivatives used in the Qur'an are not used in a political sense, but only in the sense of "succession" "successor", etc. Despite this the state that the Prophet established came to be called the *Khilafah,* after his death, meaning simply the successor regime. It is universally agreed in Sunni tradition that the Prophet (P.B.U.H.) did not nominate anyone to succeed him, so that *Khilafah* cannot mean representation in a political sense. Moreover, even if the Prophet (P.B.U.H.) had nominated anyone such a person could not represent him, because a living person cannot represent a dead one. Therefore, *Khilafah* cannot mean anything but succession. And this sense of the word is certainly derived from the Qur'an. But succession is not meant in a mere temporal sense; in the historical context of Islam it means the political state that was established by the Muslims after the death of the Prophet (P.B.U.H.) to enforce the rule of the Shari'ah as he himself did in his life-time. This sense is, of course, not implied in the word *Khilafah* philologically but was acquired by it in the political situation that developed immediately after the death of the Prophet (P.B.U.H.).

In later history, as long as the Arab influence continued, great states, like those of the Umayyads, the 'Abbasids and the Fatimids, preferred to call their regimes *Khilafah*. But when other races, like the Turks and the Mongols, appeared on the stage of history, and built great empires, e.g., the Ottoman Empire and the Mughal Empire, the term was entirely discarded and replaced by the word "*Saltanah*" (rule, govern-government, kingdom, empire). One reason for discontinuing the use of *Khilafah* was of course, the insistence of *Sunni* theology that this institution can only be presided over by a Qurayshite. The real historical explanation is, however, that the idea of representing the Prophet in his administrative functions had by this time vanished from the minds of state buil-ders. But in Islamic history the concept of the *Khilafah* reflecting the regime of the Prophet (P.B.U.H.) has continued to persist until this day. From the days of the Orthodox Caliphs down to the fall of Baghdad the supreme Muslim political powers were always called the *Khilafan*, and were never known as the *Imamah*, in spite of the philosophizing of the jurists and the theologians. The conclusion is therefore that the *Khilafah* as the highest political institution in the Muslim world continued to flourish, at least theoretically, until the days of Ibne Taymiyah, The adoption of the term *Khalifah* by Abu Bakr was only fortuitous, because there was no express command for it, and in fact no better word to depict his status. The title occurs consistently in all the official documents signed by him. But after 'Umar had adopted the new title of *Amir al-muminin* (Commander of the believers) the use of the word *Khalifah* was completely discarded. Ibne Jarir al-Tabari writes; "The first person to be called *Amir al-muminin* was 'Umar bin al-Khattab; afterwards it became the common practice and the Caliphs use it to this day."[8] So the institution of the *Khilafah* remained but the use of the title *Khalifah* was dropped because it was inconvenient, as 'Umar once remarked, and the term *Amir al-maminin* became the official title for the head of the State. The "Abbasid al-Mamun added a further title of *Imam* to his office,[9] but the institution of *Khilafah* retained its name until the fall of the 'Abbssids and even in later days.

Now, Ibne Taymiyah does not accept the institution of the *Imamah* during the life-time of the Prophet, either as a theoretical or historical fact; we have already examined his arguments in the previous chapter.

About the *Khilafah*, too, his opinion is very much different from the traditional view, for he does not admit the classical theory of the caliphate at all. He contends that though the regime of the Prophet (P.B.U.H.), fulfilled all the requirements of the state, yet it was no state (*Imamah*) but only *Nubuwwah*. Discussing the problem of the *Khilafah*, he says that the necessity for it arose only after the death of the Prophet (P.B.U.H.). Following this he makes a detailed study of the meaning of the word *Khilafah*, and then examines it as a political term as applied in history.

Quoting Ibne Hazm in defence of his argument, he says the *Muhajirun* and the *Ansar*, after, the death of the Prophet (P.B.U.H.) agreed to call Abu Bakr "the *Khalifat* al-Rasul" (the successor of the Prophet). "And philologically the word *Khalifah* means one whom a person has nominated to succeed him, after his death, and not one who simply succeeds him after his death without having been nominated. In the idiom of the language the word does not mean anything else; there is no difference of opinion about it. It is said: So-and-so nominated so-and-so and the latter became the *Khalifah* and successor of the former. But if the second took the place of the first without being nominated by him it will be simply said that the second has occupied the place of the first and will be merely called a *Khilif*—the aftercomer"[10] and not the *Khalifah*—the successor.

Ibne Hazm further argues that the Companions called Aba Bakr *Khalifah* because they had certainly heard his nomination by the Prophet (P.B.U.H.). And this nomination cannot refer to his appointment as the leader of the prayer for two reasons. One is that, although Abu Bakr had been nominated as the *Khalifah* the never earned this title in an absolute sense during the life of the Prophet (P.B.U.H.). And secondly many persons acted in his behalf, like 'Ali during the Battle of Tabuk, Ibne umm Maktum during the Battle of the Ditch, and '*Uthman* during the Battle of *Dh*at al-Riqa', and many others in the Yaman, al-Bahrayn and al-Ta'if, but none of them was ever called the *Khalifah* of the Prophet. And it is impossible that the Companions would have agreed in calling Abu Bakr "*Khalifat al-Rasul*," were he not nominated as such by the Pro-phet. So it is proved that the word *Khalifah* means one who succeeds to the office of his predecessor by the latter's nomination.

Ibne Taymiyah takes up the inquiry once again and says that there are two schools of thought about Abu Bakr's nomination; one believes that the evidence for it is manifest (*Jali*) in the fact that the Companions agreed to call him *Khalifah*. For these people the word *Khalifah* means one who is nominated by another person to succeed him. So here *fa'il* is used in the sense of *maf'ul*; that is *Khalif*, agreeing with *fa'il*, means the nominated one. And the second school believes that the evidence is implied (*Khafiy*), According to it *Khalifah* means one who is nominated to succeed and also one who succeeds without nomination. So here *fa'il* is used in the sense of *Fa'el*, and hence *Khalifah* means *Khalif*, that is, one who takes the place of another, whether he is nominated to it or not.[11]

It is in this sense that the Prophet said, "One who provides the necessary equipment for the fighter (*Ghazi*) is as if he himself goes to fight; and one who takes the place of the fighter in his family with goodness (*Man Khalafa fi ahlihi*) is also as if he himself goes to fight." [12] The same sense can be noticed in another tradition. The Prophet (P.B.U.H.) said, "O Allah! Thou art the Companion in journey and the *Khalifah* in the family; O Allah! Accompany us on our journey and be in our family (in our absence)." [13]

In these two traditions the word *Khalifah* has been used in the sense of one who takes the place of another.

And it is in this sense of succession, that is, taking the place of previous agents, that the word *Khalafa* and its derivatives have been used in the following verses of the Qur'an:

1. Then We made you successors (*Khala'if*) in the land after them, so that We might see how you act. [14]

2. And when thy Lord said to the angels: I am going to Place a successor (*Khalifah*) on the earth."

3. And He it is Who has made you successors (*Khala'if*) in the land, and exalted some of you in rank above others. [16]

4. David! Surely We have made thee a successor (*Khalifah*) in the land; so judge between men with equity. [17]

(Commenting on this verse, Ibne Taymiyah observes: "Here *Khalifah* means successor to the previous generation of people, and it does not mean that he (David) is *Khalifah* of Allah; nor does it mean that he is related to Allah as the pupil is related to the eye, as say many heretics who believe in incarnation and union,")[18]

Ibne Taymiyah is here making the point that *Khilafah* carries no religious or spiritual significance, it is mere succession in time, and "the use of this word (*Khalifah*) as found in the Book and the *Sunnah* indicates that this word applies to one who succeeds another, whether the latter has nominated him or not." [19] For instance the Qur'an says: "And Allah makes him succeed, as he makes the night succeed the day and the day the night. The sense is not that one is the *Khalifah* (successor) of Allah as some people imagine." [20] To support his argument, he further cites the following verses, in addition to the ones we have already quoted:

1.  And if We pleased, We could make among you angels who would succeed (you) on the earth. [21]

2.  And remember when He made you successors after the people of Noah.[22]

3.  And remember when He made you successors after 'Ad. [23]

4.  And Moses said to his brother, Aaron: Take my place among my people. [24]

5.  And He it is Who made the night and the day to succeed each other, for him who desires to be mindful. [25]

6.  And Allah says, "In the succession of day and night" that is, this succeeds that and that succeeds this, so they follow each other. [26]

7.  He said: It may be that your Lord will destroy your enemy and make you succeed to them in the earth, then He will see how you act. [27]

8.  Allah has promised to those of you who believe and do good that He will surely make them successors in the land as He made those before them successors. [28]

In all these verses the word *Khalifah* is used in the general sense of *Imam* or sovereign without any idea of reference to divine commission or prophetic nomination. [28]a

People call their rulers *Khulafa*. Indeed the Prophet (P.B.U.H.) himself has said; "You must follow my *Sunnah* and the *Sunnah* of my upright and rightly-guided *Khulafa'* (successors)." He did not nominate these successors but enjoined that their example should be followed if they were good Muslims. It is also known that 'U<u>th</u>man did not nominate 'Ali. 'Umar, too, did not take the responsibility of nominating any one person because he could not decide between the two examples he had before him—one of the Prophet who did not nominate his successor and the other of Abu Bakr who did nominate one *Umar*. But despite this hesitation he addressed Abu Bakr as "*Ya Khalifat Rasul Allah*" (O successor of the Prophet of Allah). Similarly many of the Umayyad and 'Abbasid rulers were called' *Khulafa'* although they were not nominated by their predecessors. Therefore, it is established that the word is commonly applied to one who succeeds another.

It is also reported in a tradition that the Prophet (P.B.U.H.) said, "May Allah bless my successors (*Khulafa*)", When the people asked, "And who are your *khulafa*", he replied, "Those who revive my *Sunnah* and teach it to the people." If this *Hadith* is genuine, it is the best argument in the issue; even if it is not genuine, it at least indicates that the word was generally used to mean one who succeeds another, whether nominated or not. That is to say, when a person takes the place of another and performs his functions in certain matters, in those matters he is his *Khalifah*. [29]

The purport of this entire discussion is that the word *Khalifah*, as used in the Qur'an and the *Sunnah*, according to Ibne Taymiyah, does not carry any religious or political significance. Now so far as his opinion refers to the Qur'an it is certainly correct; but so far as it refers to the *Sunnah* it seems to reveal a contradiction in his own argument. For he faithfully accepts a large number of traditions in which the words *Khilafah* and *Khulafa'* have been expressly used in a political sense, and he gives no other name but *Khilafah* to the regime of the first four successors of the Prophet. It is true that for him the *Khilafah* existed only for thirty years (see below) after the death of the Prophet. But the point is that it existed; so whatever name we give to it, even Ibne Taymiyah had to recognize that the *Khilafah* has existed in history as a political institution.

The standard jurists and theologians always define the *Imamah* and the *Khilafah* both as the representation (*Niyabah*) of the Prophet. Nevertheless, a parallel political theory has developed in Islamic history, which defines the *Khilafah* as the viceregency of Allah, And in recent times this concept has gained great approval and even juristic and theological recognition in the Muslim world.

This theory enunciates that man is the *Khalifah* (vicegerent) of Allah on earth. If he believes in the mission of the Prophet he is a true *Khalifah*, otherwise he loses the *Khilafah*. Thus all the Muslims are the true *Khalifahs* of Allah, and it is to them that He has delegated his authority to rule in this world and enforce His decrees. But since individuals are incapable of doing so, they must choose one of them to act on their behalf. This chosen one is called *Khalifat*[30] *al-Muslimin*, although he ought to be called *Khalifat al-Khulafa'*.

But, the theory goes on, the *Khalifah* is a mere

vicegerent; he is not the sovereign. The *Khilafah* is, therefore, not a sovereign institution, because it is mere delegated authority, above which stands the real sovereignty of Allah,' Hence in the "Islamic State" (which is a modern term and, on strict logical grounds, cannot be accepted as the equivalent of *Khilafah*) the sovereignty resides neither in the people nor in the head of the state, but in Allah alone. The government and the people both are only agents of Allah, and they can function only under the limited conditions of delegation. Also they cannot legislate; their duty is no more than to enforce the law of the Book and the *Sunnah*. Man-made law can be of no use in the Caliphate. Commenting on this aspect of the problem, a leading Muslim jurist of today writes: "And the error lies in the analogy when they compare the positive law, which is made by man, with the Islamic *Shari'ah*, the responsibility for whose legislation rests on the Creator of man; in doing so they but compare the earth with the heaven and men with the Lord of men; how can it come in the mind of a sane person to compare himself with his Lord and his earth with his heaven?" [31]

The advocates of this theory, in order to prove their thesis, quote the same verses, which Ibne Taymiyah has quoted to prove that *Khilafah* only means succession. They say that *Khilafa* and all its derivatives, as used in the Qur'an, mean delegation of authority. This is not the occasion to refute this concept in detail. It will be sufficient to say that in the Arabic language, classical or modern, the word *Khilafa* does not carry even the slightest sense of nomination, representation or delegation. Therefore giving it an arbitrary meaning and building on it an important political theory would be violating the purpose of revelation and falsifying the fact of history.

It is impossible to prove that the Qur'an has any where used the word *Khilafah* in a political sense. There are many passages in the Qur'an where the whole context would become meanin-gless if it were interpreted in a political sense. For instance, consider the following verses:

1. And remember when He made you successors after the people of Noah.[32]

2. And remember when He made you successors after 'Ad.[33]

3. But they rejected him, so We delivered him and those with him in the ark, and We made them successors and drowned those who rejected Our message.[34]

In all these places 'successors' means 'survivors' and the reference is to the fact that the previous peoples have been destroyed because of their intransigence and others have been allowed to take their place. No other meaning is admis-sible.

The concept that Allah has made man his own *Khalifah* is not only linguistically wrong but inherently absurd, as Ibne Taymiyah observes, "...no one can succeed Allah, because succession takes place only after the absentees, but He is ever present, administering the affairs of His creation: He does not need anyone else to administer them in His place."[35] It is also not understandable how these people reconcile this theory of delegation with the juridical and theological dictum that *Khilafat Allah* (vicegerency of Allah) is inconceivable. So even if it were admitted that *Khilafah* means vice-gerency, in the opinion of strict theology and jurisprudence, it cannot be recognized to emanate from Allah.

Historically it is admitted on all sides, even by Ibne Taymiyah, that Abu Bakr (R.A.) refused the compliment of *Khalifat* Allah and said, "No! I am the *Khalifah* of the Prophet of Allah, and this suffices for me."[36] The classical theory of the caliphate is essentially based on the practice of the Orthodox Caliphs; so consistency demands that on an important issue such as this it should not be made to deviate from its original basis. In-deed, the idea of the vicegerency of Allah was so much abhorrent to the early Muslims that the historians not only one approvingly refer to 'Abd al-Malik, the first Muslim ruler to adopt the title of *Khalifat* Allah, but regard this event as a great *bid'ah* (heresy) and something very shocking to the Muslim conscience. [37]

If the *Khilafah* really meant the *Khilafah* of Allah, it could have been restricted to be mentioned in the Qur'an, in view of its importance, but it is not mentioned even in passing. The word *Khalafa* and its derivatives occur in the Qur'an at more than one hundred places but not in a single instance does the Book represent Allah as saying, "I have made you my caliphs." And how could have Allah said it, for if He said it, it would have meant the denial of His own existence? Further, how can it be believed that Allah has revealed such an important command in a highly shrouded and mystified language, unintelligible even to scholars, when referring to the Qur'an He Himself says, "And this is clear Arabic language." [38]

Hence, to quibble on the words of the Qur'an in order to prop up a political thesis not only outrages the dignity of the Book but also challenges the wisdom of Allah, Who did not will the thing that we should will on His behalf. In fact, the truth must be acknowledged frankly that there is no constitutional theory in the Qur'an. The Qur'an, however, declares that the acceptance of the prophecy of Muhammad (P.B.U.H.) is a paramount responsibility, for it involves the acceptance of the great *Shari'ah* revealed by God through him. It contains numerous injunctions, calling upon the Muslims to establish prayer, collect *Zakat*, make arrangements for the *Hajj*, establish justice, eradicate evil, enforce the laws of marriage and divorce, distribute the inheritance equitably, punish the criminals, propagate the mission of religion, fight the enemies of Islam, command the doing of good and forbid the doing of evil, etc. These are certainly great responsibilities and cannot be fulfilled without the aid of the political machinery known as state; but Ibne Taymiyah argues that the acceptance of these responsibilities cannot be termed as delegation of divine authority to man. [39]

Again, political authority is a physical concept, that is, it actually and really exists in this world, and therefore a superior can delegate it to his inferior. But the divine authority or sovereignty is a moral concept and therefore it cannot be transferred on to the physical plane. In other words, political sovereignty in the Islamic State is not delegated but original, and it does not belong to God but to the people. Besides, since the acceptance and rejection of the divine authority is a matter of free human choice, it becomes totally ineffective in the political sense, for it does not exercise the coercive power to impose its will on the recipient of delegation. That is to say, it becomes manifest only when it is desired by another will. But this is a negation of the attribute of sovereignty; hence the idea of the vicegerency of God does not seem to be tenable from any point of view.

The political order that was set up in Madinah immediately after the death of the Prophet is called *Al-Khilafah al-Rashidah* (the Orthodox Caliphate'). This name was, however, given to it long afterwards by religious leaders and then by historians. But it should be noted that *Khilafah* was never the official title of the head of the state, except during the reign of Abu Bakr (R.A.). We might add that Muslim historiography was started in the beginning of the third century of the *Hijrah*, when many contemporary terms in political theory were pro-jected back to earlier times. As a matter of fact, no special term was used for the state in the beginning, for even the term *Imamah* was employed very late during the 'Abbasid period.

It is also true that Muslim political theorists have invariably used the term *Imamah* and not Khilafah, yet the fact remains that supreme political authority in the Muslim world, after the death of the Prophet, has always gone under the name of the Khilafah.

Ibne Taymiyah also calls the regime of the first four caliphs after the Prophet *Khilafah*. But his concept of the Khilafah is very much different from the classical theory. As regards the idea of vicegerency of God, he repudiates it in strong language, as we have already seen. He also believes in the *Hadith* in which the Prophet is reported to have said, "You must follow my *Sunnah* and the *Sunnah* of my Orthodox and guided caliphs." Yet he does not call the regime of the first four caliphs *Al-Khilafah al-rashidah*, but calls it Khilafat al-Nubuwwah, the Prophetic Succession.[40] He does not use the word Khilafah in the generally misunderstood sense of vicegerency, but in its real sense of mere temporal succession. The succession of the first four caliphs, however, carries a special significance for him, for there is a well-known *Hadith* from the father of Abu Bakrah who says, One day the Prophet asked: Has anyone of you seen a dream? I said: O Prophet of Allah, I dreamt that a scale descended from the sky and you were weighed in it against Abu Bakr and you weighed heavier than Abu Bakr; then Abu Bakr was weighed against 'Umar and he weighed heavier than 'Umar; then 'Umar was weighed against 'Uthman and he weighed heavier than 'Uthman, and then the scale was raised above. Then the Prophet said: This is Prophetic succession, after which Allah will give sovereignty to whomsoever He likes."[41] Ibne Taymiyah quotes a number of other versions of this *Hadith* and then concludes that these immediate successors of the Prophet were destined to take his place under divine dispensation, but since they were not nominated by him, it is more correct to call them *Khulafa'* (successors) than vicegerents. And they were specially selected by the wisdom of God to succeed the Prophet in the polity of the Muslims, so that they were called not mere successors but the successors of the Prophet. They were thus distinguished from the other *Khulafa'* who had to govern the affairs of the Muslims in later times. To support this idea he quotes a *Hadith* from the *Sahihayn*: "The Prophet said: The Israelites were guided by their prophets; whenever a prophet died another prophet took his place. But there will be no prophet after me: there will be successors (*Khulafa'*) and they will be in great numbers."[42] So the other *Khulafa'* will continue to come until the end of time but they will be mere *Khulafa'* and con not be accorded the title of the Successors of the Prophet.

This argument is further reinforced by another famous *Hadith* which Ibne Taymiyah cites again and again. It is reported by Sufyanah that the Prophet said, "The Prophetic Succession will be for thirty years, after that Allah will give sovereignty to whomsoever He likes."[43] So according to him all those *Imams* who governed the affairs of the Muslims during this period, though not actually nominated by the Prophet (P.B.U.H.), represented his will, and spread his mission in the world as he desired. And the limitation of the period of *Khilafah* amounts to indirect nomination, that is, the men who ruled during that period as caliphs were really providentially appointed.

This *Hadith* on which Ibne Taymiyah has built a whole political theory is of a spurious origin. In the first place, he no where indicates as to what is the difference between *Khilafat*

*al-Nubuwwah* and ordinary *Khilafah*. It is true he calls the
ordinary *Khilafah* "*Mulk*" (dominion, sovereignty, kingdom,
etc.) but this differentiation is neither clear nor valid, because
the *Khilafah* also, even according to him, possesses the attribute
of sovereignty and it is a form of state. Then in a well-known
passage in the *Minhaj* he quotes a *Hadith* of the Prophet, who
said, "Blessing of Allah be on my *Khulafa'* (successors)." When
they asked "And who are your *Khulafa'*?" He answered, "Those
who revive my *Sunnah* and teach it to the people."[44] According
to this report all those *Imams* who perform these functions
rightfully belong to the prophetic succession. And logically also
it must be accepted that persons other than the early caliphs
may be equally capable of representing the Prophet, if Islam
claims to be practicable in all times and the final message of
God to man. But from the tone of Ibne Taymiyah it appears that
the *Khilafat al-Nubuwwah* cannot go "beyond thirty years after
the death of the Prophet, because he (the Prophet) is alleged to
have prophesied it. He does not realize the logical and historical
contradiction involved in the *Hadith* from which he takes his
sanction.

On one occasion, however, referring to 'Ali, he remarks,
"Neither was the *Khilafat al-Nubuwwah* established during his
regime nor *Mulk*"[45] This opinion he expresses again and again
about 'Ali.   This means that he has in his mind some special
image of the *Khilafat al-nubnwwah* which he has never presented
in a denned form in his writings. If he means that this special
*Khilafah* was ideal, and it is capable of being realized again in
history, although actually it has never been realized again, it
may be admitted as a rational opinion. But if he means that it
was a special dispensation, willed by God or the Prophet, and
incapable of being realized again, this view cannot be accepted
on rational grounds. He is not explicit on this issue but seems
overwhelmingly inclined to the second view.

In an important passage in the *Minhaj* he discusses the conditions for the election of the *Imam*;[46] these are :

1. The *Imam* should be a Qurayshi.
2. He should be appointed by the consultation of the Muslims.
3. He should receive the oath of allegiance from the Muslims
4. He should possess the quality of justice.

Basing his opinion on this passage, Abu Zahrah observes: "Like the *Ahl al-Sunnah;* Ibne Taymiyah also divides the rulers into two categories: the rulers who are *Khulafa' al-Nubuwwah* (successors to prophecy) and rulers who are kings, who have secured authority over the majority of the Muslims with the word or by other means."[47] Elaborating the issue further he says that those who fulfil the above mentioned conditions belong to the second category. This view, he says is also supported by history, because actually the *Khilafat al-Nubuwwah* did not last more than thirty years, and is also confirmed by the Prophet when he says; "The *Khilafah* after me will last only thirty years, after that it will become dominion (*Mulk*)."

But there is no justification for this conclusion of Abu Zahrah. He has torn a number of passages from their contexts and huddled them together to arrive at an opinion. In the passage referred to above Ibne Taymiyah is discussing the general conditions of the *Imamah* and expressing his overall conformity to the classical view: but he is not considering the *Khilafat al-Nubuwwah*. In another passage, already quoted, he cites a number of traditions from the Prophet to prove that the *Khilafat al-Nubuwwah* will not last more than thirty years after the Prophet, and seems to rule out its reappearance in history. And then he says that the regime of 'Ali was neither *Khilafat al-Nubuwwah* nor *Mulk*. Yet in another passage, commenting on

Yazid, he remarks, "The *Ahl al-Sunnah* believe that he was the king of the majority of the Muslims, their *Khalifah* of that time and the wielder of authority, as there were others of his kind, from the Umayyad and Abbasid[48] caliphs." Here he simply means to convey that even the rulers, who come after the thirty-year period, can be called *Khulafa'*, because the term only carries the sense of temporal succession and not of any religious sanctity. These rulers are called *Imam, Khalifah* and sultan in the sense that they wield real authority and power, they appoint and dismiss, reward and withdraw favours, issue orders and execute them, enforce the penal laws of the Qur'an, fight against the infidels, and collect and distribute the revenues. So we see that the *Khilafah* is not differentiated from *Mulk*.

Ibne Tayimyan is not very sure of the four conditions mentioned above. Even if all these were realized, the *Imam* would not be recognized as such until he were supported by people who are effective (*Ahl al-shawkah*). And nowhere does he say that the *Khilafah* becomes *Mulk* when it lacks one of the four conditions enumerated.

Further it should be observed that his exclusive work on political science, *al-Siyasah*, gives a detailed discussion of administration according to the *Shari'ah*, but does not use the term *Khilafat al-Nubuwwah* in the book even once. This may be deliberate, because he most probably believes that this institution will not come into being again.

Ibne Taymiyah has written in great detail about *Khilafat al-Nubuwwah* in the *Minhaj*. Yet, as we have tried to show above, he has not explained what it is precisely. His cue, was, however, taken a few centuries later by Shah Wallyullah al-Dihlawi, who, in a voluminous treatise entitled *'Izalat al-Khafa' 'an Khilafat al-Khulafa'*, has covered almost the same ground that Ibne Taymiyah has surveyed in the *Minhaj*. Wallyullah says that the

*Khilafah* is of two kinds: *al-Khilafah al- 'ammah wa 'l-Khilafah-al-Khassah* (the general caliphate and the special caliphate).[49] The general caliphate is the same as enunciated by the classical theorists, like al-Ash'ari, al-Baqillani, al-Mawardi, 'Abd al-Qahir al-Baghdadi, Ibne Hazm, al-'Iji, and others. As regards the special caliphate, its discussion is spread over six hundred pages. We shall, however, note briefly only the definition and the chief characteristics of this type of caliphate.

Waliyullah says: "The will of God which descends from above the seventh heaven to spread the prophetic guidance among the people, to perfect the prophetic light and make it dominant, and to effect the execution of the promises made to the Prophet, creates an urge in the heart of the *Khalifah*. There may be thousands whose hearts are filled by divine inspiration, with the urge to help the religion of the Prophet, but this *Khalifah* is among them as the heart is among the organs of the body. First of all, the divine inspiration enters the heart of the *Khalifah* and then from there it reaches the hearts of other persons"[50]. This inspiration enters the heart of the *Khalifah* through the agency of the Prophet and urges from inside, and unless it urges from inside no one can become special *Khalifah*.

Then this *Khalifah* must have spent long years under the training of the Prophet and cultivated unbounden love for him; excelled in offering his life and possessions in the service of the Prophet; regarded the obligations of *Jihad* not as an act of obedience to the Prophet but as a realization of truth; accompanied the Prophet through thick and thin and thought that he had suffered on his own account and not on account of the Prophet. He must be the one whom the Prophet might have tried frequently and seen that he could perform only such acts as led to salvation and could not do mean and pernicious things. He should be the one about whom the Prophet might have said on numerous occasions that he would enter paradise and occupy high office in this world, and whose greatness and capability for the _Khilafah_ might be manifest from the word and conduct of the Prophet. When a person possesses these qualities, he can endure the divine inspiration referred to above, enforce the religion of the Prophet and fulfil some of the promises made to him by Allah. And this is indeed a blessing of Allah and He confers it on whomsoever He desires. This Special Caliphate is part of the period of prophecy.[51]

On another occasion, quoting from the "*Isti 'ab*" of Ibne 'abd al-Barr, Waliyullah writes that the Special Caliphate is based on three fundamental principles: [52]

1.   The prophets are created with the purest and noblest souls and it is on account of this quality that they become the recipients of divine revelation and are given the charge of guiding mankind. Only God knows as to who among men Possess this pure and refined nature, for the Qur'an says, Allah knows the soul to which He assigns the commission of Prophecy."[53] Similarly, in the *Ummah* also there are some people whose soul is created almost as pure and noble as that of the prophets, and these are the people who, because of the goodness of their nature, become the real successors of the prophet. They get the spiritual illumination from the Prophet which others cannot get. And whatever knowledge they receive from him they believe in it as if they have seen its truth and realized its essence independently and the Prophet has only confirmed it by giving its details. So the special caliphate means that just as the _Khalifah_ is the head of the Muslims in the temporal sense he is also their head in the spiritual sense.

2.   The real successor of the Prophet is like a pipe. When

someone plays on a pipe and produces a sweet melody in the atmosphere this performance is attributed not to the pipe but to the piper. Similarly God had promised to do many things through the Prophet but He called him back before all of them were realized. The remaining things were then performed by his successors, and this performance will be attributed to the Prophet rather than to these people, because they are, like the pipe, his mere organs. Thus the special caliph is one who complements the works of the Prophet which have been explicitly and implicitly mentioned in the Qur'an and *Hadith*.

3.    The *Khilafah* is an office of great responsibility. But satisfaction of the uncontrolled physical desires and devilish tendency are ingrained in the very instinct and blood of man. Therefore, if the *Khalifah* is elected by the people, the possibility is there that he may do tyranny and injustice. Hence there must be some factor to remove this possibility, so that normally it might be impossible for the *Khalifah* to be negligent or tyrannical in performing his duties. This fear, however, cannot be removed except by the text (*Nass*) of the Book or the *Sunnah*. So the special caliph is one whose knowledge and sense of equity are guaranteed by God and His Prophet.

Shah Waliyullah makes certain further observations and says that the special claiph must be one of the first immigrants (*Al-Muhajirin al-awwalin*), and he should have been present at the Truce of Hudaybiyah and participated along with the Prophet in Badr, Tabuk and other major campaigns.[54]

After making these categorical statements Waliyullah brings forth a good number of verses from the Qur'an and hundreds of traditions from the Prophet to substantiate his thesis.

And when he has fully established his thesis, he observes that a large number of the Companions of the Prophet possessed the qualities required for the *Khilafah Khassah*, and some of them actually enjoyed the status of *Khalifah* in special fields; for instance, Ibne Mas'ud in Qira'at and fiqh (Qur'anic reading and law), Mu'adh b. Jabal in the adjudication of litigations (*Fasl al-khusumat*) and Zayd bin Thabit in the law of Inheritance (*al-fara'id*). There were others who were competent to assume the responsibilities of the Absolute Caliphate (*Khilafah mutlaqah*). "Now these persons entitled to the absolute caliphate are waiting upon the presence of the Lord to see whom the divine grace actually selects for this august office. But in fact only these four are appointed to this office and the rest are ordered to serve under them."[55]

This exactly seems to correspond to the *Khilafat al-Nubuwwah* concept of Ibne Taymiyah. And from the clarifications of Waliyullah it is abundantly clear that this institution cannot reappear in history. Logically speaking, therefore, it cannot serve as a basis for political theorizing in Islam. This is obviously the attitude of Ibne 'Abd al-Barr, Ibne Taymiyah and Waliyullah. The majority of Muslim political thinkers, however, regard the regime of the first four caliphs as the ideal which is always realizable.

In this concept of the special caliphate, according to Waliyullah, the *Khalifah* is not only a successor of the Prophet in point of time, but he is really chosen To this office by divine grace and prophetic laws of the state, otherwise this divine choice would be of no avail. For instance, in the opinion of both these scholars, 'Ali was capable of the special caliphate, but these laws were not observed in his case and so the *Khilafat al-Nubuwwah* was, in fact, not realized in his regime. To this subject Waliyullah has devoted a full chapter entitled "About the fact that the special caliphate did not materialize in the regime of

'Ali, although he possessed all the attributes of the <u>*Khilafah*</u> *khassah*"[56] And Ibne Taymiyah also observes "In his ('Ali's) regime neither the <u>*Khilafat al-Nubuwwah*</u> was realized nor absolute political power (*Mulk*),"[57] although he frequently says that 'Ali was one of the <u>*Khulafa' rashidun.*</u>[58] So the idea of delegated authority, even with reference to the, <u>*Khilafat al-Nubuwwah*</u>, is absent from Ibne Taymiyah and Waliy Ullah both. And as regards later political development in Islamic history, Ibne Taymiyah calls it *Mulk* and Waliy Ullah calls it <u>*Khilafah*</u> *'Ammah,* but neither of them says that authority in this form of the state is delegated by God or His Prophet.

Waliyullah defines the <u>*Khilafah*</u> *'ammah* as "the general state which has been actually founded for the establishment of religion, representing the Prophet in the performance of the following functions: establishment of the pillars of Islam; organization of *Jihad* and other matters connected with it, like the training of the armed forces, fixation of the salaries of soldiers and apportionment of booty to them; organization of the judiciary, enforcement of the penal provisions of the Qur'an (*Hudud*), hearing of appeals and the commanding of good and forbidding of evil."[59] It is very clear that the authority is to be originally created by the Muslims and not received from the Prophet. At another place he says, "And we regard the <u>*Khilafah*</u> as the rule and authority of the Muslims."[60] A little further in the same context he says, "And in the language of the *shari'ah* the <u>*Khilafah*</u> means an Islamic state which has been founded for the establishment of religion, and comes into being to perform the functions of the Prophet."[61] So if by delegation of authority is meant the moral sanction of the Prophet, there can be no question about it. But if what is meant is the transfer of political authority, it is neither logically true nor historically. So far as Ibne Taymiyah is concerned, he utterly rejects the idea of vicegerency, and, therefore, the problem of delegation is no problem for him.

In our opinion, it is difficult to accept the concept of the special caliphate, either from Ibne Taymiyah or Waliy Ullah. Both these authors, along with the majority of the *Ummah*, agree that the Prophet neither gave any political constitution nor nominated anyone to succeed him. Once this fact is accepted, the entire idea of vicegerency and delegation becomes untenable. Ibne Taymiyah has come nearer to the truth than Waliyullah, for, unlike the latter, he altogether rejects the classical theory of the caliphate, and gives a general theory of the state which stands more to reason than anything else that has been written on this subject by any Muslim political thinker. His insistence, however, to call the first four successors of the Prophet *Khulafa' al-Nabiy'* and not to give this title to others has no justification. He is of the view that even if the other rulers fulfilled all the conditions which were realized in the regime of the early caliphs, they would still not receive this title, simply because the Prophet is alleged to have said that the ideal regime of his successors would not last more than thirty years, or because there are faint and veiled references in certain traditions to the goodness and virtue of the early caliphs. No sound political theory can be built on these weak traditions. Moreover, if the *Khilafat al-Nubuwwah* is limited in time, it would in-volve an impossible conclusion for any Muslim to accept, that the ideal pattern of the Islamic state is incapable of functioning in history for more than thirty years. And it is impossible to believe that the Prophet (P.B.U.H.) himself would have pronounced this dictum.

Now the question is: why did Ibne Taymiyah propound such an impossible theory, when his other political speculations seem to be quite sound and reasonable? The answer is not far to seek. He wrote the *Minhaj*, which is the main source of this idea, only to counter Shi'ism, which was menacing the world of Islam seriously in his day, under the patronage of the Mongols.

The very basis of *Shi'ahism* is the concept of the *Imamate*. As against the idea of the specially chosen, guided and infallible *Imams*, Ibne Taymiyah built up the concept of *Khilafat al-Nubuwwah*. History was on his side; all that he has written about the early caliphs is factually true. He subsumed these facts under a theory and proved that the regime of the orthodox caliphs is the ideal of Islamic polity and it is no longer possible for anyone in history to excel them and give a better performance. If this opinion is accepted the *Shi'i* concept of the *Imamate* is automatically nullified and this is what Ibne Taymiyah wanted to achieve.

Another aim in Ibne Taymiyah's view was to revive faith in early Islam. Ibne Taymiyah lived in the age of universal despair and specticism resulting mainly from Mongolism and Shi'ism. He felt it necessary to take back the people to the glorious age when the *Sunnah* of the Prophet served as the ideal basis of social and political organization. He is, therefore, less interested in political theory than in emphasizing the fact that the *Sunnah* of the Prophet can be translated into practice as it was done under the early caliphs. But being brought up and trained in the strict Hambali School, he could not utterly throw off the weight of tradition. He was a great fighter against *Bid'ah* (innovation) and falsehood, yet he could not detect the deceit hidden in many a spurious tradition that carried with it the authentication of long ages of history. He faithfully believed in the traditional saying that the *Khilafah* of the Prophet would not last more than thirty years and also in the dreamtraditions which limit the *Khilafah* to the first three or four caliphs. He also believed that the law of the *shari'ah* can function in every age as efficiently as it did in its early career. But somehow, partly instinctively and partly because of the weight of tradition, he thinks that personalities like Abu Bakr and 'Umar shall not emerge again in history, although the *shari'ah* may rule supreme.

In the end it may be observed that the idea of an irrepeatable special caliphate did not exist in early Islam. Especially under the Umayyads, the opposition always demanded that the regime of the early caliphs should be restored; and it could not make this demand unless it believed that such realization was possible. It was given a maystical religious sanctity and exclusiveness under the 'Abbasids, when the opposition had, for fear of dreadful persecution, withdrawn its claim. This latter idea was, continually nourished in history as a romantic vision to feed the spiritual susceptibilities of the believers. And Ibne Taymiyah could not be immune from it.

## Notes

1.  *Minhaj*, vol. I, p. 17. What Ibne Taym'yah means by this assertion is not that there was no political authority during the regime of the Prophet. He only wanted to emphasize that this political authority was subject to his moral authority and it did not depend for its power on any other source except the moral will of the people. And as the Prophetic regime did not rest on the ordinary attributes of the state, Ibne Taymiyah refused to call it by this name and demanded that it must be termed only as *Nubuwwah*.

2.  Ibne Khaldun, *Muqaddimah*, translated by Franz Rosenthal, New York 1958, vol. I, pp. 388-89.

3.  Ahmad bin Yahya al-Baladhuri, Ansab al-ashrsf, edited by Hamidullah, Cairo, vol. I, p, 582.

4.  Ibid., p. 585.

5.  Ibid., p. 587; 'Abd Allah b. Muslim b. Qutaybah, al-Imsmah wa'l-siyasah, Cairo, p. 16.

6.  Muhammad b. Jarir al-Tabari, Tarkh, Cairo, vol. 3, p.

209; *Al-Imamah wa 'l-siyasah* (op. cit.) p. 9.

7.  Abu Yusuf, al-Radd 'ala Siyar al-Awza'i, edited by Abu'l-Wafa' al-Afghani, Cairo 1938 A.C. p. 23: "then the leaders of guidance (*'Immat al-huda*) are agreed to give a share to one who has died or is slain (*In Jihad*)"; (here the word *a'Immoh* refers also to the scholars and the jurists although it can also mean the political authority.); page [47]: "If the *Imam*, after dividing the booty of war among his combatants, says: "anyone who has slain a person (from the enemy) can take his belongings', then he is right and permitted in making this decision"; (here the word *Imam* obviously means the commander of the army): p. 4: "When the *Imam* appears at a place and fights and defeats its people then his order shall be obeyed in that place, and there is no harm if he distributes the booty before returning"; (here too the word *Imam* clearly refers to the local commander); p. 80: "When an army fights in an enemy territory and is headed by an *Amir* then he shall not enforce the hudid (Qur'anic punishments) hi his troops, except when he happens to be the governor of Egypt, Syria, Iraq or a similar province, in that case he can enforce"; p. 20: "The *Imams* gave no share for mules before the outbreak of civil war, following the assassination of Walid bin Yazid))"; (here *"Imams"* certainly means caliphs and heads of state).

8.  Al-Tabari, *op. cit.*, vol. 5, p. 22; Ibne Khaldun, *Muqaddimah*, Cairo edition, p. 227; the Encyclopaedia of Islam, New edition, Leiden 1960, vol. I, p. 445 reports, "From this time (Umar's time) until the end of the caliphate as an institution, *Amir al-mu'minin* was employed exclusively as the protocollary title of a caliph."

9.  T.W. Arnold, The Caliphate, Oxford 1942.
10. *Minhaj*, vol. i.p. 135; Ibne Hazmt al-Fisal, vot.4, p. 107.
11. *Minhaj*, vol. i, p. 137.
12. Quotation: Hadith.
13. Quotation: Hadith.
14. Al-Qur'an, ch. 10:14.
15. Ibid., ch. 2:30.
16. Ibid., ch. 6:166.
17. Ibid.,ch.. 38:26.
18. *Minhaj*, vol. 1, p. 137.
19. *Minhaj*, vol. 3, p. 131.
20. *Minhaj*, vol. 3, p. 131.
21. Al-Qur'an, ch. 43:60.
22. Ibid., ch. 7:69.
23. Ibid., ch. 7:74.
24. Ibid., ch. 7:142.
25. Ibid,,ch. 25:62.
26. Ibid., ch. 10:6.
27. Ibid., ch. 7:129.
28. Ibid., ch. 24:45.
28a. *Minhaj*, vol. 3, p. 131: Majd Ad-din Ibne al-Athir in his
     "*Al-Nihayah fi gharib al-Hadith*" quotes a large number
     of traditions to prove that <u>Khalafa</u> means "to succeed"
     or "come afterwards" and "<u>Khalifah</u> is one who takes
     the place of one who is gone and performs the func-tions
     which the former used to perform, (vol. 1, pp. 349-50).
     The same sense of <u>Khalafa</u> can be found in all the
     standard classical dictionaries of Arabic, like the *Lisan
     al-'Arab* and the *Taj al-'arus*.
29   Ibid., Ibne Taymiyah takes up the discussion once again
     in the vol. 2, pp. 460-61.

30 Abu'l-Kalam Azad, *Khilafah* (Urdu); Abu'l-A'ls al-Mawdudi, The Islamic Concept of State (Urdu). It is a small tract published frequently from Lahore, in several languages.

31 'Abd al-Qadir 'Awdah, al-Tashri' al-jina'i al-Islami, Cairo 1959, vol. 1, p. 13.

32 Al-Qur'an, ch. 7:69.

33 Ibid., ch. 7:74.

34 Ibid., ch. 10:73.

35 *Minhaj*, vol. 1, p. 137.

36 Ibid., p. 138.

37 Ibne 'abd Rabbihi, al-'Iqd al-farid, vol. 3, p. 241.

38 Al-Qur'an, ch. 16:163.

39 No Muslim commentator, jurist or theologian has interpreted the verses of responsibility (*Taklif*) in the Qur'an in the sense of delegation of authority.

40 E. J. Rosenthal has also made the same mistake by translating *Al-inabah al-nabaviyah* into "prophetic vice-gerency," (Political Thought in Medieval Islam. Cambridge, 1958). The word vice-gerency carries the sense of delegation but Ibne Taymiyah does not mean this. According to the Sunni theory, the Prophet did not nominate anyone to succeed him; therefore the question of delegation of authority does not arise. Nor does the word *Inabah* carry any political significance for one can be *Na'ib* of (to deputize for) only a living person, so none of the Muslim rulers who came after the Prophet can be termed as his *Na'ib*, because they wielded sovereign power and were not subject to any superior authority. *Inabat al-Nubuwwah*, therefore, must be taken in the figurative and moral sense of establishing the law of the *Shar'ah* as the Prophet did. And this is the

meaning given to it invariably by all Muslim political thinkers. The well-known tradition: "The *'Ulama'* are the inheritors of the Prophet", is meant to convey the same idea.

41   *Minhaj*, vol. 1, p. 134, p. 138.
42   Ibid., p. 28.
43   Ibid., p. 28, p. 144, p. 145; vol. 2, p. 239.
44   *Minhaj*, vol. 3, p. 131.
45   *Minhaj*, vol. 1, p. 86-89.
46   *Minhaj*, vol. 2, pp. 138.
47   Abu Zahrah, "Ibne Taymiyah", Cairo, p. 345.
48   *Minhaj*, vol. 2, p. 239.
49   Waliyullah, *Izalat al-Khafa' 'An Khilafat' al Khulafa'*, (Urdu translation by 'Abd ush-Shakur, Karachi), vol. 1, p. 27.
50   Ibid., pp. 121-22.
51   Ibid., p. 123.
52   Ibid., p. 40.
53   Al-Qur'an, ch. 6:124.
54   Izalah, vol. 1, p. 43.
55   Ibid., p. 59.
56   Ibid., p. 632.
57   *Minhaj*, vol. 1, p. 138.
58   *Minhaj*, vol. 2, p. 204.
59   Izalah, vol. 1, p. 28.
60   Ibid., p. 506.
61   Ibid. p. 507.

# CHAPTER V

## THE GENEARL CONCEPT OF THE STATE

### 1. *The theory of Compromise.*

To understand Ibne Taymiyah's attitude toward a general theory of state, it will be necessary to examine the historic past against which he reacted so sharply.

Islam started as a community of believers in Makkah. After a bitter and protracted struggle, it shifted to Ya<u>th</u>rib, where it succeeded in establishing a *political* state of its own. After the death of the Prophet (P.B.U.H.) this state came to be known as the Caliphate. But before Islam the Arabs had no idea of nation, nationality or state. The idea was born out of this new religion, and it was very much different from existing ideas on the subject. The state of Madinah was not conditioned by geographical limits or race or colour or nationality. It represented the general will of an organized community of believers which transcended the clan, the tribe and the nation. The *Ummah*, which established this state, was potentially international, and the only cohesive force, which bound together men of differing traditions, customs, race and nationality, was the message of Allah sent to mankind through His Prophet Muhammad (P.B.U.H.).

It is now a completely exploded theory that "material inducements of booty and landed property as a result of the holy war (*Jihad*) on behalf of Allah succeeded in winning the allegiance to Islam of independent, proved, born warriors."[1] The real secret of the rapid expansion of the Islamic power in Asia, Africa and Europe and its eager acceptance by large number of pagans, Christians, Jews, and Zoroastrians lies in the fact that Islam alone inherently possessed those virtues and qualities, which fulfil the spiritual and material aspirations of man. It proposed a comprehensive law for the guidance of man;[2] this law actually and dominantly controlled and guided civilized life on this earth for more than one thousand years, and still provides guidance for more than six hundred million people in the world. This law is known as the *Shari'ah*, the road leading to Allah. The *Shari'ah*, the law of the Islamic state, is derived from the Qur'an, the *Sunnah* of the Prophet and the *Ijma'* (consensus) and *Ijtihad* (systematic reasoning) of the *Ummah*. The constitutional law of Islam is derived from the same sources, and is discussed in all the standard works on *fiqh* and politico-juridical treatises.

Much doubt has been cast in modern times on the nature and essence of the *Shari'ah*. It is often said that the Islamic law underwent a long period of development before it was codified into the four schools of law. Also much of the law is based on fabricated traditions projected back to the Prophet to seek religious sanction. No one can deny that a large number of traditions were forged during the formative period of the Islamic law. And no one can question the fact that the Islamic law passed through a continuous process of growth and orientation, before it was formally organized. But one must bear in mind that the Qur'an did not any process of development. And the *Sunnah mutawatirah* (the practice of the Prophet reported by his generation to the next generation) did not experience any mutation in its essentials. And these two are the bases of the *Shari'ah*. So the fundamentals of the Islamic law have always remained intact. The questions of interpretation and application arc, however, different matters. Further the principles of *Ijtihad* and *Ijma'* are given by the Qur'an and the *Sunnah* themselves. These principles provide continuous development and progress within the framework of the Shari'ah. Therefore in early history when Islam expanded rapidly over the globe and was confronted with thousands of problems of daily importance the Muslim jurists were faced with the task of meeting this challenge and integrating the political, social and economic life of their age into the religious life of Islam. They performed this task with marvellous success. Indeed, it was this principle of dynamism and growth that kept the Shari'ah alive and universally applicable.

From the very beginning in Islam politics was so intimately interwoven with religion that the one could not be divorced from the other. The state and Islam were certainly not equivalents, yet the state was regarded as the agent of religion. The *Fuqaha'* (jurists) were, therefore, under obligation not only to keep the authority of the Shari'ah unimpaired but also develop the constitutional theory in line with political reality. The Prophet (P.B.U.H.) was the spiritual and temporal head of the community and so the political order that was established after him followed his *Sunnah*, and the caliph became the supreme political leader of the community and executor of the Shari'ah. This was the real situation under the Orthodox Caliphs, the Umayyads and the early 'Abbasids. But in the middle of the third century of the *Hijrah* the conditions greatly changed. The caliph became extremely weak and real power was wielded by the *Amir al-umara* who later on acquired the title of *Sultan*. In theory, however, the caliph remained the supreme authority in the State, because all the usurpers of real power were Qura shites, who could not appropriate the caliphal dignity, and if they did they would do violence to the religious susceptibilities of the Muslims and would not be recognized. The *Fuqaha'* were thus forced to effect a compromise between theory and practice. The Islamic law insisted on the unity of the *Ummah* and its authority; therefore, the weak caliph was nominally allowed to hold supreme authority while the *Amir* was granted effective power to rule. Hence, Rosenthal is not quite right in observing, "Muslim law does not differentiate between authority and power."[3] According to the *Shari'ah* there can be only one supreme authority, the caliph. He can of course delegate all or part of his authority to his *Amirs*, governors, ministers, judges and other agents. So when the Turks, the Buwayhids and the Saljuqs usurped power in Baghdad and became the actual rulers of the vast 'Abbasid empire, they were theoretically regarded as were agents of the powerless Caliph. To maintain the dignity of the *Shari'ah* a formal investitute ceremony was held in which the Caliph delegated all his powers to the *Amir* and awarded him a written diploma (*Sanad*) to rule in his name. And it often happened that the diploma was given in return for the *Amir's* recognition of the Caliph. This is how the facade of unity was maintained in the Muslim world. This unity was a legal fiction but it was real in the sense that it saved the Muslim world from political disintegration for long centuries.

The concepts of the spiritual and the temporal did not exist in Islamic polity as it was in Christendom.[4] The reasons are twofold. One is that in Islam there is no scope for an organized church in the Christian sense; that is, the Muslim clergy, as such, does not represent a special class against the rest, of the *Ummah,* and it is not invested with any authority to control the spiritual life of the believers. The Caliph is not the vicar of the Prophet, he only represents him in the enforcement of the *Shari'ah*; he neither communicates with God nor is he entitled to make any basic change in *Shari'ah*. The second reason is that Islam does not recognize two laws for the community. It has only one law, that of the *Shari'ah*, which is all-pervad ng and all-embracing, guiding and controlling the entire life of the believers. The head of the Islamic state is, therefore, the religious as well as the political head of the community, and the question of a clash' between the two forces does not arise. This is indeed the theory. In practice, however, the lay power has occasionally acted independently and arbitrarily although it has never challenged or abrogated the *Shari'ah*. And it is a fact that if constitutional problems are accepted, the law of the *Shari'ah* that almost ruled supreme in all Muslim states throughout history. And even in constitutional developments the dominant role and dignity of the *Shari'ah* has been remarkably maintained.

But the Sunni theory of the Caliphate, as enunciated above, leaves very little scope for the development of an independent political philosophy in Islam. This accounts for the monotony and extreme deficiency of new thought in the numerous political treatises written by Muslim thinkers. The weight of tradition is so great that even an unusually independent thinker like Ibne Khaldun does not deviate from the main thesis of the classical theory. Commenting on this issue Rosenthal observes; "The existence of the state as the political organization of the *Ummah* or *Jama'ah*, the Muslim community, is taken for granted. The jurists do not ask whether and why there must be a state; they are only concerned with the application of the *Shari'ah* to the body-politic."[5] It is admitted that the *Sunni* theory is hardened and inflexible, but it is impossible to accept this statement of Rosenthal as it stands. The Islamic *Ummah* like any other *Ummah* has certainly always felt the necessity of establishing the state to preserve its existence and identity, but it has never *Ipso facto* assumed the existence of the Islamic state in the Muslim community. The infidel Mongols ruled over the lands of Eastern caliphate for one and a half centuries, yet the Muslims did not recognize that there was any Islamic state in subjection. Similarly during the nineteenth century almost the whole of the world of Islam was occupied by the colonial imperialist powers of the West but no Muslim had the illusion that despite this situation 'the Islamic state continued to exist, if not to function, in these enslaved territories. And to say that the Muslim jurists never think whether and why the state is necessary is simply closing one's eyes before glaring facts of history. We have discussed this matter in some tie-tail in Chapter Two and shown that on the contrary, it has been one of the most critical problems of Islamic history, and has seriously engaged the attention of the Muslims throughout history. If, however, certain ideas about it have become dogmatic, that is another matter. And the last remark that jurists are concerned only with the application of the *Shari'ah* and nothing more, is not at all true. In fact it is these jurists who have, without respect to history, continuously maintained the idealism in Islamic polity. Un-doubtedly their principal aim is the application of the *Shari'ah*, but they have always felt and advocated that the *Shari'ah* can not function properly and ideally except in a rightly constituted political organization.

By Ibne Taymiyah's time, the compromise in the classical theory had gone too far. The fall of Baghdad marked the practical extinction of the caliphate, but the Mamluks immediately revived the institution in Egypt. One of the refugee 'Abbasid princes was installed in Egypt as the Caliph of Islam, and the dynasty theoretically continued to rule for the next two and a half centuries, until the advent of Ottoman power in the West But the 'Abbasid Caliph in Egypt enjoyed no real power or authority, and his claim to original and central authority was not even seriously considered by anyone. Ibne *Jama'ah's*[6] efforts to maintain the old fiction, that under the *Shari'ah* the caliph wielded supreme authority and the Mamluks exercised effective power only through delegation, remained a mere bookish formula which nobody believed. The spurious Caliph was no more than a shadow, a mere device to obtain the obedience of the Muslims outside the clutches of the Mongols, and to inspire rebellion m the Muslims who had fallen prey to the Mongol invaders. For all practical purposes the institution of the Caliphate became a futile idea; it really did not exist anywhere. Indeed there was always a Caliph, but he enjoyed absolutely no authority, power, influence, dignity or respect from the public. He was mostly confined to the place and was taken out in the open only on rare ceremonial occasions, and often the common people did not ever know who the caliph of their time was. The compromise theory, therefore, could not be extended any further and there was not the least advantage in backing the dead horse. The evil implications of the theory had by now fully come to the surface; and everyone could understand that:

1.  The lay power was the real power and it was completely independent of the religious authority of the Caliph.

2.  The Caliph had become almost a non-entity, even a mere nuisance; the theory of delegation had utterly failed.

3.  Political power in the world of Islam had passed into non-Arab and non-Qurayashite hands long since. It was no use harping on the Qurayashite hegemony any more. And to recreate the unity of the *Ummah* it was high time to abandon the theory of the supremacy of the Arabs over non-Arabs.

4.  Through seven hundred years of Islamic polity it loud not be shown, either by theorizing or from the actual practices of history, that the theory of the caliphate had any real religious foundation.

5.  The dualist theory was doing positive harm to the *Shari'ah,* in the sense that arbitrary and oppressive secular power was continually flouting its authority, yet it was always justified and tolerated in the name of

religion. As a consequence, the *Ummah* was seriously threatened by the forces of disintegration. The only thing that could keep it together and sustain it as one moral and social order on earth was the cohesive force and authority of the *Shari'ah,* which had by now almost completely lost its status as the basic guiding principle in Muslim polity.

This political impasse was broken by Ibne Taymiyah. He (rejected the compromise for good, and gave to the *Ummah* a new political ideal that was Islamic, real, practicable and enduring.

First of all, he considers the social order under the Prophet and refuses to call it a state (*Imamah*). He says it is true that the Prophet was obeyed in all matters by members of the community but he was obeyed only as a Prophet, and not as the head of a state. He issued judicial decrees, collected revenues, waged wars, concluded treaties, and entered into international relations, but all these functions he performed simply as a prophet. These achievements were not a condition to his prophecy, but the natural and necessary outcome of it. And then he was obeyed even when he possessed no power just as much as when he became the leader of a powerful community. And he was obeyed when he was alone and shall be obeyed by his followers until the end of time. These, are not attributes of political sovereignty which is the very basis of the state. Further, he was neither chosen nor inducted into power by his people, nor was he responsible to them for his conduct. In other words, if we use the word sovereignty in relation to him it must be admitted that it was not derived from the consent or will of the people, it was conferred on him by God. And finally, the Qur'an has on numerous occasions clearly defined the aims and objects of his prophecy, but nowhere mentioned that the establishment of political authority is also one of his duties. From all this it follows that no constitutional theory in Islam can be built from the political practices of the Prophet (P.B.U.H.). Ibne Taymiyah does not deny that there was some kind of political authority during the regime of the Prophet, What he insists upon is that the Prophetic regime is a *Sui generis* institution and as such it cannot serve as the basis of a political theory in Islam.

Further, Ibne Taymiyyah regards the political order that came into being in Madinah after the death of the prophet as a special dispensation of Allah and calls it *Khilafat al-nubu-wwah*. And this caliphate too, in his opinion, possesses a *Sui generis* character, and is not realizable again in history. For the Prophet has declared that it will last only thirty years after which there will be dominion, that is, general political order and not prophetic succession. It is true that the Umayyads, the 'Abbasids and others called themselves *Khulafa'*, but we accept them as such because they possessed actual power and authority and "were the Kings of the Muslims and masters of the earth."? They did not rule as the vicegerents of the Prophet, but only came after him in point of time and enforced his *Shari'ah* as the fundamental law of the state as best as they could, and so were popularly called *Khulafa'*. Historical practice of the Muslims, therefore, offers for Ibne Taymiyah no basis for a political philosophy. He does not fall into the error of justifying actual political power as authority delegated by a shadowcaliph. And since he does not see the indication of a constitutional theory in the Qur'an or the *Sunnah* or the practice of the Orthodox Caliphs, he ignores the classical theory of the caliphate altogether.

After discussing, in the *Minhaj*, the role of the Prophet as the guide and leader of men and of the Orthodox Caliphs as the successors of the Prophet, he abandons the thought of the Caliphate and theorizing about it for good, and is not the least interested in the form or pattern of government. He knew very well the mistakes of the *Sunni* concept of the *Khilafah* and the

Shi'ah concept of the *Imamah*; he knew the shaky foundations of both the concepts; he had read with a bitter feeling about the scramble for power in the early history of Islam and the long and destructive conflict between the weak 'Abbisid Caliphs and their powerful *Amirs* and *Sultans*; and had finally watched with pain the mockery of the spurious caliphate set up in Egypt by the Mamluks. He clearly saw that all the claims of the jurists and the theologians about the institution of the ideal Islamic *Imamate* were empty talk and the ever increasing modification in the theory of the Caliphate was a perpetual concession to the stark facts of history. This was, therefore, no idealism but mere opportunism. These lessons of history convinced him fully that to propound a permanent constitutional theory for the Muslim world can neither be realistic nor practicable. Moreover, there was no demand for such a theory either from the *Shari'ah* or from the circumstances of his time. Also he realized that if he launched a new theory he would be confronted with a stiff and ,violent opposition from the traditionalist school. He was continually persecuted for his other ideas there was no need to indulge in a new fruitless controversy. He, therefore, abandoned the idea of the constitution but seriously concerned himself with the ideas of state and government.

## 2. *The Community (Ummah)*.

The concept of an *Ummah* professing the religion of Islam as given by the Prophet Muhammad (P.B.U.H.) is defined and discussed in much greater detail and clarity than any state theory in the works of Ibne Taymiyah. As a matter of fact, he emphasizes it in almost everything that he has written. In addition to the numerous statements he has made on the subject in the *Minhaj, al-Siyasah* and the *Hisbah*, he has given it exclusive treatment in the famous tracts (*Rasa'il*) that he has written to define the Islamic faith. The most important of these are:

(1) *Al-Wasiyah al-Kubra,*

(2) *Al-'Aqidah al-Hamawiyah al-Kubra,*

(3) *Al-'Aqidah al-Wasitiyah,*

(4) *Al-Furqan bayn al-haqq wa'l-batil*

(5) *Iqtida' al-Sirat   al-mustaqim and the Qa'idah fi tawahhud al-millah wa ta'addud al-Shara'i.*

This emphasis seems to be born out of the feeling that the *Ummah*, being the recipient of the message of God, holds overall responsibility for the preservation and propagation of the faith; and the state-organization is only one of its functions and, therefore, deserves less attention and proportionate importance.

The idea of a unified and universal Muslim community has been co-existent with Islam. The political and social milieu of Ibne Taymiyah, however, compelled him to give it a different and original orientation. Internally he was worried by the Shi'ah heresy which was undermining the very basis of Islam, and by the treason of the Jewish and Christian minorities. Externally he was deeply moved by the memory of the Crusades and the Tartar invasion. These dangers were a standing threat to the free Muslim world of which the Mamluk Empire in Egypt and Syria formed the nucleus. This historical situation dictated a unity of front, severe discipline and mutual understanding among the Muslims. And Ibne Taymiyah stands out as the unique figure of that age who endeavoured to realize these ends.

The word *Ummah* is derived from the root *Amm,* meaning to aim at or to intend. "*Ummah*" therefore carries many senses denoting this original meaning of intending. Primarily, however, it means the people who intend to follow a leader (*Imam*) a law (*Shari'ah*), a religion (*Deen*) or a path (*Minhaj*), and also the thing intended. Hence the two principal concepts denoted by the term *Ummah* are "community" and "religion," and they are used separately and are also combined to denote a religious community. We shall now investigate the sense in which it has been employed in the Qur'an, because that would give us a direct clue to the understanding of the historical *Ummah* of Muhammad (P.B.U.H.). First, it is used in the sense of a nation without any qualification, as in the following verses:

1. Those are an *Ummah* that have passed away; for them is what they earned and for you what you earn. (2:134).

2. And certainly We raised in every *Ummah* a messenger.[9]

3. And every *Ummah* has a term; so when its term comes they can neither delay nor overtake it in advance by a single moment.[9a]

4. And if Allah had pleased He would have made you a single *Ummah*.[9b]

Secondly, it is used in the sense of a party or group of people, as in the following verses:

1. And from among you there should be an *Ummah* who invite to good and enjoin the right and forbid the wrong.[9c]

2. And of Moses' people there is an *Ummah* who guide with truth and therewith they do justice.[9d]

3. And when an *Ummah* of them said: Why preach you to a people whom Allah would destroy or whom He would chastise with a severe punishment?[9e]

Thirdly, it is used in the sense of a religion, as in the following verses:

1. Nay, they say: We found our fathers on an *Ummah* (course, religion) and surely we are guided by them.[9f]

2. And thus, We sent not before thee a Warner in a town, but its wealthy ones said: Surely we found our fathers

following an *Ummah* (religion), and we follow their footsteps. [9g]

Fourthly, it is used to deonte period of time, that is, the duration for which a thing is intended, as in the following verses:

1.  And if We delay for them the chastisement for a stated period (*Ummah ma 'dudah*), they will certainly say: What prevented it?[9h]

2.  And of the two, he who had found deliverance and remembered after a long tune, said: I will inform you of :ts interpretation, so send me.[9i]

Fifthly, it is used to combine the first and third senses, that is, to denote a religious community. It is especially in this sense that the Qur'an speaks of the Followers of Muhammad (P.B.U.H.) when it addresses them as an *Ummah*, as in the following verses:

1.  You are the best *Ummah* raised up for men; you enjoin good and forbid evil and you believe in Allah. [9j]

2.  And thus We have made you an exalted *Ummah* that you may be the bearers of witness to the people and (that) the Messenger may be a bearer of witness to you.[9k]

There is abundant evidence to show that thd Qur'an frequently uses the word *Ummah* in the absolute sense of a nation.   This is why when Abraham was building the Ka'bah with the help of his son, he prayed to God, "Our Lord!  Make us both submissive to Thee, and (raise) from our offspring a nation submissive (*Ummah muslimah*) to Thee."[9L] An *Ummah* may be Muslim as well as *Kafir,* neverthe-less, when the Qur'an uses the word *Ummah* for the followers of Muhammad (P.B.U.H.) it exclusively refers to the believers (*Mu'minin*). In other words, according to the Qur'an, the *Ummah* of Muhammad (P.B.U.H.) are only the *Mu'mins* and the Muslims. This concept we consistently find in the Qur'an; in recent times, however, some doubt has been cast on it by Muslims and non-Muslims alike. The doubt is engendered not by any text in the Qur'an but by a historical document, i.e., the Pact of the Prophet with the Jews of Madman. In this Pact there occurs a statement; *"Inna Yahud Bam 'Awf ummatun* ma'a *'l-Mu'minin.*" Montgomry Watt translates it: "The Jews of Banu 'Awf are a community (*Ummah*) along with the Muslims," meaning that the Jews and the Muslims together from one *Ummah*. He writes, "There in Article 1, it is stated that the believers and Muslims of Quraysh and Yathrib are one *Ummah*: and this community presumably includes also those who follow them...The *Ummah* is thus the complex community at Madinah to which Muhammad (P.B.U.H.) believed himself to be sent. The later article (Art. 25), which affirms that certain Jews are an *Ummah* along with the believers, though it could conceivably mean that they constituted a community parallel to that of the believers, presumably means that they are included in the one *Ummah*. As they are specifically allowed to practice their own religion, however, this suggests that the *Ummah* is no longer a religious community."[9]m

In the next paragraph he remarks, "To the external observer is dear that the *Ummah* as described in the Constitution of Madinah in fact has a territorial basis." It is impossible to accept these observations of Watt; for, in the first place they violate the concept of the *Ummah* in the Qur'an, and secondly, they contradict the first article of the Constitution. The protocollary para with the first article reads: "This is a writing of Muahmmad the Prophet between the believers and Muslims of Quraysh and Yathrib and those who follow them then join them and fight along with them:

1.  "That they are a single community to the exclusion of the rest of mankind." Watt has wrongly interpreted the

word *"Tabi'ahum"* making it mean the infidel tribes
outside Madinah who made themselves a party to this
political covenant but have not been specifically
mentioned in the document. But the clarity and emphasis
of the first article utterly precludes this interpretation.
He has also incorrectly translated the words *"Falahiqa
bihim"*. The letter "fa" indicates that "following the
*Mu'minin* and the *Muslimin"* was not a mere physical
act but conformity with them in faith. Further, there is
no syntactical or philological necessity to translate the
words *"Ma'a'l-Mu'minin* in art. 25 as "along -with the
believers." Grammatically as well as considering the
unequivocal declaration in the beginning of the
Constitution, art. 25 should be properly translated as
"The Jews of Banu 'Awf are a community (*Ummah*) by
the side of the believers," that is, they are a distinct
community who has entered into a political alliance with
the Muslims.

The concept of the historical *Ummah* of Mohammad
(P.B.U.H.), that is, a community following a definite religion
and ideology, is undoubtedly the same as the concept of
Muhammad's (P.B.U.H.) *Ummah* in the Qur'an. In support of
our view we quote only one example from one of the most
important and reliable documents of the early history of Islam-
the Pact of Arbitration between 'Ali and Mu'awiyah. The pact
was concluded in 37 H. The word *Ummah* occurs thrice in it,
exclusively in the sense of the Muslim *Ummah*. The relevant
clauses are: [9n]

"Clause 7. And the *Ummah* (community) shall support
them on whatever decision they (the two arbitrators) take
righteously in accordance with the Qur'an."

"Clause 11............ And if they violate (the conditions

of the pact) and do excess then the *Ummah* shall be free from their judgment and shall have no obligation or protection for them."

"Clause 17. And the *Ummah* guarantees this pact because of the obligation it Owes to Him and the covenant it has made with Him."

In recent times the idea of a composite *Ummah* was strongly pleaded by the *'Ulama'* of India before its partition into the independent states of Pakistan and India. They principally took their inspiration from the Pact of Madinah. The many Muslims of India, in general, however, rejected this theory and their very struggle for the establishment of a separate homeland for themselves was based on the concept of a separate *Ummah* and religious unity.

The real truth is that on Principle, the Muslim never coerces the non-believers to embrace Islam. Hence non-Muslims have always been tolerated and protected in the Muslins society more than confessional minorities elsewhere. They have lived, often happily, in the midst of the Muslims, although they were not regarded as a constituent part of the *Ummah*.

The pressure of circumstances, however, compelled Ibne Taymiyah to develop the notion of a confessional solidarity. He knew the juridical position well that non-Muslim groups can live with complete freedom in the Muslim state; tort experience of history had shown that these extraneous elements were never loyal and sincere. During the Crusades the Christians of Egypt and Syria served as spies and fifth columns for the European invaders, and they were fully helped by the Jews and the Shi'ahs. And the same triangular alliance worked against the Muslims during the Tartar invasion It is well-known that Qazan Khan, the Mongol conqueror, had given a pledge to Ibne Taymlyah that the city of Damascus would not be stormed if the Muslims ceased to resist. But the pledge was soon broken and when Ibne Taymryah wanted to see the emperor to ask him to stop the carnage and plunder in the metropolis, his Jewish minister stopped him from doing so and[10] the orgy continued. The Christians on their part persuaded the Mongols to show no mercy to the Muslims. They took the actual administration of the city into their own hands under Mongol patronage. They occupied the central mosques of Damascus and held drinking parties in them and sprinkled wine on Muslim passers by in the streets to injure their religious feelings.[11]

Ibne Taymtyah, therefore, condemns every principle of union other than Islam, and denounces every union that marks the triumph of multiplicity over unity, of the part over the whole. The sectarian solidarity which groups men around the distinctions of birth, race and religious deviationism, he denounces in the degree in which it works against the larger interest of Islam and hinders the good exercise of social and political life. He further says that this pernicious solidarity is often responsible for the failures of the functions of the state, for the partiality with which the agents of the state are appointed, for the dishonest distribution of the goods of the community, and for intercessions (*Shafa'ah*) in public affairs. This evil therefore must be rooted out if the community is to be preserved and to prosper.

Internally Ibne Taymiyah regards the Rawafid as the greatest obstacle in the expansion and progress of Islam and often remarks that they are far worse than the infidels and the pagans. He similarly denounces all the heretical sects in Islam and advocates a perpetual war against them.

To the solidarity of the *Ummah* he gives a fresh basis, going back to the Qur'an, and calls it the solidarity in goodness and God-fearing (*Al-birr wa'l-taqwa*), and in the sentiments of unity and fraternity. This basis combines, in the same ideal and for the same destiny, the mass of the believers from the mission of the Prophet Muhammad (P.B.U.H.) to the Day of Judgment. The community forms a grand organism in which each generation owes a moral debt to the preceding one for the good legacy it has received from it, and to the coming one to which it has to bequeath its own contribution.

This solidarity in the view of Ibne Taymlyah, is reflected in two forms, in the unity of faith and in the unity of language. The unity of faith consists in the recognition of homogeneous beliefs, belief in one God in one Prophet and in a core of common doctrines. This unity of faith practically applies only to the *Ahl al-Sunnah wa'l-Jama'ah*, who are the repository and custodians of the thought and practice of the Prophet and his Companions, and who represent the original Islam. The majority of the Muslims in the world belong to this category. They are called *Ahl al-Sunnah* because they follow the *Sunnah* (practice) of the Prophet, and are distinguished from those who follow the tradition of the family of the Prophet (*Ahl al-bayt*) and from those who follow other modes of knowledge than *Sunnah*. And they are called *Ahl al-Jama'ah* in opposition to the <u>*Kharijis*</u> and other dissident sects.[12] The *Ahl-al-Sunnah wal-Jama'ah* represent a cultural and doctrinal continuity from the time of the Prophet (P.B.U.H.). They are the moderate people, the only sect among the seventy three sects of the *Ummah* that will be saved from the fire of the hell. Their chief characteristics are that they agree on the main doctrines of the and for general purposes remain united and maintain a harmonious religious and social life and differ among themselves only on points of detail (*Furu'*)."[13]

The term *Ahl al-Sunnah wa'l-Jama'ah*, however, does not refer to a well defined or fixed group of Muslims. The expression really denotes an ideal group whose doctrines constitute the golden mean between extremes. Ibne Taymiyah however, says that he has nowhere seen a clear and positive exposition of *Sunnism*; even al-Ah'ari and al-Ghazali have failed in this endeavor. The *Ahl al-Sunnah* are in Islam, the middle group (*Ummah wasat*). [14] On the question of 'Ali's merits; they are in the middle course between the Khawarij and the *Rawafid*. On the question of '*Uthman*, they are between the Marwanids and the Zayditcs. Likewise on the question of the Companions, they are between the Kharijis and the Mu'tazills on the one hand and the Kharijis and the Murji'is on the other; and on predestination between the Qadri Mu'tazills and the Qadri Determinists. Similarly, on the question of attributes, they occupy a middle position between the partisans of denudation (*Mu'aftilah*) and those of equivocation (*R'ushabbihah*).

The *Ahl al-Sunnah* are also the middle *Ummah* in relation to the Jews and the Christians (*Ahl al-Kitab*). The Jews give to God attributes of imperfection which are the characteristics of creatures. For instance, they say that, God is avaricious. He is Poor; He got fatigued after making the heavens, etc. But the *Ahl al-Sunnah* believes that God is generous (Ghani) and knows no avarice: He is rich and needs nothing, and He is powerful and gives shelter to all those who are weak. The Christians, on the other hand, give the attributes of God to his creature, and say, that Jesus, son of Mary, is one of the Trinity, and the son of God. Also they have given divinity to their priests and monks. The Muslims alone believe in the oneness of God and give Him the attributes of perfection. Similarly Ibne Taymiyah carries out the comparison in the concepts of prophecy, law and other matters with a view to establishing that only the *Al al-Sunnah wa'l-Jama'ah*  among the Muslims constitutes the *Ummah wasat* in this world.

As regards the *Sunni* internal differences, especially in the legal schools (*Al-madkahib al-fiqhiyah*), Ibne Taymiyah attaches no importance to them for he believes that these differences are of a superficial nature, and arise mostly because of the fragmentary knowledge of the texts that the *'Ulama'* possess and because of the excessive importance (*Ghuluww*) that they give to certain points. The four schools of law do no harm to the unity which exists in the original condition of Islam. These differences can be tolerated as long as they are not imposed as final truths. In several of his tracts, especially in the *Qa'idah fi tawah hud al-millah,* [15] he lays down the detailed method by which these differences can be reduced or removed. If the relevant verse of the Qur'an or the particular *Hadith* can be found, the problem can be easily settled. Moreover, it is well-known that these differences do not touch on fundamentals; they mostly pertain to recommendations (*Mustahabbat*) or disagreeable (*Makruhat*). Ibne Taymiyah has not himself attempted to recreate a unified code of Islamic law, as Henri Laoust has rightly observed, but it can be easily proved from his writings that on most of the controversial issues in dogmatic and in the *Shari'ah* he has given his independent opinions which have been largely accepted by latterday religious and political reformers. These opinions have been gathered in a separate volume, entitled *Kitab al-Ikhtiyarat al-'ilmiyah* and published at the end of the third volume of his *Fatawa.* This book comprises about two hundred and fifty pages and does represent a tremendous effort towards the unification of the Islamic law, or at least teaches the methodology to achieve this purpose if a modern attempt is made at the problem.

The unity of language is another basic factor that con-tributes to confessional solidarity of the Muslims. He is the one jurist who strongly advocates the methodical Arabisation of the Muslim world. He regards Arabic as the only language of religion "because the Arabic tongue is the symbol (*Shi'ar*) of Islam and its followers." Everyone who can learn it must do so.

A foreign tongue may be learned and used but preference must be given to Arabic because God chose it as the medium of His revelation and made it the language of the last Prophet (P.B.U.H.). He discusses in detail whether a non-Arabic tongue can be used in the prayers and after quoting the principal authorities says that so far as the Qur'an is concerned it is not allowed to be translated. Only Abu Hanifah and his followers differ on this issue. Then he quotes a number of *Athar* (*Hadiths* of the Companions) and traditions of the Prophet condemning the use of Persian in preference to Arabic. If the Muslims adopt another tongue and use it in their homes, in their market, in state affairs and in legal business it is undoubtedly not liked by Islam. "This is why when the early Muslims occupied the land of Syria and Egypt, where Greek was spoken and the land of Iraq and Khurasan, where Persian was spoken, and the land of Maghrib, where the Berber tongue was spoken, they imposed Arabic on the inhabitants everywhere so that it became the dominant language of all the people in these areas, Muslims as well as infidels."[19] The same happened in Khurasan originally, but because of the negligence of the authorities, people readopted Persian which in due course drove away Arabic. So the best way is to cultivate the habit of Arabic speech so that children may become accustomed to it at home and in the school, and Arabic may become the language of the state and of daily business, and it may become easier for Muslims to understand the Qur'an and the *Sunnah* and the words of the classical authorities (*Salaf*). But if one accustoms oneself to another language and then studies Arabic for business purposes one cannot understand the niceties of expression and cannot realize perfectly the deeper meaning of the faith and the law. "It should be noted that the habit of a language does influence the mind, manners and religion very strongly, and the association with Arabic generates a similitude with the first pioneers of this

*Ummah* the Companions and the Successors, and this similitude makes the mind, religion and manners improve." [20] More-over, acquiring the knowledge of religion is obligatory, and this entails an understanding of the Qur'an and of the *Sunnah*, and this is not possible without understanding the Arabic language; and what is necessary to realize an obligation (*Wujub*) is itself obligatory (*Wajib*), therefore the learning of Arabic becomes a personal obligation (*Fard 'ayn*).

Ibne Taymiyah does not want to destroy other languages but he feels that the spiritual and cultural unity of Islam demands that Arabic should be imposed as the state language in all the Muslim lands. This linguistic unity will, on the one hand, preserve the true religion, and on the other, tend to reduce political difference and maintain the *solidarity* of the *Ummah*.

But, finally, this Muslim solidarity is not a mere mechanical solidarity depending only on the community of territory, believers and language. It is also an organic solidarity which supposes the existence of a common purpose, in the realisation of which all members of the community must participate to the best of their capacity. The Muslim community is the best of communities, the *Ummah wasat* (balanced community), which commands the good and forbids the evil. Some theologians regard this injunction as the most important element in the prophecy of Muhammad (P.B.U.H.). And the *Kharijis* think it to be one of the principal duties of the Muslim. In the system of Ibne Taymlyah it assumes the same importance for the life of the community. [21] It is this function that creates the moral solidarity in the *Ummah*.

Ibne Taymlyah has emphasized this function in most of his principal works. First he gives the Qur'anic authority that Allah has made it obligatory that the Muslims should because of the unity of ideological purpose; befriend one another, and not the non-believers. Allah says: "O you, who believe, take not the Jews and the Christians for friends; they are friends of each other. And whoever amongst you takes them for friends, is indeed one of them. Surely Allah guides not the unjust people...[22]. Only Allah is your friend and His Messenger and those who believe, those who keep up prayer, pay the *Zakat*, and bow down (to Him).[23] And whoever takes Allah and His Messenger and those who believe for friend — surely the party of Allah shall triumph.[24]

"Thus", Ibne Taymiyah comments, "Allah has informed that the friend of the Muslim is He himself and His Prophet and His servants who are Muslims. And this applies to every Muslim, who carries these attributes, whether or not he is a relation, or belongs to the same city or the same school or the same path." Allah says: "And the believers, men and women, are friends of one another." [25] And He says: 'The believers are brethren, so make peace among your brethren, and keep your duty to Allah that mercy may come to you."[26] These verses clearly indicate that the Muslims are an organic whole and are morally and materially bound to one another in an intimate and inalienable way.

Ibne Taymiyah, continuing his argument, supports still furthers the concept of moral solidarity from *Hadith*. "It is reported in the *Sihah* that the Prophet (P.B.U.H.) said: The Muslims, in their reciprocal pity, and in their mutual sympathy, resemble a single body; whenever a single member of it complains the other members respond to it and the entire body get insomnia. There is another report in the *Sihah* in which the Prophet says: A believer is to another believer like an edifice all the parts of which reinforce one another, and he interlinked his fingers (to demonstrate it). And there is another report in the *Sihah* which the Prophet says (P.B.U.H.): By Him in whose hands is my soul; no one of you can be a believer unless he wishes for his brother the same that he wishes for his own self." The Prophet (P.B.U.H.) has also said: "The Muslim is the brother of the Muslim; he will neither abandon him nor hurt him." [27] Such texts are numerous in the Qur'an and the *Sunnah*. This same thesis Ibne Taymiyah has again developed in *Al-'Aqidoh al-Wasitiyah* in a more compact but equally forceful manner.

Very important results follow from this concept of solidarity. [28] First, there are social consequences. Each member of the Muslim community has the right of existence; if his personal means are known to be insufficient it will be the imperious obligation of the community, under the form of the state or of private initiative, to provide him with material possibilities to live. To allow one of the faithful to remain in destitution is to violate the rights of God by depriving Him of one of His servants. Also politically there exists only a difference of degree, and not of nature, between the functions exercised by the members of the community.

This ideal community, which in the beginning practiced real *Tawhid*, did not require any political organization. The individual virtue of the members of the society sufficed to maintain a social cohesion, and there was no need to set up a coercive force to maintain the solidarity of the *Jama'ah*. But like all societies this society also eventually suffered from ignorance and injustice and could no longer exist without a chief who would guard the maintenance of this order. To justify this necessity Ibne Taymiyah, like his predecessors, easily found scriptural as well as rational arguments.

In a famous verse, [29] the Qur'an has ordered the believers to obey God, His Prophet "and those who from amongst you are in authority." The text (*Nass*) gives the argument for obeying the authority but it does not discuss the form of the government or the problem of sovereignty. That is why the theologians have resorted to *Ijma* to prove the theory of the caliphate. Ibne Taymiyah is, however, not interested in the caliphate, but is concerned with mere authority and with the problem of obedience, and therefore for him this verse suffices, because he is not to establish any theory. This is why he opens his famous tract *Al-Siydsah al-Shar'iyah* with this verse. He realizes the necessity of a strong government, for he says, "the political organization of the affairs of men (*Wilayah*) is one of the greatest obligations of religion, rather there can be no religion without it, because the good of mankind cannot be fully realized without a social order, as their needs are interlinked, and a social order must have someone at its apex." [30]

Along with this sociological argument, he repeats the traditional argument of the jurists and theologians that the general demands of religion (which we have discussed in Chapter Two) cannot be met without a political organization. And he feels the necessity of political authority so keenly that he eagerly admits the veracity of the proverbial sayings: That the sovereign is the shadow of God on earth, and that sixty years of rule under a tyrant sovereign is better than a single night without a sovereign. This idea appears again and again in the *Minhaj*. [31]

But this authority need not be one single unit Ibne Taymiyah for the first time in history endeavours to justify juridically that it may be divided. The vicissitudes of history have actually divided the Muslim world into a large number of independent states, whose political unity is very difficult to accomplish. Their real unity in fact resides in the confessional solidarity, where each state, having the feeling of its own autonomy, has the consciousness of being the member of an organic whole. The ideal community is a confederation of states. [32]

Ibne Taymiyah naturally does not use the modern terminology to express this idea, but he is very clear on the issue. In the beginning of the *Siyasah*, discussing the famous verses of the Qur'an, dealing with the question of trust (*Amanah*), authority and obedience, he observes, "The 'ulamd' say: the first verse is revealed about the rulers; it is obligatory on them to return the trusts to their owners and to adjudicate among the people with justice. And the second verse is revealed about the subjects who constitute the army and other sections of the population; it is obligatory on them to obey the rulers who perform all these duties of distributing the goods among them, adjudicating their cases and organizing their wars." [33] Here obviously Ibne Taymiyah is considering the possibility of many Muslim states at a time; that is why he is talking of rulers and not of one supreme ruler of the community. This idea is dominant in the book. In another passage he says: "The important thing in this connection is the knowledge about the best person, and this can be attained by knowing the purpose of *Wilayah* and the method of attaining this purpose; and once the ends and the means are known the (ideal) state is created." [34] This can obviously happen even when numerous Muslim states co-exist. In another passage he writes; "And the wielders of sovereignty are of two kinds: the rulers (*Umara'*) and the scholars (*'Ulama'*)." [35] Here again he envisages a multiplicity of Muslim states. In yet another passage he says, "So these are the sovereigns (*Wulat al-amr*) after them (the orthodox Caliphs), and these are the rulers and the scholars." [36]

But the question is how to reconcile this hierarchy to the concept of equality which is a basic and distinctive feature of Islam. Ibne Taymiyah solves this problem by defining the relation between individual aptitude and obligations. Writing about the Qur'anic injunction of commanding the good and forbidding the evil, he observes that this is the very end of religion and of all governments "and this is enjoined on every capable Muslim, and it is a communal obligation, and it becomes a personal obligation for a capable person if others do not rise to fulfil this duty. And capability means authority and sovereignty. So people in authority are more capable than others; therefore they have more obligations than others. Thus obligation is measured by capability." [37] In other words, the social hierarchy is the generator of obligations.

As regards the confessional minorities, Ibne Taymiyah seems to be very hard on them, because they constantly betrayed the Muslims against the non-Muslim invaders. He advocates their complete exclusion from the government. They must also be kept out of the army. [38] Commenting on this issue Laoust remarks, "The ideal community as it was conceived in the beginning had to be homogeneous. This explains why Ibne Taymiyah conceived a politics of reduction and absorption of the minorities in the long term." [39] This is only partly true. Islam as an ideal does indeed conceive a homogeneous society, as does every other religion or social philosophy; but neither does the Qur'an nor the *Sunnah* advocate an extermination of minorities to achieve this end. The Prophet offered equal status to the Jews in the state of Madinah. The Christians of Najran were offered most favourable terms of citizenship in the Islamic milieu. 'Umar's treaty with the Bishop of Jerusalem is a landmark in religious toleration. The reason why Ibne Taymiyah is so hard is not far to seek. As already pointed out, the Jews and the Christians in the Mamluk empire proved to be the worst traitors during the Crusades and the Mongol invasion. For about two centuries the Muslim world had fought a war of life and death with the European Crusaders and the pagan Tartars. During this long period the minorities had behaved most irresponsibly and treacherously and done incalculable harm to the Muslims. They did intense espionage work for the invaders, and often betrayed the Muslims in critical moments of conflict with the enemy. Indeed they secretly invited the Europeans and the

Mongols, and insulted and tortured the Muslims after an area was occupied by the invaders. [40] Such a state of affairs even the most liberal modern state could not tolerate. And Ibne Taymiyah, being a great realist, saw no alternative to restraining these minorities and laying down a policy of their systematic long-term reduction.

### 3.  The Judicial Necessity of the State.

We have discussed this subject briefly in Chapter Two at a general religious level and also incidentally in section two of this chapter. We shall now consider it again in a strict juridical sense. All treatises on Muslim political science and all discussions on the theory of the Islamic State open with the question: Is the institution of an *Imam* a juridical obligation? If it is answered in the affirmative, it is further asked: Does this obligation of appointing the *Imam* fall on God or on the believers?

All the sects in Islam except some Kharijis answer the first question in the affirmative. But in the answer to the second question there are two broad divisions. The Shi'ahs say, the responsibility of appointing the *Imam* falls on God; and the *Sunnis* say, it is an obligation of the *Ummah*. The Shi'ahs believes in the theory of grace. They say: God has created men for their own good, and He knows their frailties and failings, and since He is the Provident (*Rabb*), the Sustainer, the Guardian of all creation, and has asked men to behave correctly, it is His duty to provide them with the proper guidance. For, if He does not do so, people will only grope in the dark and never attain the real truth. Since the mission of prophecy terminated with the last Prophet, Muhammad (P.B.U.H.), God must create another system of perpetuating His grace to mankind. This system is that of the infallible *Imamah*. And it is for God to designate the

*Imam*, because men, who are subject to error, cannot make an impeccable selection. And necessarily this *Imam* is infallible, perfectly just, the protector and the only reliable interpreter of the law. These attributes of the *Imam* very much resemble those of the Prophet (P.B.U.H.), yet the <u>Shi</u>'ahs vainly differentiates between the two. This theory has, however, not worked, because, even according to the <u>Shi</u>'ahs, the succession of the *Imams* ended at a certain juncture in history. Centuries have elapsed since and the world has continued without the grace of an *Imam*, and is perhaps not the poorer for it.

The *Sunni* doctrine, without exception, is agreed on recognizing the obligatory character of the *Imamah*, although the nature of this obligation is differently interpreted by different scholars. We have discussed these differences in detail in chapter two above. Here it may only be pointed out that Ibne Hazm is alone in seeking the juridical necessity of the *Imamah* from a text, not of the Qur'an which is silent on the subject, but of a *Hadith:* "He who dies without knowing the *Imam* of his time dies as if he has died in the *Jahiliyah* time." Ibne Taymiyah has discussed this *Hadith* at length[41] and declared it to be doubtful, and even if its authenticity were accepted it proves nothing. The context in which it occurs in the Sahih of Muslim simply proves that under no circumstances should the people take up arms against the *Imam*. In fact, in the orthodox *Sunni* doctrine the *Imamah* is established only through *Ijma'*.

Al-<u>Gh</u>azzali's position on this issue is very peculiar. First, he observes that the consideration of the *Imamah* is not an important problem, nor does it come within the purview of reason; it is strictly a question of law. Then he says that it has often raked up fanatical quarrels in the *Ummah*, so it is better not to discuss it at all. But since it is the custom of theologians to close their treatises with a consideration of this issue, he, too, would follow their *Sunnah*. [42] This reflects the trivial importance that he attaches to the traditional theory of the Caliphate. He says it is not proper to regard the institution of the *Imamah* as a rational necessity; it is certainly a legal necessity. But the argument from *Ijma'* is not sufficient. The basis of this *Ijma'* is that the Prophet (P.B.U.H.) wants the order of this religion to be established but this cannot be done without an *Imam* who is universally respected. From these two premises it follows that the institution of the *Imam* is a legal (*Shar'iy*) necessity. [43] Thus we notice that the consensus theory of the <u>Khilafah</u> received only luke-warm support from Al-<u>Gh</u>azzali, the last great political thinker before Ibne Taymiyah. The only other thinker of importance to support the old theory of the Caliphate is Fa<u>kh</u>r ul-din al-Razi, but he is essentially a compiler and offers little original on the subject.[44]

Ibne Taymiyah's method is very much different. He never treats of the <u>Khilafah</u> as an institution in Islam and thus mentions it only rarely in his discussions.[45] As regards the regime of the Prophet, he refuses to call it *Imamah*, and insists only on calling it *Nubuwwah*, and says that the question of the *Imamah* arose only after the death of the Prophet.[46]

Elaborating on this point, Laoust remarks; "His theodicy, however, prevents him from seeing in prophecy an obligatory grace, although in fact the generosity of God is in his eyes so perfect and His providence so extensive that the sending of infallible Prophets, and to a certain degree of *Imams*, is as indispensable to him as is to <u>Shi</u>'aism the investiture of the infallible *Imam* of God."[47] This observation is basically incorrect. According to Ibne Taymiyah, the Prophet is infallible in a limited sense— in the sense that he most faithfully conveys the message of God to man. The Prophet does not say anything out of his own invention. He is in immediate communion with God and, therefore, whatever he says or does constitutes the final truth. But the Shi'ah *Imam* is not only infallible but also absolutely impeccable in his own right. Therefore, the concept of infallibility in Shi'ism differs intrinsically from the concept of infallibility in Ibne Taymiyah. And as regards the other *Imams* Ibne Taymiyah denies their infallibility in most emphatic terms. To reinforce his thesis, Laoust refers to a passage in the *Minhaj*: "If by the *Imam* they (*Shi'is*) mean the conditional *Imam* (*Al-Imam al-muqayyad*) then the *Ahl al-Sunnah* do not enjoin any obedience to him if he orders something which does not conform to the order of the ideal *Imam* (*Al-Imam ai-mutlaq*)." [48] This very passage is enough evidence to show that the other *Imams* have no locus *Standi* without reference to the Prophet. Moreover, there is nothing in the passage to show that the epithet of *Imam* for the Prophet has been used in a political sense.

We have already seen that according to Ibne Taymiyah the regime of the Raghidun was a special dispensation of God, never to be repeated in history. This explains why he does not treat of the *Khilafah* as other jurists have done. Of course he uses the Sunni methodology but his purport is often different from the traditional concept. For instance, in *Al-Siyasah* he introduces a chapter "The obligation of instituting the *Imarah* (i.e. government)." [50] Here he deliberately uses the word *Imarah* (i.e. government or rulership) and carefully avoids the use of *Khildfah* and *Imamah*. Similarly, in the same text, when he describes the qualifications and functions of *Wilayah* he has in view rulers in general, and not caliphs and *Imams*.

The unitary and universal Caliphate disappeared after the *Rashidun* and multiplicity took the place of unity. The Muslim world was broken into numerous divisions. The principal aim, therefore, of dogmatic and juridical evolution in Islam has been to restore this unity. But history seldom follows the dictates of theology, and Ibne Taymiyah realized very early that the unitary character of the Caliphate could not be maintained even as a fiction. But it is a highly ironical coincidence that his political theory is, in no small measure, inspired by Kharijism of which he was a vehement opponent.

As already mentioned, Ibne Taymiyah follows the *Sunni* method of inquiry. The Qur'an makes no mention of the *Imamah*, neither does it lay down the obligation of instituting it nor determines its form. The *Sunnah* is equally silent on the matter. Hence there is no valid juridical concept of the *Imamah*. And even the Companions of the Prophet were never unanimous in recognizing the necessity of political authority for the good order of religion. This authority, however, may take any Suitable shape, and at one and the same time there may be a number of independent Muslim states. The verse of the Qur'an "obey God; obey the Prophet and those among you who hold authority" does not limit the number of *Imams* (rulers). Even the Companions believed that there can be more than one *Khilafah* at a time.[52] Ibne Taymiyah has strengthened his thesis by citing a number of traditions, apparently of *Khariji* inspiration. It is reported in he *Shahihayn* by Abu Hurayrah that the Prophet said, "The Israelites were guided by their Prophets; when one Prophet (P.B.U.H.) died he was succeeded by another. But there will soon be my successors (*Khulafa'*) and they will be numerous." When they asked; 'What do you then order us to do?" He replied, "Abide by your oath of loyalty to the first and after him to the second." [53] In another report in the Salilhayn 'Abdallah bin Mas'ud says, "The Prophet said to us, 'After me you will soon see preferences and things which you will not like.' When they asked, 'O Prophet, what do you order us to do then?' he said, 'Pay their dues to them and pray to God for your own dues.'" [54]

The truth is that Ibne Taymiyah was not influenced only by Khariji ideas. His original and impartial researches in the Qur'an and the *Sunnah* and in Islamic Law necessarily led him to the position where he ultimately stands. He found no juridical authority for the Caliphate and, therefore denied its necessity.

Also the political climate of his time did not permit him to advocate this necessity, for it would have imposed on' the Muslims the duty to seek the unique leader of a community which had lost its original cohesion. But above all Ibne Taymiyah was an iconoclast. He could not tolerate a fiction whose dry formalism was undermining the political and social life of the community. He, therefore, stoutly preached the necessity of law and order and of a strong government. The Muslims, he thought, should form independent sovereign states wherever feasible and everywhere make the Islamic *Shari'ah* the directive law of the state. When all these states accept the same moral law and the same *Shari'ah* they would ultimately confederate and achieve the unity of the Islamic *Ummah*.

## 4.   *The Appointment of the Imam.*

Since Ibne Taymfyah does not recognise the additional theory of the caliphate, the problem of the appointment of the *Imam* does not concern him. Also, what he has written about the *Khilafat al-nubuwwah* does not apply to later times. However, he frequently talks about the choice and appointment of rulers (*Wulat al-umtir*) and mostly uses the same terminology which the other *Sunni 'Ulama'* employ. Laoust seems to have failed to understand this, and while writing on this point has argued throughout on wrong premises.[53] For the sake of contrast and evaluation of Ibne Taymiyah's viewpoint a brief notice of the traditional concept is, however, necessary.

On the mode of designating the *Imam* the previous Muslim theologians are divided into two principal groups: the *Ashab al-Nass*, who say that the *Imam*s are chosen for all eternity by explicit scriptural text; and the *Ahl al ikhtiyar* (election) who believe that the *Imam*s are appointed by a free choice of, the community. Ibne Taymiyah has written on this point mainly in his refutation of the arguments of the Shi'i al-Hilli. The Shi'ah doctrine as propounded by al-Hilli says that it is logically incumbent on God to appoint, by an explicit text, the infallible *Imam*, who, after the death of the Prophet, acts as the supreme preserver and the only reliable interpreter of the law and the intermediary between God and man. Since men, because of their own failings and their imperfect reason, cannot recognize the infallible *Imam*, he must be clearly designated by God. In his *Minhaj al-Kardmah*, al-Hilli has cited some forty verses of the Qur'an and a dozen *Hadith*s to prove the nomination of Ali, the first *Imam* by the Qur'anic *Nass*. Ibne Taymiyah has devoted the whole of the second volume of his *Minhaj* to the refutation of this divine right theory. It is during these discussions that he has frequently presented the *Sunni* doctrine and his own viewpoint.

The *Ahl al-Sunnah* also admit the validity of *Nass* but their concept of *Nass* is fundamentally different. They say that no such text is found in the Qur'an or the *Sunnah*, but if there were any it would have been certainly binding on the Muslims. But some scholars believe that Ab'ı Bakr was nominated by the Prophet (P.B.U.H.) to succeed him.[56] Among the *Sunnis*, however, few believe that the Prophet made any categorical declaration about his successor. Moreover, this nomination has nothing to do with the Shi'ah theory of grace. As for Ibne Taymiyah, he does not think that Abu Bakr or anyone else was directly nominated by the Prophet, but he believes that the Prophet (P.B.U.H.) had given enough hints and indications that the first four Caliphs would succeed him in the order in which they actually succeeded in history. However, the knowledge of these hints and indications did not qualify the Persons concerned for the Caliphate until they were actually elected by the Muslims. Thus the hidden or indirect nomination to which some *Sunni* writers refer carries no significance political or spiritual.

The main thesis of the *Ahl al-Sunnah*, naturally, is that it is the duty of the Muslim community to give to itself a supreme chief. The institution of the *Imamate* is a collective obligation (*Fard 'ala al-Kifayah*). The *Imam* is elected by the consensus of the community, but this consensus, on one view, is constituted only by the *'Ulama'*, who because of their knowledge and piety, impose on themselves the duty of electing the *Imam*. Likewise it is said that the obligation of electing the *Imam* lies on the shoulders of those who hold the supreme power to bind and unbind (*Ahl al-hall wa'l-'aqd*). Here the question of sovereignty crops up. This is definitely a modem concept; nevertheless it did exist in the minds of the people in the classical and medieval times too. The nearest equivalent in Ibne Taymiyah's vocabulary is the word *Sultan* or the sovereign. He often writes that obedience is due to one who holds supreme power (*al-Sultan al-niutlaq*). But the phrase *Ahl al-fall wa'l-'aqd* does not mean those who hold supreme power; it is not equivalent to the modern sovereign parliament. Moreover it is nowhere defined or claimed that the *Ahl al-hall wa'l-'aqd* are the representatives of the *Ummah*. The *Sunni* doctrine does not say that the sovereignty belongs to the *Ummah*. Some modern Muslim writers have tried to show that sovereignty resides in the *Ummah* as a whole. [57] This theory, however, gets no support from classical juridical opinion. The main plank of the *Sunni* theory is that it is God who designates the *Imam* through the infallible voice of the community. This voice is the voice of *Ahl al-hall wa'l-'aqd*. But no one has ever considered whether at all and how these people are chosen to represent the *Ummah*. The phrase was unknown in the early history of Islam; and came into vogue long after the installation of the 'Abbasid dynasty, which was based oh a principle resembling that of divine rule, and in whose regime the *Ahl al-hall wa'l-'aqd* could not dream of enjoying any sovereignty (*Sultan*).

Ibne Taymiyah is most critical of the institution of the *Ahl al-hall wa'l-'aqd*. In theory it constitutes a body which enjoys juridical supremacy; it can make and unmake the *Imam*. But all the arguments of the theologians fail to convince Ibne Taymiyah, for he does not know from where this body draws its authority and how it is constituted. In fact, the Electoral College formed by them to elect the *Imam* is a pure fiction. A real election has never taken place in Islamic history: "whenever they have tried it, it has always been only to ratify, by a juridical comedy, a dictatorship of fact."[58] This explains why Ibne Taymiyah throws into the waste-paper basket with scorn al-Mawardi's sterile and subtle discussions on the minimum number of candidates necessary for the election. [59] Ibne Taymiyah is also afraid that the concept of *Ahl al-hall wa'l-'aqd* creates a veritable clergy as in *Shi'asm* and Christianity and excludes all lay element from the electoral college.[60] Besides, he knew from history that often the usurpation of an adventurer was legitimized by the *Ahl al-hall wa'l-'aqd* by the application of the minimum of juridical principles. To acquiesce in such a theory was, therefore, impossible for him.

Because of his special methodology he apparently agreed with the *Sunni* doctrines of *Nass* and election both, but both these terms denoted for him very different concepts. "Some theologians (*Ahl al-Kalam*) hold that the *Imamah* is instituted by the allegiance of two persons, and still others say it is instituted by the allegiance of only one person. But these are not the opinions of the leaders of the *Ahl al-Sunnah*. The *Imamah* is, according to these, established only by the allegiance of those who hold supreme power (*Ahl al-Shawkah*). And a person does not become *Imam* until he is supported by the *Ahl al-Shawkah*, by whose obedience accrues to him the purpose of the *Imamah*, because indeed the purpose of the *Imamah* cannot be realized without power and authority. So when a person receives a pledge of allegiance which confers on him power and authority he becomes an *Imam*. This is why the *Sunni Imams* say: one who obtains powers and dominion (*Qadrah wa Sultan*) and utilises them to realise the purposes of the State, he is counted one of those rulers whose obedience Allah has enjoined as long as they do not command disobe dience to God. So the *Imamah* is sovereign power (*Mulk*) and authority; and sovereign power is not realized by the support of one or two or four persons, except when the support of these persons commands the support of others in such manner that the state is established. And thus any matter which requires cooperation is not realized until those for whom it is possible offer this cooperation." [61] So all those matters— like a person becoming a ruler or a judge or a governor, etc.—which depend on power and authority, are realized when power and authority are established, otherwise not; because the aim of these offices is the realization of certain functions, which are not realizable without the aid of authority. When the authority which makes these functions possible is established the state is established. He further argues: if one does not get the power to act one is not called the doer. And the authority to rule over people is obtained either by their willing obedience to the *Imam* or by his compulsion over them. And when he becomes able to rule over them, either because of their allegiance or because of his compulsion, he becomes the ruler, to whom obedience is due, as long as his orders obedience to Allah."

Thus, Ibne Taymiyah has destroyed the fiction of election and the amorphous, ineffective and largely fictitious institution of *AM al-hall wa 'l-'aqd*. For him the State comes into being by cooperation of the members of the community; and the sovereign is chosen by *the people who command real power* and authority in the community. Abu Bakr, for example, who deserved the office of the *Imam* and whose title, according to some scholars, is proved by *Nass* also, became *Imam* only by the allegiance

(*Mubaya'ah*) to him of those who possessed power (*Ahl al-Shawkal*). Similarly, 'Umar became *Imam* when he was nominated by Abu Bakr and the people declared their allegiance to him. But supposing they did not accept Abu Bakr's nomination, and did not declare their allegiance to him, he could not, in that case, have become *Imam*, whether this were right or wrong, for rule and authority are defined as actual power is realized. Or, if 'Umar and a few others with him had offered their loyalty to Abul Bakr and the rest of the Companions had rejected him he would not have become *Imam*. So the view that a person becomes *Imam* by the support of one, two or four individuals, who are not *Ahl al-Shawkah*, is simply erroneous. The fact is that the right religion (*Al-din al-haqq*) must stand by the guiding Book and the helping sword (*Al-Kitab al-hadi wa 'l-sayf al-nasir*). What Ibne Taymiyah means is that the State is not founded by the allegiance of a few *'Ulama', the Ahl al-hall wa 'l-'aqd,* but by the cooperation of the entire community, and particularly by the support of those who wield real power (*Ahl al-Shawkah*), because political authority cannot be established without physical force.

The rightful *Imamah* is one which is instituted by the oath of obedience (*Mubaya'ah*), by which the sovereign and the community bind themselves to each other. The *Mubaya'ah* is a contract, and like all other contracts, it, too, has its aim (*Maqsud*), which is the common will to obey God and His Prophet, and presupposes two parties: namely, the *Imam*, on the one side and on the other the *'Ulama'* and, in the most general manner, all those who by their knowledge, latent, fortune, and personal ascendancy, hold an authority in the community. Finally this *Mubaya'ah* must be interpreted in terms of common profits. It assures to all the blessing of obedience to God: to the *Imam* effective authority and the happy perpetuity of a power which could not be founded on mere force; to the subjects the social peace and constitutional guarantees of the law. [64]

Al-*Shawkah* in the doctrine of Ibne Taymiyah is not brute force, because he does not admit the idea that an *Imam* who imposes himself with force, becomes legitimate by the sanction of a few scholars and supporters. For him *Ahl al-Shawkah* are all those persons who, irrespective of their profession and station in life, command the respect and obedience of the community. He writes: "So the *Khilafah* is not conditioned by anything except the support of the *Ahl-al-Shawkah*; and as regards the common people (*Jumhur*) by whose arms the State comes into being, they are only the means by which the purposes of the *Ummah* are realized." [63] Thus, in his opinion, the common people do cooperate in achieving the fundamental aims of the state, but so far as the institution of the *Imamate* is concerned it is only the *Ahl al-Shawkah* who counts.

The idea of *Shawkah* seems to have been developed first by al-Ghazzali. He swrites: "Then indeed according to us the *Imamate* is instituted by the *Shawkah* and the *Shawkah* is established by the *Mubaya'ah.*" [66] In another passage he declares: "The *Shawkah* cannot be achieved except with the support of the majority of the reliable persons of the age (*Mu'tabari Kull al-Zaman*)." [67] But al-Ghazzali developed it for a different purpose. In his time the Saljuq Turks were the real masters of Bagdad, who ruled with the title of *Sultan*. To maintain the integrity of the Muslim world, he endeavoured to strengthen the compromise theory of the caliphate. He says that the *Khilafah* can be instituted either by a text from the Prophet or by a will by the reigning Caliph for his successor, or by the delegation of authority (*Tafwid*) to a powerful person whose obedience and delegation may be able to command the agreement of others and hasten them towards *Mubaya'ah*. [68]

The idea of *Shawkah* was put into its proper perspective

only by Ibne Taymiyah, who rejected the traditional theory of the Caliphate and developed an independent theory of the State. This same concept was subsequently to be transformed by Ibne Khaldun into his famous theory of the *'Asabiyah* (solidarity), [69] and there is nothing basically new in Ibne Khaldun, except his elaboration of the *'Asabiyah*-structure.

But the question remains: what is the role of the *'Ulama'* as regards the determination of sovereignty and the institution of the *Imamah*? The second part of the question has already been answered. According to Ibne Taymiyah, the *'Ulama'* do not constitute a sacred clergy and do not enjoy special privileges. Their cooperation for the institution of the *Imam* is as essential as of other effective elements in the community. This is why he scrupulously avoids calling them the *Al-hall wa 'l-'aqd*. And the *Hadith* to the effect that the scholars are the inheritors of the Prophet does not mean that the professional men devoted to the study of theology and law are the only inheritors. The word *'Ulama'* has been used here in its widest sense, and it includes all those who, because of their knowledge and learning, interpret the *Shari'ah* correctly and adapt it to new conditions of time and place. In the light of this definition, the *'Ulama'* do, indeed, occupy a high place in the estimation of Ibne Taymiyah. It is only in this sense that he writes: "The holders of authority are of two kinds: rulers and the scholars (*'Ulama'*); these are the people when they do well the people also do well." [70] The sense of this passage is not as Laoust and Rosenthal have averred, that the *'Ulama'* in the Islamic state enjoy individual magistracy [71] or collective sovereignty. [72] What Ibne Taymiyah intends to say is rather that the *'Ulama'*, because of their knowledge of the law and their custodianship of the legacy of the Prophet, constitute the premier directive class in the community, and the rulers must rule with their advice and cooperation. He is not considering here the formal problem of sovereignty but that of the general effectiveness of administration. He has made the above statement under the chapter of consultation (*Al-mushawarah*) and the trend of his argument is that in the day-to-day administration the rulers must take the help and advice of the *'Ulama'*. This passage has unnecessarily confused Laoust, who, commenting on it, observes: "The Sovereignty, in the doctrine of Ibne Taymlyah, is a diffuse sovereignty; it is as a result of this that the *'Ulama'* constitute, in law, the premier directive class of the community and the state." [73]

The second part of the observation is true, but not in the narrow senses in which Loaust is using the word *'Ulama'* here. Ibne Taymiyah has nowhere professed the concept of diffuse sovereignty; on the country, he very frequently advocates the strongest concentration of sovereignty. He is so serious about it that when discussing the qualifications of rules he does not repeat those meaningless phrases of al-Mawardi, al-Baghdadi and others, but gives unusual importance to power and honesty (*Al-quwah wa'l-Amanah*) .[74] The position of the *'Ulama'* is, however, most clearly determined by Ibne Taymiyah in another impotant passage. He writes "And the *Imam*s have said: Indeed the holders of authority are of two kinds, the scholars and the rulers. In this authority are included the leaders of religion (*masha'ikh al-din*) and the King of the Muslims. Each one of them shall be obeyed in matters which relate to him. The former (*masha'ikh*) shall be obeyed when they order about worship (*'Ibdat*), and to them shall be referred the interpretations of the Qur'an, the *Hadith* and the messages of Allah; the latter (the Kings) shall be obeyed in matters of *Jihad*, enforcement of canonical punishments (*al-hudud*), and similar acts the execution of which is enjoined on them by Allah." [75] The role of the *'Ulama'* is, therefore, clearly interpretative and advisory, and one should not be misguided by the use of the word *"Amr"* with reference to them.

In the last analysisi it can be said that Sovereignty in

*Shi'aism* is a divine gift; in traiditional Sunnism, it is the *Ijma'* of the *Ahl al-hall wa'l-'aqd,* and ion the system of Ibne Taymiyah, the cooperation of the entire *Ummah.* He observes, "For indeed the *Imam* is not to lord (*Rab*) of his subjects so that he may dispense with them, nor is he the messenger of God towards them so that he might serve as the intermediary between them and God; on the contrary, he and the subjects are parters cooperating in the interest of the religion and the world; thus their help is indispensable for him and his help indispensable for them."[76] The same idea is better expressed in a famous *Hadith*: "Everyone of you is a shepherd and everyone of you is responsible for his flock."[77] As a matter of fact, the principle of cooperation is best illustrated by the injunction of commanding the good and forbidding the evil which is the very purpose of religion and government. [78]

## 5. *The qualifications of the Imam*

With this question Ibne Taymiyah is not concerned directly because he does not accept the idea of the universal *Imamate.* But in the course of his refutation of al-Hilli's concept of the *Imam,* he is constantly preoccupied with one aspect or another of the problem. The fundamental quality which the Shi'ahs attribute to their *Imam* is that of infallibility (*'ismah*), from which flow all other qualities. The *Imam* is the grace of God and the shelter against all error and against all forms of injustice. Al-Hilli assigns to the *Imam* the same qualities, which Plato and Al-Farabi assign to the chief of the ideal city. He is to the community what the heart is to the human organism; like the heart he is the source of life, the principle of order and organization. Even more than Plato, al-Farabi, under the influence of the social conditions of his age, when Muslim thinkers worked in the courts of princes and exalted their achievements and personalities, attaches extreme importance to the chief of the ideal city (*Al-madinah al-Jadilah*) and places in him all his hopes.

The *Imam* of Farabi (339 H. /950 A.C.) is really the prophet duly Platonized. He demands of his chief the sum total of qualities which it is well-nigh impossible for a single person to possess. Physical qualities of health and robustness of body are necessary for governing the perfect city. And equally necessary are the moral-intellectual qualities: a profound intelligence, a prompt memory, a grand eloquence, a taste for study, horror of evil thought, love of justice, nobility of soul, a temperance which guards against the pleasures and seductions of fortune, a tested and firm will and an extraordinary power of persuasion. Then the chief must supplement these qualities by attaining the highest degree of happiness (*Al-sa'adah al-quswa*). And this he can do only by uniting with the active intellect (*Al-'aql al-fa'al*). God will inspire him, through this intermediary, i.e. the active intellect, to implement the necessary laws of social and moral life. This collection of qualities, where the Qur'anic and Hellenistic notions intermix, can be found across a long series of theologians, and philosophers; with Ibne Miskawayh, al-Ghazzali. al-just and his pupil al-Hilli; But strangely enough, the biographies of the Shi'ah mams are impregnated with an asceticism which regards as the foremost virtue of the chief rather the renunciation of the world than an aptitude to direct it.[79]

Al-Hilli is to be sure, deeply influenced by al-Farabi and his school. His *Imam* is none other than the chief of the best city. He deduces the principal arguments for his infallibility from the functions he assigns to him. Only the infallible *Imam* can render justice among men and offer to the weak shelter against oppression. Only he can serve as the guide of the community and inspire everyone with the rule of life that conforms most to his interest. *Shi'ism* demands that the *Imam* be infallible, and if he is not then rebellion against him is necessary. Further, the

*Imam* is the preserver of the *Shar'* and the only correct and responsible interpreter of the law. The Qur'an and the *Sunnah* by themselves cannot unfold their truth they must be explained by one who knows them with certainty. Even the *Ijma'* is incapable of knowing the truth, because those who constitute it are not infallible, and it is illogical to attribute to the whole a quality which does not exist in its parts. And the *Qiyas* is strictly personal and unreliable thing (*Zann*). Examples of irrationality are not lacking in Muslim law, which establishes a difference between similar things, and then identifies different things as one. For instance, the hand of a thief is cut for a small amount but that of a pick-pocket is not cut for a big amount.[80]

A fallible person is bound to commit injustices, and an unjust person cannot be worthy of the *Imamate*. For this reason the *Imam* is the best person of his age, and conversely the best man of an age is the legitimate sovereign according to the *Shari'ah,* and yet he may not in fact be the *Imam*. Thus the Shi'ah messianism offers to the community a constant possibility of revolt.[81]

Ibne Taymiyah discusses these arguments in great detail and breaks them to pieces. He agrees with al-Hilli that the community requires a chief, but the chief needs the help of the people more than the people of the chief.[82] He traces the Shi'ah political history at length and conclusively establishes their practical performance does not in the least reflect their theoretical idealism. "The good that is required of the *Imam*s possessed with authority and might was never obtained from any of them; so it is clear that the grace and the benevolence which they mention with the names of their *Imams* are mere deception."[83] "Except 'Ali, none of them were able to establish political power for themselves, and none of the purposes of the *Ummah* were realized at their hands."[84] And even 'Ali was a failure. "The Muslims did not agree in owing their allegiance to him, rather the entire period of his reign was sunk in civil war, and throughout this period the sword remained withdrawn from the infidels and drawn against the followers of Islam,"[85] and thousands of Muslims were killed by Muslims. Now if most of the purposes of the *Imamah* are not realized by such an *Imam*, either because of his non infallibility or his actual inability, how can human reason reconcile itself to the fact that it is obligatory on Allah to create an infallible *Imam*, who can do no good to His servants? And how can he be recognized when He has created him so weak that he can achieve no good; rather he becomes the cause of much evil on this earth? Obviously, if Allah had to created this *Ma'sum* there would have been much less evil m the world. Now, why did the Wise (*Hakim*) create such an *Imam* through whom no good, but only evil obtained? and if it be said that this evil was the result of the tyranny that the people wrought on him, it may be answered: then the Wise, who created him to stop their tyranny, knowing at the time of this creation that it would increase them in tyranny, did not perform an act of wisdom but of foolishness.[86]

Then Ibne Taymiyah examines in detail the days of Shi'ah political power and proves that their sovereigns were the worst heretics, several of whom claimed personal divinity, and did their utmost to disgrace the honour and prestige of Islam, and hence were finally wiped out by the true followers of the religion.[87] The *Shi'ah* according to Ibne Taymiyah, have, on the whole always played a negative and destructive role in Islamic history. They abuse the illustrious Companions of the Prophet, and the leading '*Ulama*', jurists, theologians of Islam, and befriend *Musaylimah al-Kadhdhab* and Abu *La'lu'ah*, the murderer of 'Umar;[88] they helped and cooperated with the Mongol invaders and the Crusaders, who under their protection plundered and massacred the Muslims in Syria and Iraq.[89]

As regards the expected *Imam* (*al-Imam al-muntazar*)

he has no utility; for he is nonexistent, and holds no power of constraint (*Shawkah*), "Rather if his existence were supposed, it would be a pure evil for the people of the earth; because the Muslims have not benefited from him at all, and no grace and no good has accrued to them from him; and they believe that those who disbelieve him shall be punished for their disbelief; so he is pure evil and there is no good in him."[90] In short "they have in hiding (*Fi'l-batin*) the nonexistent *Imam* and in the open the most infidel and the most tyrant *Imam* (*Kafur wa zalum*)." [91] Thus Ibne Taymiyah pulls down the entire edifice of al-Hilli's sociology and political doctrines.

He is equally critical of the *Sunni* doctrine, which seems to be a reaction against and an adaptation of the Shi'ah position. Al-Mawardi, the chief spokesman of the classical school, says that there are seven conditions necessary for the election of the *Imam*: 1. Justice, with all the conditions pertaining to it. 2. Knowledge, which enables one to from an independent judgment in problems which present themselves for solution. 3. Integrity of the physical senses, hearing, sight and speech, so that the *Imam* may have a direct knowledge of things. 4. Integrity of the physical organs, so that he may move freely and rapidly. 5. Wisdom, necessary for administering the affairs of the people and expediting the affairs. 6. Bravery and the energy necessary for defending the Muslim territory and fighting against the enemy. 7. Lineage, that is, he should be of Qurayshi descent. [92] From this list al-Ghazzali omits justice (*al-'adalah*) and adds to it piety (*al-wara'*); he also adds a list of natural qualities, which are generally not considered by other writers. In any case in the traditional *Sunni* doctrine the *Imam* is always imagined as the model of a Muslim, in who is concentrated a much idealized union of physical, intellectual and moral qualities.

Ibne Taymiyah does not admit the *Sunni* doctrine of the qualities of the *Imam*. This ideal and perfect union of personal qualities, so diverse and so often complementary, is historically found only in the first era of Islam. Only the *Rashidun* Caliphs, and to a lesser degree Mu'awiyah and then 'Umar bin 'Abd al-'Aziz, were able to combine in their person the humility of the ascetic, the juridical competence of the *Mujtahid*, the military aptitude and the political sagacity of the *Amir*.[94] But the *Sunni* thesis, which was realized under a providential dispensation, will not be reenacted. That historical context has disappeared and, therefore, those conditions of the investiture of the *Imam* do not exist. Hence to demand that union of ideal qualities in the *Imam* is to find fault with the work of God; which apparently means to compel His creatures to an impossible task and deprive the law of its subtleness for adaptation.

And as regards the Qurayshi descent Ibne Taymiyah is extremely critical of it also. This condition is most incompatible with his egalitarian spirit. He stood firmly for the great principles of brotherhood and equality, the basis of Islamic social order, and was, therefore out to break the temporal and spiritual pre-eminence of a clergy, of a clan or of a family. He clearly agrees with the Khariji thesis that Qurayshism is not a condition for the *Imamate*, but this doctrine applies only to the post-Rashidun period. To support his stand he digs up from the great classical collections of traditions, a good number of *Hadith*s of Khariji inspiration. Some of these *Hadith*s have already been quoted above. The most famous of them is the one in which the Prophet is reported to nave ordered obedience to an Abyssinian slave, even if he had mutilated features, in the limits of respect which the Qur'an testifies for him.[95] Also in another place he points out that there is a great difference of opinion about the meaning of Qurayshite and hence its application is impossible.[96]

His own idea on the subject is very modest, realistic and supple. In the first place, he is not thinking of the *Imam* of the unitary universal Caliphate. In his opinion there may be as many independent and sovereign *Imam*s as the exigencies of time and place may require. The qualities which he considers, therefore, may apply to the selection of any Muslim *Imam*. In fact, he does not demand more qualities of the *Wali* (ruler) than the Muslim ordinarily demands of the credible witness.[97] The state is a cooperative institution in which all the members share according to their natural faculties, resources and station in life, so that the ideal qualities, which the Rashidun Caliphs united in their person, can be realized by the community as a whole, and, therefore, any Muslim, who enjoys the confidence and support of the *Ahl al-Shawkah*, can be elected as *Imam*.

In the *Minhaj* Ibne Taymiyah considers the problem from the purely philosophic and social viewpoint, but in the *Siyasah*, which is definitely a later work, he considers it from the practical-administration-angle and lays down a few more qualifications for the *Imam*. Here he defines the cooperative nature of the state once again and says that the term *Wilayah* includes all the officers of the state— the *Imam*, ministers, governors, judges, military commanders, revenue secretaries, *Imams* of *salat, Mu'adhdhins*, teachers, intelligence men, technicians tribal agents, and town and village representatives.[98] There is only a difference of degree rather than of nature between the different agents; that is why Ibne Taymiyah calls the head of the state *Al-mutawalli al-Kabir* (i.e. the chief responsible administrator). Therefore the qualities which he discusses here apply to all the *Wilayahs* (incumbents), especially to the highest, the *Imamate*, because obligations are the consequence of administrative hierarchy.

Among these additional qualities the foremost is trust (*Amanah*). The *Sunnah* of the Prophet informs us that the *Wilayah* is a trust which must be placed where it belongs. The Prophet said to Abu Dharr about *Imarah*: "Indeed it is a trust, and on the Day of Resurrection it will cause shame and disgrace, except to one who accepted it with its conditions and fulfilled

the obligations which were due on him because of it."[100]
According to another report given by al-Bukhari the Prophet
(P.B.U.H.) said; "When the trust is violated, wait for the last
Hour. When he was asked: O Messenger of Allah, what is the
violation of it? He replied: When the government is entrusted
to the undeserving, wait for the Last Hour."[101] In still another
*Hadith* the ruler is compared to a shepherd of the sheep. The
Prophet (P.B.U.H.) said: "Everyone of you is a shepherd, and
everyone of you is responsible for his herd; thus the *Imam* who
is the shepherd of the people is responsible for his herd; and the
wife is the shepherdess in the home of her husband and she is
responsible for her herd; and the child is the shepherd of the
goods of his father and he is responsible for his herd; and the
slave is the shepherd of the property of his master and he is
responsible for his herd; and beware, everyone of you is a
shepherd and everyone of you is responsible for his herd."[102] It
is also said that once Abu Muslim al-Khawlani, a famous
"Successor" who was born during the lifetimes of the Prophet,
visited the court of Mu'awiyah bin Abi Sufyan and saluted him:
"Peace be on thee O wageearner!" The courtiers said: "say, O
*Amir*". But he repeated the original salutation and the courtiers
repeated their demand. Then Mu'awiyah intervened and said:
"Leave Abu Muslim alone, he knows best what he says." At
this Abu Muslim remarked, you are a wageearner, the Lord of
these sheep has employed you to look after them, if you smear
coaltar on the itch-stricken and give medical help to the diseased,
and keep them from the first to the last within your charge, their
Lord shall pay you your remuneration; and if you do not smear
coaltar on the itch-stricken, and do not give medical help to the
diseased, and do not keep them, from the first to the last, within
your charge, their Lord shall punish you."[103] Ibne Taymiyah adds:
this is easy to understand, because the people are the servants
of God, and the rulers are the agents (*Nuwwab*) of God over His

servants and they are also representatives of the people over their souls, and in them are united the concepts both of guardianship and representation (*Al-Wilayah wa'l-wikalah*).

In another passage Ibne Tamiyah says: "The *Wilayah* (government) is based on two fundamentals, power and trust (*Aliquwwah wa'l-Amanah*), just as God has said: "Surely the best of those that you can employ is strong, the faithful one;"[105] and the king of Egypt said to Joseph: "Surely you are in our midst today powerful and trusted."[106]

Further, power for each function (*Wilayah*) is measured according to its nature. Thus power for the command of war (*Imarat al-karh*) is derived from the bravery of heart, the experience of battles, the practice of stratagems, from the ability to launch different kinds of war, etc.; and power for adjudication between the people is derived from the knowledge of justice, as defined in the Book and the *Sunnah*, and from the ability to enforce decisions.[107]

Trust is derived from the fear of God, from not selling His instructions for paltry sums, and from abandoning the fear of men; these three things God has made incumbent on everyone who judges among men. And *Qazi* (judge) is a word that applies to anyone who adjutants between two persons, and decides between them, whether he is a Caliph, or a *Sultan* or his deputy, or a governor. Even a school-master who decides between the writings of two children as to which of them is better is a *Qazi*. [108] And the supreme *Qazi* (*al-Qazi al-mutlaq*) must be learned, just and powerful, and this indeed applies to every ruler of the Muslims. But learning being a vague term Ibne Taymiyah asks: "Is it necessary that he (the ruler) should be a *Mujtahid* (capable of forming independent legal judgemnts), or is he permitted to be a *muqallid* (dependent on the decisions of *Mujtahids*), or is it obligatory to appoint the most competent, and then the next best, according to availability?"[109] He answers the question in another passage and says that in the school of Ah mad bin Hanbal all the three alternatives are permitted.[110]

Finally, in a highly pregnant passage he declares: "Thus, in all the offices of the state (*Fi sa'ir al-wilayat*) when the desired purpose is not realized by the appointment of one person, more than one may be appointed, because either the most competent should be selected, or a multiple charge should be instituted, when one person is unable to fulfil his obligations alone." [111] It is not clear whether Ibne Taymiyah means to apply this principle to the headship of the state as well. There is no other evidence to this effect in his entire work, but from the tenor of his thought it appears least probable that he means a council of rulers, because he is a great advocate of concentrated, effective central authority, as is indicated in numerous passages in the *Minhaj* and elsewhere.[112] And considering the age in which Ibne Taymiyah lived, when half the Muslim world was enslaved and the other half was constantly threatened by the Mongol invaders and the Crusaders, and when the ambitious Mamluk aristocracy in Egypt posed a serious danger to internal peace, it is too much to think that he should have advised the institution of a weak central government, wherein sovereign power rested in a number of individuals.

### 6. Duties of the Imam and the aims of the state.

Here, too, Ibne Taymiyah is first confronted with the Shi'ah doctrine of the function of the *Imam*. According to al-Hilli the *Imam* is the political chief and the supreme legislator. He is the model to be imitated and the example to be followed; it is in trying to resemble this *Imam* that the members of the community attain sanctity (*Karamah*) and happiness (*Sa'adah*). The function of the *Imam* is at once social and moral. He unites the function of regulating and legislating with that of ascetic elevation. Already with al-Farabi the function of the chief in the perfect city was comparable to that of God in the universe; the separate intellects and the celestial spheres acquire their force and perfection only by inclining towards the First Existent; so also is the chief in the community, being the interpreter and executor of the law, the centripetal force of perfection. This Hellenized Shi'ah conception is the same which one finds, with some attenuation, in the *Sunni* doctors who, like al-Ghazzali, have formed it by contact with Hellenis-tic philosophy and Shri'ism.[113]

Ibne Taymiyah rejects both the Shi'ah as well as the *Sunni* assertions about the *Imam*, and views the problem principally as a jurist. He is not primarily interested in the pattern or the mode of formation of the state, or in the person or privileges of the *Imam*. Whatever be the form of the state, and m whatever manner it may have come into being, he wants that the *Shari'ah* should rule supreme in it. This is why he has entitled his exclusive work on political science as *"Al-Siiyasah al-Shari'ah"* (The Rule of the *Shari'ah*), and its very first chapter opens with the statement: "This is a brief tract containing the of divine government and prophetic representation."[114] The duties of the *Imam* are, therefore, objectively determined by the functions and aims of the *Shari'ah*. He is in fact invested with a social function, permitting the exercise of a force of constraint which differs from other functions of the community, not in nature but in degree, by the greater power and authority he wields, because tile quantity of obligation is measured by the ability one possesses, which, in turn, determines the position in administration. And every *Wilayah* can be defined by its purpose. The end of all *Wilayahs* in Islam is to act in a way that all religion comes to be for God, and that the word of God triumphs, that is, "all submission is due to God alone."[115] This is the principal aim of all state-craft, and all political thinking of Ibne Taymiyah moves around this master idea. All the social functions in Islam tend towards this same end: the whole of religion must belong to God; the word of God must be sovereign; God has created the world for this very purpose, and sent His messenger to struggle for the same end. God says: "And I have created the jinn and men only to serve Me;" and also: "We never sent before you a Prophet without revealing to him that there is no God but Me, therefore serve Us;" and: "We have sent a Prophet to each nation ordering him to say: Serve God and shun the devil." Here Ibne Taymiyah observes, "It is only the service of God that is the essence of religion."[116] It is for this purpose that God sent Muhammad (P.B.U.H.) with the best of ways and ordinances, revealed to him the best book, deputed him towards the best *Ummah* chosen for the guidance of men, and perfected the religion for him and his *Ummah*, and gave all His blessings to them.

To implement this mission practically, the basic aim of the *Wilayah* is further defined as ordering the good and forbidding the evil. This is the fundamental aim of religion and all governments. [117] So the foremost duty of the *Imam* is to enforce the <u>Shari</u>'ah, in its totality, in the *Ummah*, and establish the institutions of ordering the good and forbidding the evil, so that the purposes of God may be realized, and social peace and individual rights may be guaranteed. Ibne Taymiyah often stresses that social hierarchy is the generator of obligations. So the *Imam* who possesses the highest power and authority in the *Ummah* carries the main responsibility on his shoulders in this behalf. The *Imam* is, therefore, responsible for the good execution of all the religious obligations which constitute the emblems (*Sha'a'ir*) of Islam: keeping of fast, observance of pilgrimage (*Hajj*) and juridical feasts (*'Ids*), the collection of *Zakat*, application of legal sanctions (*Hudnd wa ta'adhir*), equitable distribution of the goods of the community, assistance of the oppressed, good functioning of all the public services, and finally observance of the social and economic prescriptions which guarantee to each the respect of his person, honour and property. These functions are at once temporal and spiritual because he must render account to God not only about the material prosperity of his people but, even more, of the rectitude of his own and their moral and religious position. The *Wilayah* is a trust which the *Imam* must deliver to those who are entitled to it. Trust and justice are the two pillars of equitable and righteous government.[118] Trust (*Amanah*) means the proper fulfilling of one's obligations, and there is the strict command of God: "O believers, be not unfaithful to Allah and the Messenger, nor be unfaithful to your trusts, while you know."[119] So those who fail to deliver their trusts will face shame and disgrace on the Day of Judgment. The *Imam* is, indeed, comparable to the guardian of the orphans, to the manager of endowments (*Qwqaf*), and to the legal representative to whom has been entrusted the administration of an estate. Just as all these persons must act in a way that is most profitable for their charge, so must also acts the *Imam*.[120] Further the *Imam* is the shepherd of the community arid he will have to account before God for his proper service to the flock. In a well-known report already quoted above, the caliph Mu'awiyah is addressed by a famous Successor as a wageearner engaged by the Lord to look after His sheep.

The *Imam* also must combine in himself leniency with firmness. There are some brilliant examples of it in the early history of Islam. According to a report 'Umar said; "O God I complain to Thee the hardness of the wicked and the weakness of the righteous", suggesting that these qualities are rarely combined in one person. This being the case, the selection of people for different responsibilities in the affairs of the government will depend on the nature of the charge that is to be given to them. For instance, if it is a command of war, it will be given to the able and brave; for the Prophet (P.B.U.H.) has said: "Allah will help this religion even through the wicked person." We also know that Abu Bakr was lenient and 'Umar was tough, but together they produced a good moderation and were perfect in their *Wilayah.*[122]

But the spiritual elevation of the *Imam* is not sufficient He must endeavour his utmost also to bring material prosperity to the people. The fundamental aim of government is twofold: service to the religion of the people and service to their affairs of the world. This second function is divided into two: the distribution of benefits among those who deserve it and the punishment of aggressors.[123] When the shepherd (*Imam*) has endeavoured his utmost in the service of the religion and the worldly affairs of the people, he is among the best men of his time and among the best fighters in the way of Allah. For whereas one concept of *Amanah* is spiritual and moral elevation of the people, the other concept of it is the fulfilment of the economic and material obligations towards them.[124] In a well-known passage, discussing the qualities of the best kind of people, Ibne Taymiyah says, "[they are] the third group: the middle people (*Al-Ummah al-wasat*) and they are the followers of the religion of Muhammad (P.B.U.H.) and his successors (*Khulafa'*) in the rank and file of the people. This religion is the spending of money and the creating of benefits for the people, even if they are rich, according to their needs for the betterment of their conditions, for the establishment of the religion and for the amelioration of worldly affairs which religion so much requires."[125] Religious statesmanship does not succeed except by this means; neither does religion gain nor the world except by this method. One of the best ways of cooperating with the state is to serve the people by money and social services. Indeed the material uplift of the people is always uppermost in the mind of Ibne Taymiyah because he believes that unless the Muslims are materially well-off they cannot be spiritually ennobled.

One of the fundamental aims of the *Wilayah* is also to establish the rule of justice. Indeed, Ibne Taymiyah envisages *Amanah* and justice as two essential qualities of the government by the *Shar'ah*. He says: justice is a sentiment universally shared and it is innate in the consciousness of man. The people of the Book are agreed that God will recompense the human actions in the other world. Some of the infidels believe likewise and others do not. But the people of the entire world are agreed on the necessity of punishing and recompensing human actions in this world. Moreover, justice, on account of the universal consciousness, must triumph in the end. For the same reason it has been said: "Allah helps a just state even if it be infidel, and He does not help a tyrannical state even if it be Muslim."[126] So the purpose of sending the Messengers and revealing the Books is that people should conduct themselves equitably with regard to the rights of God as well as the rights of men. But this mission could not be fulfilled without the help of the sword, as God says; "And we sent down iron, wherein lie great power and advantages to men, and that Allah may know who helps Him, unseen, and His Messengers."[127] Therefore if anyone deviates from the Book he may be set right by the iron, and so the Book and the sword are the very foundation of religion (*Qiwam al-deen*). The *Wilayah*, therefore, must allow the use of effective power which will bend the people to the respect of law. And this effective power is nothing but political authority and State, which comes into being by the support of *Ahl al-shawkah*. A real *Imam* is one who enjoys this *shawkah*. But a pretender, even if he were the best man of his time, and also infallible, would not be able to claim the *Imamate*, if he did not possess this *Shawkah*.[129]

According to Ibne Taymiyah, the State is a general cooperation between the different members of the community, hence any form of *Wilayah* is a religious duty, a pious work by means of which a man seeks nearness to God, and if he acquits himself to the best of his capacity, it would be counted as one of the most righteous deeds. As regards the *Imam*, his responsibility is the highest in the community; hence he must look upon the *Imarah* as a religious function and a means to seek nearness to God. When it is clear that the purpose of authority and property (*Al-Sultan wa'l-mal*) is to seek nearness to God and to spend in His way, then, indeed, only therein consists the good of religion and of the world both.[130]

For the best of cooperation the *Imam* has to seek the best of talent, so that the state-machinery may work efficiently and the purposes of the *Imarah* may be fully realized. In fact, Ibne Taymiyah devotes the first twenty five pages of the *Siyasah* to the study of this problem. The search for the best must be made even for the lowest office. And in making the selection no consideration should be paid to personal relationship, friendship, sectarian conformity, nationality, bribe or any other gain, and no right should be trampled for personal animosity and jealousy. If the *Imam* or wait did not act in this spirit, he would be unfaithful (*Kha'in*) to Allah, to the Prophet (P.B.U.H.) and to the Muslims. Hence Ibne Taymiyah says: for every office two things are needed, technical aptitude and loyalty; and he defines these qualities in detail, and regrets that these are often lacking in the people. But despite this dearth of proper men the principle cannot be abandoned. He suggests that if these qualities are not found in one person, a number of persons may be appointed who complement one another.[131]

He observes that when the purpose of the *Wilayah* and the method of realizing it are known, the question of selecting the best man for it can be easily settled. Then the *Imam* par *excellence* is the Muslim qualified to preside over the prayer and to direct the *Jihad*. These two functions, the two most important duties in Islam, assure his preeminence in the State. It is not difficult to find out the great importance that is attached to prayer. The Qur'an repeatedly commands the establishment of prayer, and the Prophet has said, "The prayer is the pillar of religion (*Al-Salat 'imad al-deen*), 'Umar used to write to his governors: "I regard the establishment of prayer as your foremost duty, so one who kept watch over it and saved it saved his religion; and one who wasted it wasted his other actions even more."[132] When the *Imam* has set up this pillar of religion, the *Salah* (prayer) will drive away all obscenity and undesirable things and help the people in observing other commandments (*Ahkam*).

Organization of *Jihad* is the second most important duty of the *Imam*. The permission of *Jihad* came to the Prophet when he migrated to Madinah: the Muslims were allowed to fight in selfdefense against the Makkan pagans. "Fighting is enjoined upon you though it is disliked by you; and it may be that you dislike a thing while it is good for you, and it may be that you love a thing while it is evil for you."[133] This obligation was more and more emphasized in the Madinese Surahs of the Qur'an. The purpose of *Jihad* is that the whole of religion may become for Allah and that His word may triumph.

When the *Imam* himself declares war on the enemy the *Jihad* is a community obligation (*ford 'ala'l-kifayah*); but when the enemy initiates the fight, *Jihad* becomes obligatory for every Muslim. Ibne Taymiyah regards the propagation of religion (*Al-Da'wah*) as a fundamental duty of the *Imam*, but does not use this word because the <u>Kharijis</u> called themselves *Ahl al-Da'wah*. Instead of this word he uses the phrase: *al-amr bi'l-ma'ruf wa'l-nahy 'an al-munkar*. And *Da'wah* is not possible without fighting against the *Kuffar* (infidels). So, *Da'wah* and *Jihad* must go together. He thinks that if the non-Muslims reject the call of Islam, which is, in fact, the call of God, they must lose the right of free existence; and the Muslims must fight against them to free this world only for the obedient servants of God. Explaining why the booty of war is called *Al-fay'* (return) he writes "Indeed, the truth is that God has created the (*Amwal*) to help people serve him, because He has created His creatures only for His service. Therefore, those who disbelieve in Him, He has made their souls with which they do not serve Him, and their goods of which they take no help in their service to Him, lawful for His believing servants who serve Him, and return to them what they deserve, just as what has been misappropriated from a person of his inheritance and of which he has taken no possession as yet is returned to him."[134]

The same is the explanation of the *Jizyah* and other things which the *Ahl al-dhimmah* (the protected minorities) have been stipulated to pay to the Islamic State. This is indeed the opinion of the majority of the classical jurists. It was much accentuated in the days of Ibne Taymiyah because of the sad political conditions prevailing then. In strict law however, there is no justification for this view. There is abundant evidence in the Qur'an to show that Islam does not declare a perpetual war against the infidels. The Qur'anic injunctions to fight refer only to the historical context of the Prophet or to similar contexts when they occur in history. The world is, therefore, not divided between the House of Islam (*Dar al-Islam*) and the House of War (*Dar al-harb*) but between the House of faith (*Dar al-Imam*) and the House of Disbelief (*Dar al-Kufr*).

As a matter of fact there is no Qur'anic sanction for the theological, division of the world into *Dar al-Islam* and *Dar al-harb*. According to the Qur'an the world is divided between believers and non-believers. It repeatedly says that the believers together constitute one people and the disbelievers together constitute another people, as in the following:

> The believers are brethren of one another.[135]

> Those who disbelieve are friends of one another.[136]

But the Qur'an no where demands that the Muslims should remain permanently at war with the non-believers. The verses (for instance ch. 4:89 and ch. 9:5) which seem to give the impression of perpetual war between the world of Islam and world of *Kufr*, are decidedly topical and circumstantial in their import, and cannot be taken as permanent injunctions of God. Questionable One should not have; however, the misunderstanding that the Qur'an teaches a happy communion with *Kufr*. No, it enjoins the incessant struggle until the whole world has submitted to the message of Muhammad (P.B.U.H.). But the struggle is to be done by *Da'wah* (persuasion and preaching). Resort to force is allowed only as a defensive or self protective measure.

In the famous pact which the Prophet signed with the Muslims and Jews of Madinah, he declared that "the Muslims are one community" to the exclusion of the rest of mankind. Despite this he concluded a truce for six years with the Quraysh at the Treaty of Hudaybiyah. Arguing from this event the Muslim jurists "are agreed on a peace with the polytheists—the worshippers of idols—and on conclusion of treaty relations with the people of the Book. But it is wrong to say that the rule of the Muslims would never be applied to them even if they possessed the power to fight them."[137] This is obviously political expediency and juristic literalism.

But the Prophet also maintained good relations with the Christian Kings of Ethiopia and Egypt and exchanged gifts with them. No conditions were attached to these relations, which were clearly based on the principle of peaceful coexistence. Ibne

Jarir al-Tabari seems to support this idea, for he writes:

"The Prophet also signed a treaty with the polytheists at Hudaybiyah, without demanding any tribute from them. And he said: the Romans (the Byzantines) would also sign a peaceful treaty with you soon."[138]

As a fact of history Muslim States have throughout the age's maintained friendly relations with non-Muslim states, and even entered into political alliances with them. The courts of the Umayyads in Cordova and those of the Abbasids in Baghdad often hummed with the activity of .foreign missions. But the Muslim jurists were not prepared to be convinced by these facts. They continued to preach the theory of undiluted *Jihad*. It is difficult to read their real motive but it can be easily seen that they certainly erred in their classification of the world.

Among the classical theologians, however, there was no unanimity on this issue. Al-Ash'ari after saying that people differ on this problem writes:

"And al-Jubba'i (303 H./915 A.C.) says: Any place, where one cannot "stay or walk without associating oneself with some kind of *Kufr* or showing acquiescence in it and dissociating from it, is *Dar* al-*Kufr*. And any place, where one may stay and walk without associating oneself with some kind of *Kufr* or showing acquiescence in some *Kufr* and dissociating from it, is *Dar* al-Islam."[139]

A little later another famous *Sunni* doctor observes:

"Any place where the call of Islam (*Da'wat al-Islam*) appears among its inhabitants without needing the help of a guard or protector and without requiring the payment of *Jizyah*, where the rule of the Muslims is applied to the *Ahl al-dhimmah* (the protected people) if there be any *Dhimmi*, and where the *Ahl al-bid'ah* (the people of heretical opinions) are not able to coerce the *Ahl-Sunnah*, is *Dar* al-Islam,......And any place where these conditions which we have mentioned do not obtain, is *Dar al-Kufr.*"[140]

These are authoritative classical statements on the subject. They clearly recognize the presence of the worlds of *Iman* and *Kufr* but do not assert or affirm that as a matter of principle the two must always remain in a state of mutual belligerency.

This idea of peaceful coexistence in any case did not catch the imagination of the Muslim jurists and theologians and by and large, did not awaken them to the realities of history.

By the time of Ibne Taymiyah the political situation of the world had completely changed. Islam was now definitely on the defensive. Most of the Muslim lands in the East were occupied by the pagan Mongols. In the West, too, Muslim power was undergoing a rapid decline. The Christian recon quest movement had almost wiped away all the petty Muslim States in Spain. Only the tiny state of Granada stuck precariously in a sheltered valley on the South-east coast. The Crusaders had still their settlements on the coast of Palestine, and in alliance with the Mongols, were constantly threatening to destroy the Mamluk empire, the last stronghold of Islam in the West. In these circumstances the question of formulating an aggressive theory of war did not arise. Ibne Taymiyah was a great realist. He, therefore, advocated two things: consolidation of the Muslims in their own lands and thorough preparation and determined resistance against the foreign invader. These are the keynotes in the famous *Fatwa* (juridical ruling) he gave on *Jihad*. He believed in the final reduction of *Kufr* from the world and the supremacy of Islam in it, but did not preach unprovoked aggression against the infidel world. He clearly recognizes the presence of the spheres of belief and unbelief and that the two may not be mutually in a state of war necessarily. Discussing the meaning of ignorance he says that before the Prophet it had a universal character (*Al-jahiliyah al-'ammah*):

"But after the prophethood of Muhammad (P.B.U.H.) absolute ignorance is found only in some places, and not in all places, as in the *Dar al-kuffar* (land of the infidels). And it is found in some persons, not in all persons, as in a man who lives in *Dar al-Islam,* but has not yet embraced Islam; he certainly lives in ignorance."[141]

What Ibne Taymiyah principally has in mind is that is one of the fundamental duties of the *Imam*, and a doctrine which aspires to capture the entire globe must necessarily come into conflict with the opposing forces; preparation and organization of *Jihad* is, therefore, as important for the *Imam* as *Da'wah.*

Consultation (*Mushawarah*) is also one of the essential duties of the *Imam*, because without this the cooperation of the community would not be possible.[142] The Qur'an praises the Muslims that their affairs are settled by consultation. There are also numerous *Ahadith*s of the Prophet which recommend it. The subject is treated in the treatises of Muslim public law as a common place. In the system of Ibne Taymiyah it acquires a special importance. He wants a more effective and more general consultation. The *Imam* should take the opinion not only of the *'Ulama'* but of all the authoritative representatives of the public, of all the social classes concerned, and of all those who are capable of providing a dynamic opinion. Ibne Taymiyah is always inclined to give considerable importance to any technical skill, just as he has the feeling to pay regard to the humblest member of the community.[143]

He advises the *Imam* ordinarily only to consult the *'Ulama'* in whose knowledge and probity he has full confidence.[144] From this Laoust has inferred that Ibne Taymiyah, so hostile to the existence of an official clergy, has created the juridical possibility of <u>Shaykh</u> *al-Islam*.[145] This inference is not justified because Ibne Taymiyah has never advocated that the *Imam* should confine himself to consultation with only one *'Alim*. He always speaks of the *'Ulama,* as a class, who can render more service to the state than others.

Laoust is not correct in observing further that the legislative power of the *Imam* is derived from a tradition of 'Umar bin 'Abdul 'Aziz. In the day-to-day working of the government the *Imam* can issue legislative decrees if he is a *Mujtahid*; this is not permitted by a stray tradition but the nature of the Islamic law itself and by the practice of the Ra<u>sh</u>idun Caliphs whom Ibne Taymiyah usually quotes as authority.

Indeed, in the system of Ibne Taymiyah the *Imam* acquires more power and ascendancy than in the classical tradition, but at the same time he becomes more humane and social. He is not like the illusory *Imam* of al-Hilli, but a practical leader, who, seeking nearness to God and acting on the advice of the Prophet, can offer real guidance and help to mankind. "And it should be known that the sovereign is like the market, what is demanded in it is supplied to it; thus has said 'Umar bin Abdul 'Aziz. If truth, virtue, justice, and trust are demanded in it, they are supplied to it; and if falsehood, wickedness, tyranny and mistrust are demanded in it, even they are supplied to it."[146]

## 7. *The duties of the subjects*

The state comes into being by the support and allegiance (*Mubaya'ah*) of the *Ahl al-<u>sh</u>awkah* and then under the influence of the *Ahl al-shawkah* the whole community declares its oath of allegiance to the *Imam*. This oath of allegiance, therefore, imposes on the subjects the foremost duty of obedience. It is a declaration that one would obey the *Imam* as long as his orders

conform to the injunctions of God and His Prophet. The *Bay'ah*
has two aspects; in one aspect it is a contract between a Muslim
and God wherein the Muslim offers his absolute, total and
unconditional obedience to God. In the second aspect it is a
contract between the Muslim and the administrative authorities
of the community. The second is necessarily based on the first,
and is conditioned by the fact that obedience is valid only as
long as it does not involve disobedience (*Ma'siyah*) to Allah.[147]
The celebrated verses of the Qur'an with which the *Siyasah*
opens in fact define the contents of the *Bay'ah*; on the one hand
they enjoin upon the ruler to deliver the trusts to those to whom
they are due, and to judge among men with justice, and on the
other oblige the Muslims to obey the ruler who conducts himself
in this way. Then there are numerous *Hadiths* and *'athar* in
which the Prophet and his Companions extol the most respectful
loyalty to the administrative authorities of the community. The
good foundation of the Qur'anic prescription has been explained
by reason as well as experience and pragmatic considerations.
These arguments are more or less the same which the medieval
Christian theologians put forth for a close liaison between the
church and the State.[148] The unity and integrity of the *Ummah*,
the necessity of social peace, the dispensation of justice and the
respect of the individual's rights, tellingly demand that good
administrative order must be maintained. It was this
consciousness of communal solidarity that brought in the
condemnation of the <u>Khawarij</u> and the *Rawafid* (<u>Shi</u>'*is*) and other
sects which seceded from the *Jama'ah*.[149] The Prophet
(P.B.U.H.) is reported to have said: [150] "If anyone sees in his
sovereign something which he disapproves he should endure it,
for anyone who separates from the *Sultan* even to the length of
a span and dies in that condition, dies the death of *Jahiliyah*."
Every group needs political differentiation, so the observance
of a judicial and moral law demands an external discipline of

constraint. Also for confessional expansion perfect internal cohesion is a foremost necessity. And as *Da'wah* is one of the foremost duties of the *Imam* in the system of Ibne Taymiyah, he lays more emphasis on the duty of submission to the *Imam* than Sunnism normally allows.

Obedience to the administrative authorities has, however, quite a different significance and meaning for Ibne Taymiyah than for his predecessors. He does cots believe in a resigned and passive submission. For him this submission requires the condition in which everyone can participate in the life of the community and in the cooperative management of the *'Fete*. The state is nothing but an organization in which the *Imam* and the subjects jointly endeavour to realize the purposes of God and work for the same ideal. Everyone, therefore, must strive to the best of his capacity. The function .of the *Imam* is only one of coordination and critical discipline in the members of the community. "The sovereign is only appointed to order the good and forbid the evil, and this is the very purpose of the government."[150]

Political obedience is essentially a critical obedience. Public opinion never loses its rights, and if Ibne Taymiyah demands too much of personal discipline, ibis also for granting too much to the individual. Each Muslim must practice good counsel (*Nasihah*) for the *Imam* as he does it for an ordinary member of the community. The Qur'an describes the Muslims as brothers and friends and binds them together for mutual assistance and exchange of good counsels. It declares: "Then He united your hearts, so by His favour you became brethern."[131] "And the believers, men and women, are friends of one another. They enjoin good and forbid evil."[152]

The Prophet, although infallible, consulted his Companions. The *Salaf* (the early fathers) have always advocated the same. Hasan al-Basri often used to say: "Religion is good counsel (*Al-deen nasihah*)." And in a well-known injunction the Qur'an announces: "And help one another in righteousness and piety, and help not one another in sin and aggression."[133] The good counsel also represents the attitude of the just society (*Ummah wasat*) between the S͟hi'i notion of legal dissimulation (*Kitman* or *taqiyah*) and the armed revolt (K͟huruj) of the K͟harijis.

Good counsel is finally linked up with the important injunction which calls upon every member of the community to order the good and forbid the evil, and participate in moral elevation and fraternal correction. And this good counsel can be given in all the domains of state activity where the individual feels to have a dynamic opinion and make a useful contribution. It is not a legal sanction but a moral duty for each Muslim to participate in the general conduct of the community. [154] This interpretation of the concept of obedience rules out the classic difference between the ruler and the ruled. But it is an ideal towards which the community must perpetually tend. In actual practice this ideal cooperation does not always obtain and good counsel is not always accepted. The law of obedience, therefore, frequently has to operate within narrow limits.

The question of armed revolt against established authority has been seriously discussed by the jurists in all ages. In the very beginning of Islam, however, such political conditions arose that the internal cohesion of the *Ummah* was badly damaged. Its unity was, for example, constantly threatened by the rebellion of the *K͟hawarij* and the *Rawafid*, who physically seceded from the main body of the Muslims and tried to create and maintain their own political entities. This compelled the majority party, the *Ahl al-Sunnah wa'l-Jama'ah*, to rise in selfdefense and guard their political and religious integrity by every means. The term *Ahl al-Sunnah wa'l-Jama'ah*, undoubtedly, came into vogue much later, but this political differentiation had certainly taken place in the early times. So the requirements of selfdefense goaded the *Ahl al-Sunnah* to take their argument from the *Sunnah* itself, for nothing could be more convincing to the Muslim than an injunction or opinion of the Prophet. Hence they coined a large number of *Ahadiths* exhorting the Muslims to stick to the *Jama'ah*, under all conditions, and submit to the authority of the *Imam*, even if he were tyrant and wicked. In this movement the State and the *'Ulama*, cooperated, because the danger was common. The nonconformists—the *Kharijis*, the Shi'ahs, the Mu'tazilis etc.— did the same and fabricated countless *Hadiths* to support their own respective theses. These sects refuse obedience to the tyrant and sinful *Imam* and advocate armed revolt against him. Particularly for the *Kharijis* it is an article of faith and personal obligation (*Fard 'ayn*) to fight against a wicked and sinful (*Fajir and fasiq*) *Imam*. The Shi'is also says that it is necessary to disobey the unjust *Imam* systematically. Some *Sunni* jurists seem to share this opinion, but they are neither very much vocal nor insistent, and are in negligible minority. A great majority of the *Ahl al-Sunnah* preach submission to the *Imam* under all circumstances.

Ibne Taymiyah observes that people differ about the obedience to the sinful (*Fasiq*) and the ignorant (*Jahil*) *Imam* when he governs with justice and issues orders in conformity with the injunctions of God, and says that there are three opinions on the subject. The first and the least acceptable to the *Ahl al-Sunnah* is that all his orders and decrees should be rejected and he should be frankly disobeyed. The second and the most correct opinion in the view of the *Ahl al-Hadiths* and the *Fuqaha'* is that he shall be obeyed in all that conforms to the principle of obedience to God. And the third opinion is that a distinction should be made between the supreme *Imam* (*Al-Imam al-a'zam*) and his subordinates; the latter may be disobeyed in case of notorious scandal and incapacity. But Ibne Taymiyah refuses to admit this distinction, because the removal of an officer who enjoys the confidence of the sovereign is bound to lead to conflict and civil war (*Fitnah*), and thus a lesser evil will create a greater evil. In his view, therefore, the second opinion is the best.[154] And permission to disobey can be given only when the decisions of the *Imam* go clearly against a juridical prescription founded on a precise text of the Qur'an or *Sunnah* or on the *Ijma'* of the *Salaf*. The Prophet has said: "There is no obligation to obey a creature involving disobedience to God," and, further, "If anyone orders you to disobey God, then do not obey him."[155]

But Ibne Taymiyah differentiates between disobedience and rebellion. One may disobey a sinful order of the *Imam* and be punished for it, but one is not allowed to take-up arms against him as along as he prays. He quotes a large number of *Ahadith*s, obviously the products of *Khariji* reaction, to support his thesis. For instance, 'Awf bin Malik al-Ashja'i narrates that the Prophet (P.B.U.H.) said: "The best of your *Imams* are those whom you love and who love you, and for whom you pray and who pray for you: and the most wicked of them are those of whom you are jealous and who are jealous of you, and whom you condemn and who condemn you." He says "We asked, O Prophet of God, should we not then fight them on this?" He answered: "No, as long as they pray. Beware! if anyone is ruled by a sovereign and he sees him doing something that is a disobedience to God he should disapprove this disobedience but should not rebel against the sovereign" (*Sahih Muslim*). The *Imam*s may be good and wicked but in no circumstance armed revolt against them is permitted. Even a Negro *Imam* with mutilated features must be obeyed.[156] And God sent his Prophet to order the people to do well and shun the evil (*Fasad*); and human actions are accompanied by good and evil both, but an action is termed good if good prevails in it, and is termed evil if evil prevails in it. So when a caliph, like Yazid or 'Abd al-Malik or al-Mansur or someone else comes on the throne, his accession may be either accepted or opposed. But those who think that it should be opposed with the sword certainly hold an evil opinion, because the evil of such action is greater than its good. And it has seldom happened that a rebel has brought in more good than the evil he has created. Such is the case of those who rebelled against 'Abd al-Malik in Iraq, of Ibne al-Muhallab who rebelled against his father in Khurasan, of Abu Muslim who rebelled against the Umayyads also in Khurasan, and of those who rebelled against al-Mansur in Madinah and Basrah. Even if the rebels are the most pious and righteous people and have the promise of the paradise, the sin of their rebellion cannot be expiated. Thus 'Ali, Talhah, Zubayr and 'A'ishah has not been praised for the wars they fought. And even Husayn was not justified in his revolt. He was advised by men of learning and piety not to take up arms against the government, but he did not listen. "And the events proved that their opinion was correct, because no good came out of his rebellion either for religion or for the world."[157]

The *Imam* need not be more just than an ordinary witness (who has to satisfy certain strict conditions in Muslim law), because the witness gives information about an unknown thing, and if he is not just his veracity cannot be tested. But when the *Imam* issues an order it can easily be seen whether it is submission or disobedience to God. It is for this reason that God has said; "When a sinner brings some news to you first investigate it to see the matter clearly." So the action of the *Imam* can be criticized but his authority cannot be challenged. Nor is there anything to prevent the tyrant from submission (*Ta'ah*) or ordering others to do it. [158] The exercise of a social function is not necessarily linked up with the moral virtues of its incumbent. He thus creates the important distinction between the private life of the *Imam* of which he alone is to bear the consequences, and his public conduct in which he is responsible for the social execution of the law, and which affects the entire life of the community.[159]

Another reason for the unqualified condemnation of rebellion seems to be the constant fear of the rise of the *Mahdi*. Political adventurers, posing as *Mahdi*, have more often than not raised the banner of revolt against established authority on the sham pretext of ordering the good and forbidding the evil and taking back Islam, to its classical purity.

And the strangest thing in Ibne Taymiyah is that he nowhere discusses the problem of the legitimacy of the deposition of the *Imam*. The Sunni scholars theoretically assert that the community which has installed the *Imam* has also the right to remove him. But Ibne Taymiyah seeing that this will disturb social peace and harm the unity of the *Ummah* does not even consider this issue. Also the absolutism of the Mamluks, the gulf between the governing Turks and the governed Arabs, and the serious international military situation must have persuaded him to maintain a judicious silence on this matter.

But in the final analysis it seems really sad that a free, democratic, critical and sublime spirit like that of Ibne Taymiyah should have (in spite of its practical abhorrence of power and authority) given its long hand of support to perpetual absolutism. His deep insight in the Qur'an, his superb understanding of the *Sunnah*, and his great historical sense could not make him discover one of the fundamentals of social philosophy, that to resist tyranny is one of the natural rights of man. He has quoted so many *Ahadiths* many of which are certainly not genuine, but has nowhere mentioned the famous *Ahadiths* of *Amr bi'l-ma'rūf* and *Nahy 'an al-munkar* which so abundantly guarantee the fundamental rights of man and enjoin the Muslims to fight physically against tyranny and injustice. For instance, the Prophet (P.B.U.H.) said: "Anyone of you who sees something undesirable must change it with his hand, and if he cannot do so must disapprove it with his tongue, and if he cannot do so he must disapprove it in his heart, and this is the weakest category of faith (*Iman*)."[160] Further: "And when the people see the tyranny of a tyrant and do not stop him physically it is most probable that the chastisement ( *'Adhab*) of God shall overtake them all."[161] "Indeed God does not punish the common people for the sins of the high classes until they ice an evil in their midst and are able to condemn it but they do not condemn; so when they do so the punishment of God descends on high and low both."[162]

It is obvious that persistent and universal tyrnanny cannot be endured indefinitely, either on the plea of the maintenance of the *Shari'ah* or the preservation of social peace. And there is no other effective means of curbing the inequity of a despot except to remove him physically by an armed revolt. Violence in itself has no virtue, yet wars are fought to ward off aggression or protect national honour and interest. And civil commotion is nó more destructive than foreign wars When principles are at stake, when basic rights are trampled, when the human spirit is enslaved, the resort to violence becomes not only a necessity but a virtue. It must, therefore, be admitted that the Muslim jurists have failed throughout the ages to catch this principle; this is the principal reason why democratic institutions could not develop in the Muslim community despite the thoroughly republican spirit of Islam. And Ibne Taymiyah, with all his fine qualities, does not seem to be immune from this malaise. It is, however, remarkable that his great insistence on obedience to state authority and his constant condemnation of rebellion in the *Minhaj* are no longer visible in the later work

*Siyasah.* Perhaps his faith in these principles had been rudely shaken in maturer years by the harsh behaviour of authority and the terrible political persecutions that he had suffered. This is why he adopted the indirect method of criticizing the political theory in Islam, by writing a manual of the Islamic principles of administration. If he ignored the question of the deposition of the *Imam* and paid no more attention to the question of rebellion, this was most probably deliberate. From the long distance of time it is impossible to discover the real motives which prevented him from uttering a truth of which he was not at all incapable.

## Notes

1. Rosenthal, op. cit., p. 21.
2. There can be no charm in mere claim until it is verified by real experience. All the great religions of the world, like Judaism, Chris-tianity and Budhism have made similar claims, but have practically failed in creating a cohesive and homogeneous society based on their respective principles.
3. Rosenthal, p. 22.
4. Ibid., p. 23.
5. Ibid., p. 24.
6. *Qazi* Badr ul-din Muhammad bin Ibrahim bin Jami'ah (b. 639 H. /1231 A.C., d. 733 H./1323 A.C.) was a contemporary of Ibne Taymiyah and one of the great jurists of the age. He served as the Chief Justice of the Mamluk Empire for a long time. He wrote his book: *"Tahrir al-ahkim fi tadbir Ahl al-Islam,"* especially to strengthen the power of the Mamluks. His attempt to advocate the theory of compromise was perhaps the last straw on the camel's back.

7.   *Minhaj*, vol. 2, p. 239.

8.   Al-Qur'an, ch. 2:134.

9.   Ibid., ch. 16:36.

9a.  Ibid., ch.7:34.

9b.  Ibid., ch. 5:48.

9c.  Ibid., ch. 3:103.

9d.  Ibid., ch. 7:159.

9e.  Ibid., ch. 7:164.

9f.  Ibid., ch. 43:22.

9g.  Ibid., ch. 43:23.

9h.  Ibid., ch. 11:8.

9i.  Quotation: Al-Qur'an

9j.  Ibid., ch. 3:109.

9k.  Ibid., ch. 2:143.

9l.  Ibid., ch. 2:128.

9m.  Montgomery Watt, Muhammad at Madinah, 1956, p. 241.

9n.  Hamidullah, *Al-Watha'iq al-siyasiyah*, Hyderabad 1941, p. 283.

10   Ibne Kathir, vol. 14. p. 8.

11   Ibid., MRK, col. 1, p. 35

12   *Al-Furqan bayan al-haqq wa'l-batil*, MRK, col., 1, p. 36.

13   Al-Wasiyah al-Kubra, MRK, vol. 1, p. 267; al-'Aqidah al-Wasitiyah, MRK, vol. 1, p. 394.

14   *Minhaj*, II, pp. 161-64; K. Iqtida' al-sirat al-mustaqim, p. 17; Q. fi tawahhud, p. 146; Al-siyasah, p, 17, p. 63.

15   Q. fi tawahhud al-millah, RM., p. 146.

16   H. Laoust, p. 253.

17   Iqtida', p. 96.

18   Ibid., p. 97.

19    Ibid., p. 98.

20    Ibid., p. 99

21    Laoust, p. 255.

22    Al-Qur'an, ch. 5:51.

23    Ibid., ch. 5:55.

24    Ibid., ch. 5:56.

25    Ibid., ch. 10:71.

26    Ibid., ch. 49:10.

27    Al-Wasiyah al-Kubra. MRK I, p. 307.

28    Laoust, p. 257.

29    Al-Qur'an, ch. 4:59.

30    Al-Siyasah, pp. 172-73.

31    Ibid., Minhaj Vol. 2, p. 88.

31a.  *Minhaj*, vol. 1, p.24, p. 142, p. 146; vol. 2, p. 86-87.

32    Laoust, p. 258.

33    Al-Siyasah, p. 3

34    Ibid., p. 20.

35    Ibid., p. 170.

36    Q. fi tawahhud, RM., p. 134.

37    Al-Hisbab, MB., p. 37.

38    Ibne Taymiyah has discussed the injunctions relating to
      the *Ahl al-Kitab* in detail in the Fatawa fi al-Kana'is, K.
      Iqtida', K. al-Ikhtiyarat, p. 189, Fatawa, 11, p. 152, IV,
      p. 278; etc.

39    Laoust, p. 277.

40    Ibne Kathir, vol. 13, p. 219; vol. 14, p. 8; R. Grousset,
      Tome 1, pp. 68-78; for further details of Christian
      treachery see Fatawa fi'1-Kana'is.

41    *Minhaj*, I, pp. 26-27.

42    Al-Ghazali, Kitab al-Iqtisad fi al-i'tiqad, pp. 104-5.

43    Ibid., p. 105.

44  Fa<u>kh</u>r ud-din al-Razi, Kitab al-Arba'in; the book contains a special chapter on al-*Imamah* which is a most thorough but insipid systematization of Muslim political ideas received by his time.

45  Laoust, p. 283.

46  *Minhaj*, I, p. 17.

47  Laoust, p. 281.

48  *Minhaj*, II, p. 112.

49  *Minhaj*, I, p. 17. "When the people wanted to embrace Islam the Prophet only asked them to believe in God and in His Messenger but did not mention the *Imamah* to them under any circumstances."

50  Al-Siyasah, p. 172.

51  *Minhaj*, II. p. 222.

52  Ibid., p. 223.

53  *Minhaj*, I, p. 28.

54  Ibid., Quotation: Hadith.

55  Laoust, pp. 283-88.

56  *Minhaj*, I, pp. 134-39.

57  Al-Ra<u>sh</u>id Rida al-<u>*Khilafah*</u>, Cairo, 1341, p. 13; Sakka. La Notion Islamique de Souverainete, Paris, 1922, p. 33.

58  Laoust, p. 285.

59  Ibid., p. 286.

60  Minahj, II, p. 109.

61  *Minhaj*, I, p, 141.

62  Ibid., pp. 141-42.

63  Ibid., p. 142. The Christian church also developed the idea of the secular arm to defend the faith, but at the same time it also developed the idea of the two powers, the religious and the profane; the question of the supremacy of the one over the other led to bitter conflicts

between them and ultimately reduced the church to the position of nonentity and deprived it of playing any effective role in the affairs of men. But in Islam, and especially in the philosophy of Ibne Taymiyah, the secular arm is not a borrowed arm; the fulfilment of the purposes of religion will itself produce this arm.

64  Laoust, pp. 288-89.

65  *Minhaj*, iv, p. 232.

66  Al-Ghazzali, Fada'ih al-batinlyah, Leiden 1956, p. 66.

67  Ibid., p. 65.

68  Al-Iqtisad, pp. tit., p. 106. Al-Ghazzali had in mind the Saljuqs of Baghdad who were the actual guardians of the caliphate. He therefore developed his theory of the shawkah only to strengthen the theory of delegation of authority (*Tafwid*).

69  Ibne Khaldun, Muqaddimah, pp. 125-35.

70  Al-Siyasah, p. 170.

71  Laoust, p. 201.

72  Rosenthal, p. 56.

73  Laoust, p. 202.

74  Al-Siyasah, p. 14.

75  *Minhaj*, Majmu'ah 'Ilmiyah, Cairo 1953, pp. 10-11.

76  *Minhaj*, III, p. 116.

77  Al-Siyasah, p. 9.

78  Al-Hisbah, MR, p. 37. With Ibne Taymiyah the injunction of commanding the good and forbidding the evil almost attains the Khariji concept of *Fard'ayn* (personal Obligation), because he feels that every Muslim must make individual contribution to the total well-being of the community. The cooperative state can emerge and flourish only if each individual accepts a responsibility in it.

79   Laoust, 289.

80   Ibid., p. 290.

81   Ibid., p. 291

82   *Minhaj*, III, p. 116.

83   *Minhaj*, I, p. 32; III, p. 248.

84   *Minhaj*, I, p. 146.

85   *Minhaj*, I, 145; II, 148.

86   *Minhaj*, III, p. 251.

87   *Ibid.*, pp. 133-34.

88   *Ibid.*, p.243.

89   *Minhaj*, II, p. 84, III, p, 244.

90   *Ibid.*, p. 132.

91   *Ibid.,* p. 137.

92   Al-Mswardl, al-Ahkam al-*Sultan*lyah, Cairo 1298, pp. 4-5. After al-Mswardi these qualities have been repeated almost verbatim by later writers.

93   Fada'ih, op. cit., p, 68.

94   *Minhaj*. II p. 135.

95   *Minhaj*, I, p. 136.

96   *Minhaj*, II, p. 85.

97   *Minhaj*, II, p. 88; al-Siyasab, p.l9.

98   Al-Siyasah, p. 5.

99   *Ibid.*, p. 16.

100  *Ibid.*,p.9.

101  Ibid., p. 101.

102  Ibid., pp. 9-10.

103  Al-Siyasah, p. 10.

104  Ibid., p. II.

105  Al-Qur'sn, ch. 28:26.

106  Ibid., ch. 12:54.

107  Al-Siyssah, pp. 12-13.

108   Ibid., pp. 13-14.

109   Ibid., p. 19.

110   Ibid., p. 170. With earlier Muslim political thinkers the *Imam* personified the universal caliphate; he was therefore, regarded as the ideal leader of the community, and hence *Ijtihad* was laid down as essential condition for his election. With the change of time, however, when the Caliph came to be an incapable, ineffective and ignorant person the fiction of delegation was coined. The function of *Ijtihad* was assigned to the legal experts (muftis) and the *'Ulama'* who were the servants of the caliph. Ibne Taymiyah does not re-quire this chicanery. For him duties arc the functions of personal aptitudes; every member of the community, *Mujtahid* or non-mujtahid shall perform his duty according to his talent and capacity, and the question of delegation does not arise.

111   Ibid., p. 18.

112   *Minhaj*, I, p. 19, 142,1 46, 148, 149,; II. p. 87, 135.

113   Laoust, p. 297.

114   Al-Siyasah, p. 1.

115   Al-Qur'an, ch. 8:39; al-Hisbah, p. 35; Al-Siyasah, p. 24.

116   Al-Wasiyah   MRK, I, p. 289.

117   Al-Hisbah, p. 37.

118   Al-Siyasah, p. 3. Ibne Taymiyah is the first political thinker in Islam who has explained in detail the deep political significance of the word *Amanah* as used in the Qur'an. In his view, *Amanah* is a trust which is placed in the ruler through the act of swearing allegiance (*Mubaya'ah*) by the subjects to him. And trust means doing justice and procuring to the citizens their proper rights. Obedience to the ruler is directly dependent on

the fulfilment of his obligations, that is, the delivering of this trust to those who are entitled to it. And *Amanah* means the total effort to the effect that the whole of religion becomes for Allah alone. And it means ordering the good and forbidding the evil. In a word it means that the ruler should act in a way which promotes the most efficient elevation of the community spiritually and materially.

119 Al-Qur'an, ch. 9:27.

120 Al-Siyasah, p. 9.

121 Ibid., p. 14.

122 Ibid., Quotastion: Hadith.

123 Ibid., p. 22.

124 Ibid., p. 25.

125 Ibid., p. 63.

126 Al-Hisbah, p. 36. Laoust observes: "It is to be noted that, hi the *Minhaj*, the study of the function of the *Imam* is treated much less systematically than in the Siyasab; this would confirm our hypothesis according to which the *Minhaj* would be regarded as an anterior work." p. 298.

127 Al-Qur'an, ch. 57:25.

128 Al-Siyasah, p. 24.

129 *Minhaj*, I, p. 146.

130 Al-Siyasah, p. 177.

131 Ibid., p. 18.

132 Ibid., p. 21.

133 Al-Qur'an, ch. 2:216.

134 Al-Siyssah, p. 40.

135 Al-Qur'an, ch. 49:10.

136 *Ibid.*,ch. 8:72.

137   Ibne Jarir al-Tabari, I<u>kh</u>tilsf al-*Fuqaha'*, ed. Joseph Schacht, Leiden 1933, p. 14.

138   Ibid., p. 15.

139   Al-A<u>sh</u>'ari, Maqslat, vol. 2, p. 190.

140   'Abd al-Qahir al-Ba<u>gh</u>dadi ('d. 429 A.H.) Usul al din Istanbul, 1928; p, 270.

141   Ibne Taymiyah, Iqtida', op. cit. Cairo 1950, p. 78.

142   *Minhaj*, II, p. 86.

143   Laoust, p. 302.

144   Al-Siyasah, p. 170.

145   Ibid., Perhaps Laoust has been led to make this remark by the fact that Ibne Taymiyah is often addressed by his biographers and histo-rians by this title. But Muslim writers often lavish such honorific titles on their great men, so they should not be given a juridical connotation.

146   Ibid., p. 30.

147   *Minhaj*, II, pp. 146-8; Al-Siyasah, p. 3.

148   Carlyle, Medieval Political Theories, vol. 1; Donning, History of Political Theories, vol. 1, pp. 152-188.

149   *Minhaj*, I, p. 149.

150   Al-Siyasah, p. 77.

151   Al-Qur'an, ch. 3:102.

152   Ibid., ch. 9:71.

153   Ibid., ch. 5:2.

154   *Minhaj*, II, pp. 86-7. Ibne Taymiyah is so much afraid of disorder and anarchy that he forbids rebellion even against a *Kafir* as long as he does Dot order disobedience to God, and enforces the commandments of the <u>*Shari'ah*</u>.

155   *Minhaj*, II, p. 85.

156   *Ibid*. I. p. 148.

157   *Minhaj*, II, p. 85.

158  *Ibid.*, pp. 241-2.
159  *Ibid.*, p. 88.
160  Mishkat al-masabih, ch. Al-amr Al-amr bi'l-m'aruf wa'l-
     nahy 'an al-munkar.
161  Ibid., Quotation: Hadith.
162  Ibid., Quotation: Hadith.

** ** **

# CONCLUSION

The political ideas of Ibne Taymiyah until now almost unexplored except for Laoust's work (for which see Preface), are of far-reaching importance in the history of Islamic polity. He begins with the study of the Prophetic regime and says that it was *Nubnwwah* and not *Imamah*; the *Imamah* came into being only after the death of the Prophet. There is no mention of the *Imamah* in the Qur'an or in the *Sunnah*. When the Prophet asked anyone to accept Islam he only asked him to believe in God and in His Messenger, Muhammad; he never asked him to believe in his *Imamah* too. Further, obedience to him was obligatory on his followers even when they were a handful of men in Makkah, and not only when he became the head of a powerful community in Madinah. It is true that he acted as an administrator, as a judge and as a commander, but all these functions were contained in his *Nubnwwah* (prophecy), and were the necessary and natural outcome of it. Further, the Prophet neither inherited political power from any one, nor was he chosen by his people as the head of the state, nor was he accountable before them. Finally, it must be realized that he is obeyed after death as he was obeyed in life. But these are not the attributes of a sovereign. Ibne Taymiyah, therefore, concludes that the Prophetic regime cannot be given the name of state. Notwithstanding this, he admits that the Prophet was commanded by God to build a social order where the rule of the <u>Shari</u>'ah would be obeyed; and the Prophet not only succeeded in doing so but also directed his followers to establish the *Imarah* after him, because the aims of religion cannot be fully and ideally realized without the instrumentality of state machinery. Indeed, Ibne Taymiyah very strongly advocates the institution of a powerful political order to support the *Shari'ah* and promote its fundamental objectives. For him, in fact, religion can-not exist without the state. Hence he does in effect believe that the Prophet established the *Imamah*, but is reluctant to call it so for reasons we have discussed in the preceding pages.

The *Imamah* that came into being after the death of the Prophet was the relatively ideal regime of the Rashidun caliphs, especially of Abu Bakr and 'Umar. These four caliphs were chosen, according to most scholars, including Ibne Taymiyah, by some kind of indirect *Nass* from the Prophet and were providentially helped to demonstrate the Islamic order brilliantly. This view is certainly a partial concession to the Shi'i theory and *Imamism* in disguise. On it Laoust remarks, "He (Ibne Taymiyah) considers the *Imamah* of the Prophet divinely installed. His theodicy, however, prevents him to see in the prophecy an obligatory grace, although in fact the mercy of God may be in his eyes so perfect and His providence so vast that the sending of the infallible Prophet and, in a certain measure, of the *Imams*, is as indispensable to his system as is, to Shi'aism, the investiture of the infallible *Imams* by God."[2] All the standard *Sunni* writers say that the four Orthodox Caliphs were chosen by some kind of *Ijma* but at the same time most of them believe, perhaps by conviction, perhaps as a reaction to Shi'aism, that they were also nominated by the Prophet (*Mansus*) in some direct or indirect way. The similarity between the *Sunni* and Shi'ah theories, however, ends there, for the *Sunnis* do not attach any juridical importance to indirect nomination. Moreover, they regard the *Imam* as the mere executive head of the community and do not invest him with the divine qualities and infallibility which the Shi'ah *Imam* possesses.

Further Ibne Taymiyah thinks that with the Orthodox Caliphs ended the era of the Prophetic Succession (*Khilafat al-Nubuwwah*), never to appear in history again,[3] This is indeed the classical dogmatic view which becomes more accentuated in Ibne Taymiyah. This defeatist thesis was originally invented by the disgruntled jurists to show the mirror to the ruling princes and to impress on them the necessity of cooperation with the '*Ulama*'. But it soon became the principal instrument for political adventurers who raised the head of rebellion and beckoned the people to the puritan regime of the *Rashidun* caliphs, and thus assumed the form of a religious dogma with the rank and file of the community. This is certainly an erroneous view, for religious sentimentalism has always done positive harm to a clear understanding of the working of history. And Ibne Taymiyah, although he was a great enemy of formalism, could not break away from all aspects of tradition. According to him, however, after the *Khalafat al-Nubnwwah* there will be *Mulk*, by which he means a form of government which will not be presided over by ideal personalities like Abu Bakr and 'Umar, who had the Prophetic and some divine sanction behind them. *Mulk* means power, dominion, sovereignty; it does not necessarily mean hereditary rule. So when Ibne Taymiyah uses this term he does not seem to convey, even by implication, that the *Mulk* that would be established after the Orthodox Caliphate, would be a dynastic regime or a system of tyranny. He simply asserts that this later state should not be given the name of *Khilafat al-Nubnwwah*, although it performs the same function.

In any case, Ibne Taymiyah is not interested in the origin and form of the state. It does not matter whether authority is sought to be justified by a divine designation or by the semblance of an election. When the play of historical forces has brought the state authority into existence Ibne-Taymiyah recognizes it as .a fact and does not worry how it has come into being. He is a realist and, therefore, sees no meaning in the empty formalism of the Sunni election and the messianic idalism of Shi'aism. The state is born from the double oath of allegiance by which the *Imam* and the community swear obedience to God. Ibne Taymiyah simply wants to see that the authority of the *Shari'ah* is supreme in the state. There is no question of the sovereignty of the ruler of the *Ahl al-Shawkah* or any clan or dynasty. The sovereignty belongs to the *Shari'ah.*

Ibne Taymiyah, however, does not want to carry the *Ummah* back literally to the age of the Prophet and the *Rashidun* caliphs; that idealism can no more be realized because historical conditions have vastly changed. The Shi'ah dream of the expected *Imam* who would remove tyranny from this world and fill it with justice has never been realized in history. Therefore, the purposes of the *Imamah*, which were realized in the beginning of Islam by the ideal personalities of Abu Bakr and 'Umar, will now be realized by a cooperation of all the elements in the community, particularly the *'Umara'* and the *'Ulama'*. When these two classes fulfil their obligations, the rest will follow suit. When they are healthy all is healthy in the community; their corruption carries away the health of the entire social body. And every union entails some kind of hierarchy. In this union, because of the superiority of the Law (*Shari'ah*) the *'Ulama'* occupy the highest status and serve as the directive class in the state to whose advice the sovereign must bind himself, if a perfect harmony is to be realized. By the word *'Ulama'*, however, Ibne Taymiyah does not seem to mean only the jurists and the theologians, but scholars in general whose enlightened and dynamic opinion in the various fields of human activity can promote a beneficial and systematic cooperation in the community.

The state of Ibne Taymiyah is, then, neither a divine

commission nor a power-state based on sheer military might; it is a cooperation between all the members of the community to realize certain common ideals—the recognition of *Tawhid*, one God, the Creator, the Provident, the Law-giver, and of the Prophet, the intermediary between God and man, and the submission to a common law, the *Shari'ah*. He conceives the state as an organic unity in which every member of the community must participate, as a matter of duty, to the best of his capacity. Whatever function is assigned to an individual its proper and honest execution is an act of virtue and a contribution to the collective life of the state. Then the *Imam* is morally bound to take counsel of his subjects and work for their welfare, and the subjects are equally bound to offer their good counsel to him. For religion is good counsel and everyone is a shepherd responsible for the good maintenance of his flock, the community, and everyone orders the good and forbids the evil and cooperates with others in acts of piety and Allah fearing (*Al-birr wa'l-taqwa*). The ideal of the social life is therefore not submission to the state but coopera-tion with the state.

In the traditional concept of the state—the caliphate—cooperation is limited between the Caliph and a definite group of loyalists; it does not extend to the entire community. In the eyes of the *'Ulama'*, unity of the ideal community was personified by the universal Caliph. The theory of political universalism is the main current in the political thinking in Islam right from al-Ash'ari, through al-Mawardi, Abu Ya'la, al-Ghazzali, to al-Razi, who has systematized it and carried it to an extreme. The Shi'ah theory of the *Imamate* has also developed exactly on similar lines. The fiction and hypocrisy of the theory as well as its dangers were thoroughly exposed by the time of Ibne Taymiyah. He saw no good and no purpose in it, therefore, rejected it completely, and in its place proposed a new theory which was more realistic and more viable. The geographical division of Islam is a fact; each region has become a separate political entity. The classical theory of the universal caliphate can neither accept this division nor destroy it. The desired unity of Islam, therefore, can be realized only through the automatic cooperation of these political entities. The same law of cooperation that operates in the regional communities also must cooperate in the international community. There is no imperative, therefore, to press the world of Islam into a political unity or a federal state; it can better develop through the principle of cooperation, into a confederation of free sovereign states. It will be no wonder, and there will be nothing irrational or Utopian in it, if the member groups, to do obedience to God and His Prophet and to live under the common and universal law of the *Shari'ah*, unite into some sort of effective political confederacy. They may internally demolish the artificial barrier of national prejudices, and externally become a solid international bloc, feel[1], confident of themselves, and be respected by the powers of the world.

In the great confusion created by the fall of the Caliphate in Baghdad, by the institution of the new shadowy Caliphate in Egypt, and by the fear of serious military intervention by the Mongols and the Crusaders, Ibne Taymiyah thought, with a cool and composed mind, about the urgent necessity of finding a new relationship between the *Ummah* and the *Shari'ah*. He reinstated the principal Islamic values and duties and created the conditions necessary for the reconstitution of a community guided by the law of God and the *Sunnah* of His Prophet. He rejected the theory of the Caliphate and suggested the principle of cooperation, both in the national and international polity of the Muslims, as the best solution to meet the challenge of history. His times did not understand him, but today if the Muslim world is to live as a well-knit, effective, honourable and happy community it must reinterpret the *Shari'ah*, as Ibne Taymiyah did, to suit the conditions of a modern civilization and meet the requirements of a dynamic life.

## Notes

1.　*Minhaj,* vol. I, p. 20.

2.　Laoust, p. 281.

3.　We have commented earlier that not only Ibne Taymiyah but all the great scholars, on the one hand believe that personalities like Abu Bakr and 'Umar shall not emerge again in history, and on the other energetically demand the reinstitution of the *Imamah* on the pattern of the *Rashidun* caliphs. They don't see the open contradiction involved in this view, because if the ideal institution can appear in history the ideal personalities must reappear with it, since the one is, logically, inconceivable without the other.

**　　　**　　**

# A DESCRIPTIVE BIBLIOGRAPHY OF
# IBNE TAYMIAH'S COMPLETE WORKS

## General Works:

1. Majmu' Rasa'il Ibne Taymiyah comprising nine tracts of various sizes, C. 1323.
2. Majmu'at al-Rasa'il al-Kubra, 2 vols., the first volume contains twelve tracts and the second seventeen, C. 1323.
3. Majmu'at al-Rasa'il wa'1-masa'il, 5 vols., contained in all twenty two tracts, C. 1341/49.
4. Majmu'at Khams Rasa'il, C. 1930.
5. Majmu'at al-Fatawa, 5 vols., comprising several hundred juridical rulings of Ibne Taymiyah, C. 1326.
6. Al-Ikhtiyarat al-'ilmiyah, at the end of the 3rd volume of the Fatawa; it is a collection of juridical rulings in which Ibne Taymiyah differed from all other jurists, C. 1329.
7. Tafsir Ibne T., matba' Qayyimah, comprising all that he has written by way of commentary on the Qur'an, in different tracts and at different places, Bombay. 1374 H./ 1954 A.C.

## Chief Works:

1. Al-Sarim al-maslul 'ala Shatim al-Rasul, in 693 the Christian secretary of Amir 'Assaf said something disrespectful about the Prophet which aroused popular indignation, and initiated the controversy as what punishments should be given to such a criminal. Ibne Taymiyah' wrote to an inspired and momentous book on

the subject, Land b.—Br. 35, Dam. Z. 49, 84. 5, Damadzade
548, C I, 327, printed in Hyderabad 1322.

2. Minhaj al-Sunnah al-Nabawiyah fi naqd Kalam al-Shi'ah
wa'l-Qadarlyah, written in reply to Jamal ud-din al-
Mutahhar al-Hilli's Minhaj al-Karamah fi ma'rifat al
*Imamah*, about 712-16 H. Jamal ud-din wrote this book to
please and influence Uljaytu Khudabandab, the Mongol
emperor of Persia and Iraq. Ibne Taymiyah wrote his
Minhaj *al-Sunnah* to stem the tide of Shi'ism that was
sweeping the Muslim east; 4 volumes, Bulaq, 1321/2.

3. Kitab al-nubuwwst, a highly philosophical and critical
discussion of prophecy, magic, miracle and mystery, C.
1346.

4. Tafgir al-Kawakib, 44 parts of the original 100 parts are
preserved in Dam.'Um, 13,151.

5. In Cairo jail he wrote a Qur'anic commentary in 40 vols.
Not extant but referred to by Ibne Battutah (a. a. o.).

## Small Works:

### On the Qur'an:

6. Al-Risalah al-'Ubudiyah ila tafslr qawlihi ta'fila: ya
ayyuha'l-nss u'budn rabbakum ilkh. (S. 2, 19), in Majmu',
1323, no. 1, 1340, II, 1/65. In this tract he defines the
meaning of *'Ibadah* and its details and discusses whether
the whole of religion is included in it or not, and also what
is the meaning of 'ubudiyah (submission to God).

7. Al-Fatwa at-Hamawiyah, printed in S. b. Sahman, Baysn
al-mubdi' R. fl tahqiq, al-istiwa' 'ala 'l-'arsh, Rampur I,
339, also printed in C.W. yt. It deals with the discussion of
sifat ullah as indicated in a number of verses in the Qur'sn.
These verses and some similar traditions were put before
Ibne T. in the form of a question. And when Ibne T, gave a
written answer to it he was severely persecuted for it,
because he did not agree on this problem with the

misguided opinion of many scholars of his time.

8.  Tafsir al-Mu'awwadhatayn, in Mjm, 1323, II, no. 10.

9.  Fasl fi qawlihi ta'aia: Qul ya 'ibadi ikh. (S. 39, 53). vol. V. 1169, 2.

10. Ajwibah 'ali as'ilah waradat 'alayhi fi fada'il surat al-Fatihah wa'l Ikhlas wa ba'd masa'il mushkilah.

10a. Tafsir surat al-Ikhlas C. 1323.

11. Tafsir surat al-Nur, on the margin of Jami' al-bayan fi tafsir al-Qur'an of al-ljl al-Safawi (S. 203), 11th. Delhi, 1316, C 1343.

12. Tafsir surat al-Kawthar in Rasa'il al-Muniriyah, C. 1343, no. 10.

13. Al-Kalam 'ala qawlihi ta'ala: in hadhani lasshirani (S. 20, 66), Dam. Z. 36, 99, 14.

## On Tradition:

14. Arba'un hadithan riwsyat Shaykh al-Islam Ibne Taymiyah 'an arba'in min kibar Masha'ikhihi, C. nkt. Salafiyah, w. yr.

15. Arba'un hadithan riwayat Ibne Taymiyah takbrij Amin al-din al-wani, C.1341. He gives a complete history of each tradition and in connection with each mention the full name and genealogy of his teacher Muhammad Amin ud-din al-Want.

16. Al-Abdal al-'awali, 31 hadiths from very aged traditionists, from the Ghaylaniyah of a. Bakr M. bin 'Ali bin Ibrahim (d. 359/969) and one from Fawa'id al-Muzakki (d. 362/972), written before 682/1203, Bankipur, v. 2, 462.

17. Su'al fi mashhad al-Husayn ayna huwa fi'l-sahih wa ila ayna humila ra'suhu wa jawabuhu (Autograph) Dam. Z. 25, 99, 3. 1 C.w. yr.

18. R. fi sharh hadith abi Dharr, C21, 119, C. 1324, in Khams Rasa'il Nadirah.

19. R. fi sharh hadith al-mizul, (summary appended to b.

Qayyim's Madarij al-salikin)— Sifat al-nuzul, Asaf 1, 638, 378 — 'al-Tibyan fi nuzul al-Qur'an, in Mjm. 1323, 1, no. 3. In this tract he discusses the meaning of nuzul and refutes the unwarranted interpretations of heretical sects in Islam.

20. Sharh had th: unzila '1-Qur'an 'ala sab'at ahruf, in Khams Rasa'il Nadirah, C. 1907, no. 4.

21. Fi'al al-anbiya', Heid. ZS VI, 214.

22. Al-Azahir wa'1-mulah fi jumlat ahadith fi fads'il al-galawat wa'l-ayysm al-sab'ah wa layaliha, C2 I, 88.

23. R. fi'1-a.jwibah 'an Ahadith al-qussas, in Mjm. 1323, II, no. 15 — R. fi l-ahadith al-mawdu'ah allati yarwiha 'l-ammah wa'l-qussas, c2, I, 118.

24. R. tatadamman ahadith fi su'al al-nabi 'an al-Islam, Landb.-Br. 627.

25. R. fi qawlihi: la tushadd al-rihal ills ila thalath masajid, C2 I, 118, in Mjm. 1323, II, no. 3.

26. Al-Jawami' fi'1-siyftsah al-ilahiyah wal-inabah al-nabawiyyah, Bombay, 1306.

**On Dogma:**

27. Al-Wasitah bayn al-thalq wa'1-haqq, Berl. 1994, C. 1318, in Mjm. 1323, no. 2, 1340, II, 66/87' like the al-Qa'idah al-wssitiyah in Maj-mu'at al-tawhid, Delhi, 1895, no. 6-al-'Aqidah al-Isfahaniyah, H. Kh. IV, 8249, along with sharri al-'Aqidah al-Isfahaniyah C2 I, 18,8, C. 1339. It deals with the fundamentals of faith and refutes the belief that any link is required between man and God.

28. Al-R. al-Wasitlyah with appendices, autograph Dam. 2. 35, 91, 86, 22' like al-Aqidah al-wasitiyah Asaf, 374, 486' (Urdu translation), Arabic text printed in C. 1346, in Mjm. 1323, 1, no. 9, along with al-Munazarah fi 'l-'A. al-Wast. itself with no. 10. This tract discusses briefly the fundamentals of faith according to ahl al-sunnah wa'l jama'ah, the only sect that will be saved from the wrath of God.

29. Al-'Aqidah al-Hamawiyah al-Kubra, Berl. 1996, Dam. Z.,
    31, 33, 2, in Mjm. 1323, 1: no. 11, see no. 7.
30. Al-'Aqidah al-Tadmuriyah, Berl. 1995 in Mjm. 1325. In
    this tract Ibne Taymiyah discusses tawhid and sifat in a
    masterly way and also pays much attention to free-will
    and determinism and to the theory of good and evil.
31. Al-Furqftn bayn awliya'al-Rahrtisn wa awliya' (hizb) al-
    shaytan, Berl. 2082/3, Rampur I, 355, 247, C. 1323, 1325,
    Lahore, 1321, and in Majmu'at al-tawhid li M. bin 'Abdul
    Wahhab al-Najdi, Delhi 1895, pp. 288/363. C. 1310, Matb.
    'Aliyah; In this tract Ibne Taymiyah discusses the attributes
    of the friends of God and the friends of the Satan and points
    out the method to differentiate the one from the other.
32. Al-Kalam 'ala haqlqat al-Islam wa'l-'imsn, Berl. 2089, Esc,
    2 1474— R. fi'1-Islam waViman, Hyderabad, JRASB
    1917, Ciii, 149, K. al-'Iman wa'1-Islam ed. Mawlawi M.
    a., 'Ar. M. l^imayatallah and M. 'Abdallatif, 11th. Delhi
    1311, in Majmu'at al-tawhid, C. 1325.
33. Al-Qa'idah al-Marrakushiyah written in 712/1313 in Egypt,
    on the occasion of some quarrel among Malikite
    theologians about the permissibility of discussion of the
    attributes of God, Berl. 1309.
34. Al-Munazarah fi '1-i'tiqSd, an open letter against
    Shamsuddin about the allegorical interpretation of God's
    attributes, Berl. 2310.
35. Answer to a question fi ₉ifat al-Kamfil, Ind. off., 467, 2—
    R. fi mi yajibu lillah min sifat al-Kamal, Mjm, 1349, V.
    no. 2.
36. Mas'alat al-'ulum, an answer to the question of two
    disputing Shafi'ites about the residence of God, Berl. 2311,
    Gotha 84, 2, Munch. 885,5.
37. Jawab ahl al-'ilm wa'l-'Iman bitahqiq ma abhbara bihl rasul
    al-Rah-man min anna qul huwa Allah,ahad tu'adil (ta'dil)
    thulth al-Qur'an, C. 1322, no. 25 in Mjm. 1322,1325. It is

an answer to the question: if the word of God has the same value in all cases how can one word have superiority over another? And if this reference is allowed does it not follow from it that a similar reference may be allowed in the attributes of God.

38. Answer to the question whether man out of his free-will can do well against God's predetermination. Leid. 2019.

39. R. fl 'iqa' al-'uqud al-muharramah, proof that even if a man commits sin more than once repentance can bring forgiveness to him C. 1323.

40. Idah al-dalalah fi 'umum al-risslah, C. 1341, 1343. Al-R, al-Munl-rlyah, 1341.

41. Al-R. fi'l-julus, published as an appendix to Mu'in b. Safi's Jami' al-bayan fi tafsir al-Qur'an, Delhi, 1297.

42. Fawa'id al-sharifah fi'l-af 'al al-ikhtiyariyah lillsh Làndb.- Br. 625.

43. Al-Furqan bayn al-haqq wa'l-bstil, C2. I, 200, in Mjm. 1323, 1, no. 1, Ibne Taymiyah establish that this furquan is the Qur'sn and its message.

44. Al-R. at Ba'lbakkiyah C. Mjm. 1328. In this tract Ibne Taymiyah establishes that the Holy Qur'an is the word of God and not of Muhammad (P.B.U.H.) or Gabriel.

45. Al-Tuhfah al-Iraqiyah fi'l-a'mal al-qalbiyah, printed in S. bin Sahman, al-Bayan al-mubdi', Amritsar, 1315, C. Matb. Munlriyah w. yr. It contains a fine discussion of the principles of belief and faith and on love of God, love of the Prophet, reliance on God, sincerity of faith, gratitude, perseverance, and other important functions of the heart.

46. Ma'arij al-wusul ilft anna fru' al-din wa usulaha mimma bayyanahu al-rasul, in Majmu' 1323, no. 7, Mjm. C. 1318, no. 2, 1323,1, no. 2, It is the most important contribution of Ibne Taymiyah to the interpretation of the functions of prophecy. In this tract he has proved that the prophet Muhammad (P.B.U.H.) has pointed out and explained all

the fundamentals and details of faith and its hidden and open meanings as well as its theoretical and practical aspects. It is in fact a refutation of the philosophers like al-Farabi and Ibne Sina and the Bstimyah and the Qaramitah and others who held that the Prophet talked from imagination and not from certain knowledge and that philosophy is superior to nubuwwah.

47. Qa'idah fi '1-mahabbab, Dam. Z. bo, 119, 10.

48. Al-su'al 'an al-ruh hal hiya qadlmah aw makhluqah wa dhalik wa'1-jawab 'alayh, Dam. 2. 35, 99, 7.

49. Al-'Aql wa'l-ruh, R. Mumriyah, C. 1343, II, no. 2.

50. Su'al al-Muhajiri 'anal-farq fi'l-sifat bayn al-mutashabih wa ghayrihi wa jawabuh, Dam Z. 36, 99, 11.

51. Fima 'alayhi ahl al-'ilm wa'1-iman min al-awwalinwa'1-akhinn mimma yushbih al-ittihad wa'1-hulul al-batia wa' in summiya hululan wa'tti-hada, Ibid., 39, 10.

52. Al-R. al-Madaniyah fi tahqiq al-majaz wa'1-haqiqah, in b. Qayyim, Ijtima' al-juyush al-lslamiyah, Amritsar, 1314.

53. Al-Iklil fi'1-musjitabih (*Mutashabih*) wa'1-ta'wll, in Mjm. 1323, II.

54. Al-Iradah wa'l-amr, in Mjm. 1323, 1, no. 8. It is a very important tract on the idea of divine creation.

55. Fi maratib al-iradah, Mjm. 1323, II, no. 4. It explains the Qur'anic verse: Kun fayakun. A question was raised: If God addressed a thing which already existed this command was meaningless, and if the thing did not exist how did God address a non-being?

56. R. fi'1-qada wa'1-qadar, Ibid., no 5.

57. R. fi'1-ihtijaj bi'1-qadar, ibid., no 6.

58. Al-'Aql wa'1-naql, Rampur I, 318, 273, 'A?af. II, 1322, 163/4'—(?) Dar'uta'arud al-aql wa'1-naql, C 2.1, 109.—Bayan muwafaqat sarih al-ma'qul li-sahih '1-manqul, printed on the margin of Minhaj al-sunnah, C.

59. Al-Kalam 'ala '1-fitrah, Mjm. 1323, II, no, 14. It is a

discussion of the famous tradition: Every child is born in nature but his parents make him a Jew, a Christian or a Magian. It also examines the meaning of fitrah in the famous Qurianic verse: fitrat 'llah allati fatara 'l-nas 'alayha.

60. R. fi darajat al-yaqm; ibid. no. 7—(?) al-Haqq al-yaqin wa 'ayn al-yaqln, C2.1, 290.

61. Al-Shafa'ah al-Shar'iyah wa'1-tawassul ila'llah bi'1-dhat wa'l-ashkhas, in Mjm. C 1341, 10/24.

62. Ibtal wahdat al-wujud wa'1-radd 'ala al-qa'illn biha, Ibid., 61/120.

63. Mas'alat aifat allah ta'ala wa 'uluwwihi 'ala khalqihi bayn al-nafy wa'l-ithbat, Ibid., 185/216.

64. Qa'idah fi'l-ism wa'l-musamma, vol. V, 1169.

65. Qa'idat al-Islsm, Land b.-Br. 632.

66. Qa'idah jami'ah fi'1-tawhid, Ibid.

67. Qa'idah fi '1-tawhid wa'1-ithbat wa'l-tawakkul, Rampur I, 356, 255C.

68. Al-Iman, Asaf. II, 1322, 14.

69. Wasiyat al-i'tiqad, C2.1, 376.

70. Qa'idah nafi'ah fi sifat al-Kalam, R. al-Muniriyah, C. 1343. II, no. 3.

71. Fi Bayan al-huda min al-dalal, Mjm. 1323, II, no. 8.

72. At-Wasiyah fi'l-din wa'1-dunya or al-Wasiyah al-sughra, ibid., I, no. 4.

73. Su'al fi '1-l'arsh hal huwa Kurly am la wa jawsbuhu, Dam. Z, 30,18, l, in Mjm. 1323, 1, no. 6.

74. Fi 'ilm al-fshir wa'l-batin, R. al-Munmyah, no. 11.

## Polemics:

### A. Against the Dhimmlyan.

75. Iqtida' (iqtifs') '1-sirst al-mustaqim wa mujanabat ashab al-jahim, polemic against the festivals of Jews and

Christians, Berl. 2084, Dam. Z. 49, 86, Bankipur, XIII, 903, Rampur II, 283, 11' printed C. 1907/8.

76. Takhjil ahl al-injil, Bodl. II, 45, Mukhtasar Takhjil man harrafa 'I-injil, v. a, '1-Fadi al-Maliki al-Su'udi, C2.1, H. 23, See Maracci in the Prodromus of his Refutatio Alcorani, See Nallino, Rend Lincei, ser. VI, vol. 7, 332.

77. Al-Jawab al-aahih liman baddala dm al-Masih, Leid., 2018, Bod. II, 45, yeni 732, Asaf. II, 1298, 165/6, printed C. 1322, 1325, it is a detailed answer in 4 vols. to a book against Islsm by Paul, bishop of Sidon and Antioch.

78. Mas'alat al-Kana'is, in favour of the Egyptian government, because the churches in Cairo had formed a united front, Paris, 2692, 2, Bayazid, 1141, 16.

79. Al-Risalah al-Qubrusiyah, Khitab li-Sajwas malik Qubrus, a request to the King and nobles of Cyprus to mete out good treatment to Muslim prisoners of war, reminding them of the liberal teachings of Islam and its relationship with the Christians, Berl. 2087, Munch. 885,3, Dam. Z. 87,21,4, printed in C. 1319.

80. Answer to a question about Maundy Thursday, Dam. Z. 47, 52, 6.

**B. Against Islamic Sects.**

81. Al-Mas'alah (al-radd 'aia) al-Nugayrfyah, Berl. 2085, in Nina. 1323, no. 5, 1340, a refutation of their strange and foolish beliefs.

82. Naqd ta'sis al-Jahmiyah, against Fakhr ud-din al-Razis description of his teacher, Leid., 2021—Radd al-Jahmtyah wal-zansdiqah in Ilahi. Fak. Macm. no. 5/6. 278 ff.

83. Al-Qa'idah fi'1-Qur'an, against the Jahmiyah, on the margin of Mu'in b. Safis' Jami' al-bayan fi tafsir al-Qur'sn, Delhi 1297.

84. Qa'idah fi '1-haqiqah wa'l-riealah wa ibtal qawl ahl al-zandaqah.

85. Al-R. al-(Adwiyah or al-wasiyah al-Kubra, in Mjm. 1323,

I, no. 7. It is the detailed reply to a letter from the followers of 'Adi bin Mussfir al-Umawi asking Ibne Taymiyah to define true Islam and indicate the right attitude to be adopted by Muslims with regard to events in the early history of Islam. These 'Adawiyah came to be called the Yazidiyah because in opposition to the Shi'ah they exalted Yazid and almost canonized him. Ibne Taymiyah in his reply makes a detailed study of Yazid's character and in his support quotes abundantly the opinions of the rightminded *'Ulama* of former times and advises the 'Adawiyah to follow the middle course.

86.  Ta'wil mukhtalif al-hadith fi '1-radd 'als ahl al-hadith wal-jam' bayn al-afehbar allatli'd-da'aw 'alayha ahl al-nuqud wa'1-ikhtilaf, C. w. yr,

87.  Bughyat al-murtad fi '1-radd 'ala '1-mutafalsifah wa'1-Qaramitah wal Batiniyah al-ma'rufah bi'1-Sab'iniyah, C. 1323.

88.  Al-radd 'ala al-Haririyah, the followers of M. b. 'A'. al-Hariri (d. 699/1299), Ms. Massignon, see Recension de Textes 228.

## C.  Against the Sufis:

89.  Sharh Kalimat 'Aq. al-Kilani fi K. Futtih al-ghayb, Leipz. 223.

90.  Ahl al-suffah wa aba til ba'd al-mutasawwifah fihim wa fil-awliya wa aansfihim wa'1-da'awi fihim, in Mjm. C. 1341, 25/60.

91.  Munazarat Ibne Taymiyah al-'alaniyah li-dajsjilah al-Bata Thiyah al-Rifa'iyah, Ibid.. I, 121/46, Land b.-Br. 626. The Rifa'iyah were a well-known sufi order in the times of Ibne Taymiyah, they were notorious for their heresies and ignorance, they had mixed up the true faith with magic, myth, superstition and every kind of nonsense, Ibne Taymiyah' s fight against them remains one of the most notable features of his life.

92.  Libas al-futuwwah wa'l-khiraq 'inda'l-mutagawwifah wa masa'il ufehrs fashat fihim, in Mjm. C.I., 1341, 147/60.

93.  R. ilā 'l-'arif billah al-Shaykh Nasr al-dm al-Manbiji, *ibid.*, 162/83. It is a general attack on the sufistic concept of *Tawhid*, ecstasy (sukr) and union (ittihad).

94.  Al-Sufiyah wa'l-fuqara', C. 1327. It is a criticism of the different stages of spiritual journey of the sufi.

**D.  Against the Philosophers:**

95.  Al-Radd 'ala falsafat b. Rushd al-hafid, at the back of Falsafat al-Qadi, C. 1328. It is a collection and rearrangement of Ibne Taymiyah 's argu-ments against b. Rushd given in his book: Dar' ta'srud al-'aql wa'l-naql.

96.  Fima dhakarahu M-Razi fi'l-Arba'in fl mas'alat al-sifst al-ikhtiysri-yah, Lepiz. 875 ii. Da. Z. 36, 29, 16.

97.  Nasihat al-imsn fi radd 'ala mantiq al-Yunan, Summary by Suymi, Jahd al-qarihah fl tajrid al-naaihah, Leid. 2419, 10.—Radd 'ala al-manliqiyin, Asaf. II, 1322, 14, printed in Bombay by Sharf ud-din al-Kutubi, w. yr. The real aim of this work is to dispel the idea from the minds of the people that true knowledge can be obtained only through logical reasoning. In this book Ibne Taymiyah has very clearly brought out the basic difference between Islamic thinking and Creek thinking and established the superiority of the former.

**Fiqh:**

98.  Qa'idah Jalilah fi 'l-tawassul wa'l-wasilah: on the three problems: a. whether one may swear by one other than God; b. whether one may in thikr call God by a name other than al-asma' al-fausnfi: c. whether the tradition that a person in prayer may invoke the intercession of a prophet other than Muhammad, is correct. Bed. 2088; C. 1327. Damascus 1331 'C. 1348.

99.  Fi sujud al-Qur'an, Berl. 3570.

100. Qa'idah fi 'adad rak'at al-salawat wa awqstiha; Ibid., 3511.

101. Fatwa about an open question put to him in Egypt in 708/ 1308 about different points in the performance of prayers, Ibid., 3572.

102. Fi sujud al-sahw, that somebody who forgets how often he has made the prescribed bows (sujad) has to perform two bows for the error, Ibid., 3573.

103. Fi awqat al-iwhy wa'l-niza' fi ds'wat al-asbab wa gjiayriha. It is a discussion of the breaking up and delaying of prayers, Ibid., 3574.

104. Renewed investigation of the same problem, Ibid., 3575.

105. R. whether through the course of pilgrimage to the grave of a prophet curtailment of prayer is allowed, or the whole pilgrimage would come to nothing if this concession is availed of, ibid., 4047.

106. Mas'alat al-ziysrah (ziyfirat al-qubur wal-istinjad bi'l-maqbur), written in 710/1310, Munch. 885, 2, Dam. Z. 35, 99, 8, ed. M. 'Abd al-raziq Hamzah, C. w. yr. Mum. C. 1323, no. 6.

107. His defence against the attacks because of this writing, Munch, 885,7.

108. R. Bsb al-taharah, Leid, 1835.

109. Usul al-fiqh, Berl. 4592.

110. Al-Musawwadah fi'l-usul. Dam. 'Urn. 57, 3, 4.

111. I'tibar al-niyah fi'l-nikah, Berl. 4665.

112. Iqamat al-dalil fi ibtsl al-tahlil, Leid. 1883, in Mjm C. w. yr. It is a refutation of the juristic view that a thrice-divorced woman can remarry her first husband if she has nominally, married a second person and obtained divorce from him before real sexual union.

113. Al-Farq al-mubin bayn al-talaq, wal-yamin, Leid. 1835.

114. Mas'alat al-half bi'l-talsq, C. VII, 565.

115. Lamhat al-mukhtalif (Lum'ah mukhtasarah, fi'l-farq bayn wa'l-halif, Dam. Z. 34, 72, 47, 52, 3, Laleli 376, 7, 27.

116. Fatawi, Berl. 480, 17/8, Dam. 'Urn. 53, 67, al-F. al-Misriyah, i 68, C. 1326/29, five large volumes.

117. R. fi'l-sams' wal-raqa wa'stima' al-shi'r wa ghayrih, Berl. 5507, Mjm. 1323, II, no. 13. It is a discussion of the chanting of music and dance in sufi gatherings and there is an incidental discussion of recital and chanting of poems in general.

118. Al-Siyasah al-shar'iyah fi islsh al-ra'i wal-ra'iyah, Berl. Oct., 2553. Paris, 2443/4, Dam. Z. 83 ('Urn. 887, 76, C2.1, 319, C. 1323.—K. ll-jawami'fi'l-siygsah al-Ilahlyah wa'l-insbah al-nabawiyah, Bombay, 1306. It is a small tract of 80 pages, dealing with the duties am) obligations of the ruler and the ruled, the payment of amanat (trusts), the realization and distribution of zakah, the dispensation of justice and the enforcement of hudud (the criminal provisions of the Qur'an).

119. Raf'al-malam 'an al-a'immah al-a'lfim, discussing the circumstances under which a scholar can deviate from the tradition, Pesh. 79, 61, Bank. XIX, 1, 1564, printed in Bombay 1311, in Mjm. 1323. no. 3, 1324. pp. 81/122, along with al-Wasitah C. 1318, with one ofthe works of al-Shawkani in Majmu'ah Mubarakah, Delhi, 1311. This is a valuable study of the causes of differences of opinions among the early jurists. It is also a critical examination of the causes of conflict between a juridical ruling and a tradition.

120. K. fi'l-salat, at the back of al-Nawawi's Arba'un, Delhi, 1895.

121. Al-qiyas bi Shar' al-Islam. C. 1346 — R. fl roa'na '1-qiyas, Mjm, 1323, W;, 12. It is not a study of principles of qiyas in general but of the well-known problem whether any consideration can supersede qiyas. Ibne Taymiyah first defines the true meaning of qiyas and then proves that nothing can be accepted against al-qiyas al-sahih.

122. Al-Nasihah al-dhahabiyah, at the back of al-Dhahabi's

Bayan zaghal al-'ilm wa'l-talab, Damascus 1347.

123. Al-Risalah al-Khilafiyah fi 'Ksalat khalf al-Malikiyah, Dam. Z. 32, 40 2.

124. Fi Hidanat al-gaghir al-mumayyiz hal hiya li'l-ab aw li'l-umm, Ibid., 36, 29,17.

125. Al-Jawab al-bihir fi zawr al-maqabir. (comp. 102). It is the reply to an inquiry from al-Malik al-Nasir, Ibid., 39,129, i.

126. Qa'idah Jalilah fi'l-'badah, in Majmu'ah fi 'l-tawhid, M. b. 'Abd al-wahhsb al-Najdi, Delhi, 1895.

127. R. fi 'l-niyah fi 'l-'ibadah, in Mjm. 1323, 1, no. 5.

128. Khilaf al-ummah fi 'l-ibadat, C. 1927, on the margin of Muqaddimah fi'l-mawdu' by M.R. Rida.

129. R. al-Halil, C2.1. 43 Fi'l-jawab 'an qawl al-qa'il: akl al-halsl muta-'adhdhir la yumkin wujuduhu fi hadha al-zaman, Mjm. 1323, II. This is a very interesting study and a recurring problem in Islamic society. Ibne Taymiyah's views on the subject are highly enlightening and instructive.

130. Bayan al-huda min al-dalal fi amr al-hilal, in Mjm. 1323, II, p. 152 In this tract Ibne Taymiyah has tried to prove the excellence, usefulness and superiority of the lunar calendar over other systems.

131. R. fi raf' al-imam al-Hanafi yadayhi fi 'l-salat, in Mjm. 1323, II, no. 16.

132. Manasik al-hajj, Ibid., no, 17.

133. Tanawwu'al-'ibadat, inMajmti'1323, no. 4, in Mjm. 1340, 11, 123/36. It discusses the variety and kind of 'ibadah and Ibne Taymiyah argues that all that is correctly reported from the Prophet is obligatory or lawful.

134. Al-Mazalim al-mushtarikah, in Mjm. 1323, no. 8, Mjm. 1340, II, 215/18. It is a study of the realization of communal fines. Ibne T. discusses the lawfulness or otherwise of the problem and examines the method as to how much fine should be collected.

135. Al-Hisbah fi'l-Islam, Mjm. 1323, no. 9, Mjm. 1340, II. 229/

310. It discusses the duties and functions of the state officer (Muhtasib) who looks after public morality. This tract throws a very good light on the social conditions of his times and on the respect of religion in society and on state jurisdiction in personal life.

136. Sharh al-'Umdah 1,605.

137. Al-Masa'ilal-fiqhiyah, Dam. Z. 'Urn. 53, 4.

138. Fasl al-asma' allati 'allaqa 'Hah biha'1-ahkamfi M-kitab wa'1-sunnah, Vat. V. 1169, 3.

139. Al-Najasah al-ma'fuwah. Land b.-Br., 127.

140. Qa'idah fi af'al al-hajj, ibid., 629.

141. Fatwa on whether a rich man is absolved of his obligation if bepayi out charity instead of performing the hajj, ibid., 631.

142. Jawab al-raunaqalah fi'1-waqf wa ghayrih, Asaf. II, 1710, 34.

143. Al-Ahkam al-sultaniyah, C2.I, 548.

144. R. ft sunnat al-jumu'ah, 1323, II, no. Ibne Taymiyah establishes that there is no prescribed sunnah prayer between the two adhans on Friday.

## On Personal Piety:

145. Jawami' al-Kalim al-tayyib fi '1-ad'iyah wa M-adhkar, AS 583, Cl VI, 228, 21, 140, Cat. Sarkis 1928, 47, 11, Mosul 62, 181, printed in C.1322, 1349.

146. Al-Hajj al-jamil waafh al-jamil wa'1-aabr al-jamti wa aqsamal-nas fi'1-taqwa wa '1-sabr, in Mjm. C.1341, 2/9.

147. Qa'idah fi al-radd 'ala al-Ghazali fi mas'alat al-tawakkul, Land b.-Br. 628. .

148. R. fi 'I-suluk, Rampur I, 341/2.

149. Qa'idah fi'1-sabr, Land b.-Br. 630.

150. Al-R. al-tis'iniyah fi bayan mihnatih, in Mjm. C.w. yr., Sarkis 1972, 50, included in the fifth volume of the Fatawi, C. 1326. He received a joint letter from the governors and

judges of Egypt and Syria asking him to deny direction and space with regard to Allah, that he should not say that the Qur'an consists of letters and sounds but that it is only meaning and stands by this meaning alone, that Allah should not be pointed to in a physical way, that he should not address the common people about the traditions and verses dealing with sifat should not write about this matter to people at large in the country and should not give fatwa on this problem in haste and extempore. Ibne Taymiyah reacted strongly against this demand and wrote a lengthy reply to this letter under the present title, for which he was persecuted and sent to jail.

## Poems:

151. Manzumah fi '1-qadr, in al-Rasa'il al-Muniriyah, C. 1343, 1, no. 5. It is the reply to a letter addressed to him in verse about freewill and determinism. Ibne Taymiyah also chose to answer this letter in verse.

152. 102 verses about freewill, Berl. 2054, (in Tawil meter).

153. Su'al ba'd ahl-al-dhimmah min al-Yahud fi'1-qada wa'1-qadar. It is the answer to a query from a Jew, in 8 verses in Tawil meter, uttered extempore, ibid., 2481, printed at the back of 'Abd us-salam bin A. al-Maqdisi's Tafiis Iblls, C. 1906.

154. Qasidah on the freewill, Berl. 2482.

155. Poem on the refutation of an anonymous poem whose writer tried to excuse his disbelief by holding that all he did was ordained by God, Berl. Mus., 984, i.

156. Qasidah, Paris, 344, 4.

157. Marthiya on Ibne Khidr al-Mutayyam, Ibid, 2.

## UNCLASSIFIED TITLES NOT LISTED BY BROCKELMANN

158. K. al-radd 'ala '1-Nasara, Br. Mus. quoted by Muhammad

Yusuf Kokan 'Umari, Imam Ibne Taymiyah, Lahore, 1960.

159. Sharh hadith: Innama '1-a'mal bi'1-niyyat, matb. Muniriyah, C. 2. y.

160. Bahtb harf law, an astronomical tract quoted by al-Suyuti in his al-Ashbah wa'l-naza'ir.

161. Risalat Jihad, written to persuade the Muslims to fight the Tartars, quoted by 'Abd al-Hadi in his al-'Uqud al-durriyah.

162. Fi M-radd 'ala man idda'a al-jabr, Nadwat al-'ulama', Lucknow.

163. Tabsirat ahl al-Madmah, discussing whether or not the practice of the Madinese is ijma', Jami' mosque, Bombay.

164. Ta'liq 'ala K. al-Muharrir fi'1-fiqh, Dar al-Kutub al-Misriyah.

165. Bayan Mujmal 'an 'ahl al-jannah wa'l-nar, Nadwat al-'ularoi'. Lucknow.

166. Munajarat Ibne Taymiyah ma' al-Misriyyln wa'l-Shamiyyin, Ibid. It contains an account of all the controversies Ibne Taymiyah had with the Egyptian and Syrian '*Ulama*'.

167. Burhan Kalam Musa, matb. Muhammadi, Lahore a w.y.

168. K. al-istighathah Mjm. 1323, 1, no, 12, discussing whether an invocation to the Prophet Muhammad for help is permissible or not.

169. Talkhty al-istiqghathah al-ma'ruf bi'1-radd 'ala '1-Bakarl, a refutation of the views of the jurist Nur ud-din on the above mentioned question, matb. Salafiyah, C. w. yr., pp. 400.

170. Al-Radd 'ala '1-Akhna'i, an answer to the objections of Qfidi Taqi ud-din Akjhna'i al-Malikl on Ibne Taymiyah's Risalah on istighathat., printed on the margin of the Talkhis quoted above.

171. Fi Ahkam al-safar wa'1-iqamah, Mjm. 1349. II. It is a lengthy discussion of the problem of curtailment of prayer on journey. It also contains a good discussion of the

question of combining two prayers at a time in journey or in residence.

172. Aqwam ma qila fi '1-mashiyah wa'l-hikmah, wa'l-qada wa'l-ta'lil wa butlan al-jabr wal-ta'til, Mjm. 1949, v, no. 5. It is a discussion of the difficult questions; why did God create the universe, especially man? Is His creation based on wisdom and goodwill? etc.

173. Haqiqat madhhab al-ittihadiyin, aw wahdat al-wujud, Mjm. 1349, IV, no. I. It is a very detailed refutation of the views of Muhiyy ud-din Ibne al-'Arabi on prophecy and pantheism. It is indeed one of the major contributions of Ibne Taymiyah to standard Islamic literature.

174. K. Madhhab al-salaf al-qawim fi tahqiq mas'alat Kalam Allah al-Karim, Mjm. Ill, no. 1. It is the most spirited defense, from the Sunnite view point, on the question of the created ness of the Qur'an. Ibne Taymiyah has taken up the question in a most serious manner and completely uprooted the arguments of the Mu'tazilah and the Shl'ah on it. He had also severely exposed the fallacies of Afu al-H. al-Ash'arl.

175. Qa'idah fi '1-mu'jizit waM-KarSmat, Mjra. 1349, V, no. 1. It is a fine tract on the nature and philosophy of divine revelation. Here Ibne Taymiyah argues and proves that true religion cannot but be of divine origin, and simple human reason, of its own, cannot realize the eternal truths, and so prophecy is the only true method for human guidance.

176. Tafsil al-ijmal Hma yajibu lillah min sifat al-Kamal, Ibid., no. 2, This is a running theme with Ibne Taymiyah because it is the misunderstanding of the attributes of God that has had to the emergence of different faiths and religions in the world, and that has led to serious differences within Islam itself.

177. Futyi fi'1-ghibah, Ibid., no. 4. It is a discussion of the meaning of ghibah (back-biting) and its religious and social aspects.

178.  Sharh hadith 'Imran bin Husayn: Kan Allah wa lam yakun qablahu shay'un, ibid., no. 6. It is a discussion of the Hadith: There was God (in the beginning) and there existed nothing before Him.

179.  Qa'idah fi jam Kalimat al Muslimin wa wujub i'tismihim bi-habl 'llfih al-matin, Ibid., no. 7. It is a small but very good tract on the necessity of keeping the ummah together. Ibne Taymiyah argues that all those who profess Islam and participate in its communal activity like the daily and Jumu'ah congregations the 'Ids, and similar meetings, must be respected as Muslims.

180.  Al-Madhhab al-wadih fi mas'alat al-jawa'ih, Ibid., no. 8. It is a juridical study of the law of compensation when an article brought under contract has been lost before it is handed over to the other party.

## MISCELLANEOUS

Titles of Ibn Taymiyah's works not traced anywhere as yet but quoted by Ibn Shakir al-Kutubl (d. 764 H.) in his *Fuwat al-wafayat and by Isma'il Pasha at Baghdadi* in his *Hadiyt al-'arif in—Asma' al-mu'allifin wa athar al-musaanifin* (Istanbul, 1901) which is an author wise rearrangement of the Kashf al-zunun of Hajji Khalifah with additions.

1.  Qa'idah fi'l-isti'adhah.
2.  Qa'idah fi'l-basmalah, al-Kalim 'aia al-jahr biha.
3.  Jawab al-I'tiradat al-Miariyah 'ala '1-Fatawa al-Hamawiyah, 4 vols.
4.  Ma amiahu fi'l-jubb raddan 'ala t'asls al-taqdis Ii'l-Razl.
5.  Sharh awwal al-Muhassal.
6.  Jawab ma awradahu Kamal al-din al-Sharisi.
7.  Minhaj al-istiqamah, 2 vols.
8.  Sharh awwal Kitab al-Ghaznawi fi usul al-din.

9. Zawajir, a nice volume.

10. Qa'idah fi'1-qadajya '1-wahmiyah.

11. Qa'idah fiqiyasmalayatanaha.

12. Jawab al-risaiah al-Safdiyah.

13. Jawab fi qawl ba'd al-flasifah: Inn a mu'jizat al-anbiyi' 'alayhim salara quwa al-nafsaniyah.

14. Ithbat al-Ma'ad wa'1-radd 'ala Ibn Sina.

15. Sharh risaiat b. 'Abdus H Kaiam al-imam Ahmad fi'1-usul

16. Qa'idah fi1-Kulliyat.

17. Al-R. al-Azhariyah al-Qadiriyah al-Baghdadiyah.

18. Qa'idah fi qurb al-rabb min 'ftbidihi wa da'ihi.

19. Al-Kalam 'ala naqd al-murshid.

20. Al-Tabrlr fi mas'alat jafir.

21. Jawab fi liql' Allah ta'ala.

22. Jawab fi ru'ya al-nisa' rabbahunna fi'1-jannah.

23. Jawab warada 'ala lisan malik al-tatar.

24. Sharh hadith "Fahajja Adamu Musa."

25. Tanbih al-rajul al-'Aqil 'ala tamwih al-baitil.

26. Tanasi al-shada'id fi ikhtilaf al-'aqa'id.

27. 'Ibmat al-anbiya' 'alayhim al-salat wal-salam Hma

28. Mas'alatun fi'1-muqarrabin: hal yas'aluhum Munkar wa Nakir?

29. Mas'alat hal yu'adhdhab al-jasad ma 'a'1 ruh fi'1-qabr.

30. Al-Radd 'ala ahl '1-kasrawan.

31. Fi Fadfi'il Abl Bakr wa 'Umar radly Allah 'anhumft 'ala ghayiihimi.

32. Qa'idatun fi tafdil Mu'awfyah wa fi ibnihi Yazld.

33. K. fi tafdil salihi '1-nas 'ala sa'ir al-ajnas.

34. Mukhtasar fi kufr al-Bagrtyah fi jawaz qital al-rafidah.

35. Fi Baqa' al-Jannah wal-nar wa fi fana'ihima raddan 'all mawlana qadi al-qudat Taqi al-din al-subki.

35a. Qa'idatun ghalibuha aqwal al-fuqaha' 2 vols.

36. Qa'idat kulli hamdin wa dhammin min al-aljwal wa'l-afal la yakunu ilia bi'l-kitab wa'l-sunnah.
37. Shumul al-nusus li'l-ahkam.
38. Qa'idatun fi'l-ijma' innahu thalathat aqsam.
39. jawab fi'l-ijma' wa'l-khabar al-mutawatir.
40. Qa'idatun fi kayfiyat al-istidlal 'ala al-lhkam bi'l-nass wa'l-ijma' fi awl-radd 'ala man qala inna 'l-adillah al-lafziyah la tufid al-yaqin. 3vols.
41. Qa'idatun fima oussa min ta'anid al-nass wa'l-ijma'.
42. Mu'akhadhatun 'ala Ibn Hazm fi'l-ijma'..
43. Qa'idatun fi'l-ijtihad wa'l-taqlid fi'l-ahkam.
44. Qa'idatun fi'l-istihasan fi waf al-'umum wa'l-ilhaq.
45. Qa'idatun fi anna al-mukhti' fi'l-ijtihad la ya'thim.
46. Jawab hal al-qadl yajibu 'alayhi taqlid madhhabin mu'ayyanin.
47. Jawab fi tark al-taqlid, fiman yaqul madhhabi madhhab al-nabi 'alayhi 'l-salat wa'l-salam wa laysa ana bimuhtaj ila taqlid al-arba'ah.
48. Jawab man tafaqqaha fi madhhabin wa wajada haditfean sahihaa hal ya'malu bihi aw'a.
49. Jawab taqlid al-Hanaff al-Shafi'i fi'l-masr wa'l-watr.
50. Al-fath 'ala al-imam fi'lsalat.
51. Tafdllqawa'id madhhab Malifc wa ahl al-Madinah.
52. Tafdil al-a'immah al-arba'ah wama imtaza bihi kullu wahidin minhum.
53. Qa'idatun fi tafdil al-Imam Ahmad.
54. Jawab hal lean al-nabi salla 'llah 'alayhi wasallam qabl al-risalah nabiya.
55. Jawab hal kan al-nabl salla 'llah 'alayhi wasallam muta'abbidan bishar' man qabla hu,
56. Qawa'id anna 'lnahy yaqtadi al-mudaddah.
57. Jawab masa'il waradat min Isfahan.
58. Jawab masa'il waradat min al-Salah.

59. Masa'il waradat min Baghdad.
60. Masa'il waradat min zara'.
61. Masa'il waradat min al-wajanah.
62. Arba'in mas'alah.
63. Mas'alat al-durr al-mudi'ah fi fatawa Ibn Taymiyah al-Maridaniyah al-tra-bulusiyah.
64. Qa'idatun fi'l-miyah wa'l-mai'at wa ahkamiha.
65. Taharat bawl ma yu'kal lahmuhu.
66. Qa'idatun fi hadith al-qullatayn wa 'adam rafihi.
67. Qawa'id fi'l-istijmar wa tathir al-ard bi'l-shams wa'l-rjh.
68. Jawaz 'ala istijmar ma' wujud al-ma'.
69. Nawaqid al-wudu', qawa'id fi 'adam naqihi bi lams al-nisa'.
70. Al-Tasmiyah 'ala 'l-wudu'.
71. Kheata'al-qawl bi 'adam jawaz al-mash 'ala 'l-khuffayn.
72. Jawaz al-mash 'ala al-khuffayn al-mutakharraqayn wa'l-jawribflfli wa'l-Jafa'if.
73. Fiman la yu'ti ujrat al-hammam.
74. Tahrim dukhul al-nisa' bila mi'zar fi'l-hammam wa'l-ightisal.
75. Dhamm al-waswas.
76. Jawaz tawaf al-ha'id.
77. Taysir al-'ibadat fi-arbab al-daruitt bi'l-tayammum wa'l-jam' bayn al-salatayn bi'l-'udhr.
78. Karahiyat al-.talaffu bi'l-niyah wa tahrira al-jahr biha fi'l-adhkar.
79. Karahiyat taqdim bast sajjadat al-musalli qabl raaji'ihi.
80. Al-Qunut fi'l subh wa'l-witr.
81. Tarik al-mathani wa kufruhu.
82. Ahl al-bid': hal yusallal Khalfahum?
83. Salat ba'd ahl al-madhahib khalf ba'd.
84. Al-Salawat al-mubtadi'ah.

85. Tahrim al-shababah.

86. Tahrim al-la'b bi'l-shitranj.

87. Tahrim al-hashishah al-mughibah wa'l-hadd 'alayha tanjisuha.

88. Al-Nahy 'an al-masharakat fi a'yad al-Nasara wa'l-yahud wa 'Iqa? al-niran fi'l-milad wa nisf gha'ban wama yuf'alu fi 'ashiira' min al-hubub.

89. Qa'idatun fi miqdar al-kaffarah bi'l-yamin,

90. Fi anna al-mutallaqatah bi thalathatin fa tahillu ilia bi nikah zawjhi thanin.

91. Bayan al-halal wa'l-haram fi'l-talaq.

92. Jawab man halafa la yaf'alu shay'an 'ala al-madhahib al-arba'ah thumma tallaqa thalathan fi'l-bayd,

93. Al-Talaq al-bid'i la yaqa'u.

94. Masa'il al-farq bayn al-talaq al-bid 'i wa nahwi dhalik.

95. Fi shira' al-silah bi Tabuk wa shurb al-sawiq bi'l-'Aqabah wa akl al-tamar bi'l-rawdah wa ma yalbasu 'l-muhrim wa ziyarat al-kbalil 'alayhi 'l-salam 'aqib al-hajj wa ziyarat al-bayt al-maqdis mut-laqan.

96. JabI Lubnan Kamithaalihi min al-jibal laysa fihi rijal al-ghayb wa la abdal.

97. Jami' ayman al-Muslimin mukaffarah.

98. Kashf hal al-masha'ikh al-ahmadiyah wa ahwaiihimal-ghaytaniyah, ma yaqiiJuhu ahl bayt al-shayhh 'Adi.

99. Al-Nujum: hal lahs tathlrun 'ind al-qiran wa'l-muqabaiah? wa fi 'l-muqabalah hal yuqbalu qawl al-munajjmm fihi wa ru'yat al-ahillah.

100. Tahrim aqsam al-mu'azzimin bi'l-'azfi'im al-mu'jamah wa sar' al-sahih wa sifat al-khawatim.

101. Ibtai al-kimiya' wa tahrimuha wa law sahhat wa rajat.

102. Bayftn talbis al-Humaymiyah fi ta'sis bid'ihim al-kalamiyah. 6 vols.

103. Jawab ahl al-'ilm wa'l-iman fi tafsir al-Qur'an.

104. Mas'alat ahl al-Irbiliyah.
105. Baysn hall ishkai Ibn Hazm al-v;arid ;ala hadith al-nuzul.
106. Al-Radd 'ala al-faiasifah, 4 vols.
107. Ajwibat al-Qur'an wa'1-nusq.
108. Ibtal al-kalam al-nafsani abtalahu min nahw thamanin wajhan.
109. Jawab man halafa bi'1-talaq al-thalath anna '1-qur'an harfun wa sawt.
110. Al-Muwakisiyat ₉ifat al-kamal wa'l-dabit.
111. Jawabun fi'1-istiwa' wa ibtal ta'wihhi bi'1-istila'.
112. Jawab man qala: layumkin al-jam' bayn ithbat al-sifat 'ala? ahiriha ma' nafy al-tashbih.
113. Jawab: kawnal-shay'fi jihat al-'illah ma' kawnihl laysa bijawharin wala 'ardin ma'qul aw mustahil.
114. Jawab hal al-istiwi' wa'1-nuzul haqlqah? wa hal ta'jim al-madhhab madhhab?
115. Mas'alat al-auzal wa 'khtilafihi bi 'khtiiaf al-buldsn wa'1-matali'.

# GENERAL BIBLIOGRAPHY

1. Abdallah bin As'ad al-yafi'i, d. 768 H., Mir'at al-jinan.
2. 'Abd al-Qadir 'Awdah, al-Tashri' al-jina'i al-Islarni, Cairo 1959.
3. 'Abd '1-Qahir al-Baghdadi, d. 429 H. al-Farq bayn at-firaq, Cairo 1948, Usul ud-din, Istanbul 1928.
4. 'Abd al-Rahman bin Khaldun, d. 808 H., Muqaddimah, Beirut 1886.
5. 'Abd 'I-Rahman bin Rajab, d. 759 H., Dhayl Tabaqat al-Hana-bilah.
6. Abid Salem Elie, Political Theory and Institutions of the Khawarij, Baltimore U.S.A., 1956.
7. Abu 'l-'A'la al-Mawdudi, The Islamic Concept of State, Lahore.
8. Abu Dawud, Ma'alim al-sunnan.
9. Abu al-Fida, Tarikh.
10. Abu '1-Kalam Azad, Khilafat (Urdu).
11. Abu '1-Hasan 'Ali bin Isma'il al-Ash'ari, d. 330 H., Maqalat al-Islamiyin, Cairo 1950.
12. Abu 'I-Hasan al-Nadawi, Tarikh al-da'wat wa 'azlmah— Ibn Taymiyah, (Urdu), Lucknow (India), 1956.
13. Abu '1-Hasan 'Ali bin Muhammad al-Mawardi, d. 450 H., al-Ahkam al-Sultaniyah.
14. Abu Hamid Muhammad al-Ghazali, d. 505 H. al-Iqti,ad fi '1-i'tiqad, al-Fada'ih al-Bltiniyah,
15. Abu Yusuf, d. 182 H., al-Radd 'ala Siyar al-Awzal ed. by AbQ '1-Wafa' al-Afghani, Cairo 1938.

16. Abu Zahrah, Ibn Taymiyah, Hayatuhu wa 'aaruhu, Cairo 1952.

17. 'Add ud-din 'Abd al-Rahman bin Ahmad al-lji, d. 756 H., al-Mawaqif fi 'ilm al-Kalam.

18. Albert N. Nader, La Systeme    Philosophique des Mu'tazilah, 1' Institute de Letters Orientals de Beyrouth, 1956.

19. 'Ali bin Ahmad bin Hazm, d. 456 H., al-Fiaal fi 'l-milal wa'l-ahwa' wa'l-nihal, Cairo 1317 H.

20. Ahmad bin Hajar al-'Asqalani, d. 768 H., al-Durar al-Kaminah fi a'yan al-mi'ah al-thaminah, Hyderabad (India), 1345 H.

21. Ahmad bin Muhammad bin 'Abd Rabbihi, d. 327 H., al-'Iqd al-farid. Cairo 1940.

22. Ahmad b. Yahya al-Baladhuri, d. 279 A.H., Ansab al-Arfiraf vol. 1, ed. by Muhammad Hamidullah, Cairo 1959.

23. Badr ud-din Muhammad bin Ibrahlm bin Jama'ah, Qadi, d. 1323 A.C., Tahrir al-afekam fi tadbir ahl al-Islam,

24. Carlyle, Medieval Political Theories.

25. al-Dhahabi, Tadhkirat al-huffaf.

26. Dunning, W.A., History of Political Theories.

27. Encyclopaedia of Islam, Leyden 1913.

28. Fabhr ud-din Muhammad bin 'Umar al-Razi, d. 606 H., Kitab al-Arba'in, Hyderabad (India), 1350 H.

29. Hcnri Laoust, Les Doctrines Sociales et Politiques d¹ Ibn Taymlyah, Cairo 1939.

30. Ibn Kathir, al-Bidayah wa I-Nihayah.

31. Ibn Rajab, Dhayl Tabaqat al-Hanabilah.

32. Imam al-Haramayn Abu 'l-ma'ali al-Juwayni, d. 478 H., Kitab al-Irshad.

33. Ibn-Shakir al-Kutubi, Fawat al-Wafayat.

34. 'Izz ud-din bin al-Athir, TariWi al-Kamil.

35. Jamal ud-din bin ai-Mutahhar al-Hilli, d. 726 H., Minhaj

al-Karamah li ma'rifat al-imamah.

36. Khwajah Nasir al-dinai-Tusi, "RisalahImamat", Tehran, 1333 H.

37. Mari al-Karmi, al-Kawakib al-durriyah fi manaqib Ibn Taymiyah.

38. Mir Khawand, d. 903 H., Rawdat al-safa', Tehran 1932.

39. Miskawayh, Tajarib al-umam, ed. by Amedroz.

40. Montgomery Watt, Muhammad at Madinah, Oxford 1960.

41. Muhammad bin 'Ali al-Shawkani, d. 1250 H., al-Badr al-tali'.

42. Muhammad bin 'Abd al-Karim al-Shahrastani, d. 548 H., al-Milal wa'l-nihal, ed. by Muhammad Fathallah Badran, Cairo 1910.

43. Muhammad bin a. al-Hadi, al-'Uqud al-durriyah.

44. Muhammad Hamidullah, al-Watba'iq    al-siyasiyah, Hyderabad 1941.

45. Muhammad bin Isma'il al-Bukhari, d. 256 H., al-Jami' a Uahih.

46. Muhammad bin Janr al-Tabari, d. 319 H., Ikbtilaf al-fuqaha'. ed, by Jeseph Schacht, Leiden 1933.

47. Muhammad Yusuf Kokan 'Umari, Imam Ibn Taymiyah, (Urdu), Lahore 1960.

48. Muslim bin al-Hajjaj, d. 261 H., Sahih.

49. Nu'man al-Altisi, Jila' al-'aynayn bi muhakamat al-Ahmadayn.

50. Phillip K. Hitti, Hsitory of the Arabs.

51. The Qur'an.

52. Rash id ud-din Fadi al-ullah, Tarikh-e-Mubarak-i-Ghazani.

53. Al-Rashid Rida, al-Khilafah, Cairo 1341 H.

54. Rene Grousset, Histoirc des croise des, Paris 1934.

55. Rosenthal, E.U., Political Thought in Medieval Islam, Cambridge 1958.

56. Rosenthal, Franz, Muqaddimah of Ibn Khaldun, English

translation, New York 1958.

57. Safi ud-din al-Hanafi, al-Qawl al-Jali fi tarjamat al-Shaykh Taqi al-din al-Hanbali, Bulaq (Cairo) 1881.
58. Sakka, La Notion Islamique de Souverainete, Paris 1922.
59. Al-Sayyid al-Sharif al-Jurijani, Sharh al-Mawaqif.
60. Taqi ud-uin bin a. al-Kafi al-Subki, d. 756 H., al-Durrah al-mudiyah fi'1-radd 'ala Ibn Taymiyah.
61. 'Umar Rida Kahhalah, Mu'jam al-mu'allifin.
62. Waliyullah, Izalat al-Khafa' 'an Khilafat al-Khulafa', Urdu trans-lation by 'Abd al-Shakur, Karachi 1960.
63. Waliy ud-din Muhammad bin Abdallah al-Khatib al-Tibrizi, d. 740 H., Mishkat al-masabih.